REVELATION

REVELATION

RONALD M. BARKER

AuthorHouse™ LLC
1663 Liberty Drive
Bloomington, IN 47403
www.authorhouse.com
Phone: 1-800-839-8640

Published by AuthorHouse   03/13/2014

ISBN: 978-1-4918-4447-2 (sc)
ISBN: 978-1-4918-4446-5 (e)

Library of Congress Control Number: 2013922953

This book is a record of over fifty three years of notes on Revelation.

I have worked in Home Missions; have been an interim pastor, a supply minister for our local association and pastor of one church for over 22 years.

All scripture comes from the New International Version unless otherwise noted.

All dates are AD unless otherwise noted.

We often hear that when one dies then he will face eternity. I say that when one is born he faces eternity. Our spiritual soul is eternal. Our physical body is not. When our physical body ceases to exist (we die), our spirit lives on. We might say that physical life is phase one of eternity and death is the threshold to the second phase. How we live and the decisions we make in life will determine where we spend phase two.

Yours truly,
Ron Barker

SIGNS OF THE END TIMES

When we not only read but study the Bible, we find that there are several prophesies of things that will happen in the generation of the last days on earth. Daniel, the great prophet of God, tells us in Chapter 12:1 *"At that time Michael, the great prince who protects your people, will arise. There will be a time of distress such as not happened from the beginning of nations until then. But at that time your people—everyone whose name is found written in the book—will be delivered."* He also describes it in verse 4 as a time where *"many will go here and there to increase knowledge."* We now live in a generation that has exploded in knowledge through electronics and computers, and Daniel also gives us a glimpse of a world of increased prosperity, travel and education. He sees a world that will achieve great things but it will lack meaning of purpose. Despite all of its accomplishments and its advancement, it still will be a world seeking answers.

The following are scriptural references of the end times:

- Luke, Chapter 21:26; *"Men will faint from terror, apprehensive of what is coming on the world, for the heavenly bodies will be shaken."*
- In II Timothy 3:1; *"But mark this: There will be terrible times in the last days."*
- II Peter 3:3, 4 gives us a futuristic view not only of a time of incredible prosperity, but also a time of impending doom, and spiritual blindness; *"First of all, you must understand that in the last days scoffers will come, scoffing and following their own evil desires. They will say, 'Where is this coming' he promised? Ever since our fathers died, everything goes on as it has since the beginning of creation."*
- Zechariah in Chapter 12:2, *"I am going to make Jerusalem a cup that sends all the surrounding peoples reeling. Judah will be besieged as well as Jerusalem."* During the last seven years of this earth age, Israel and Jerusalem will become a *"cup of trembling"* (KJV) for the world.

Before the ruler of this end time kingdom (Antichrist) can appear on the scene there are certain events that must occur and certain conditions that **must** prevail. In Daniel 9:27 we find that the Tribulation begins with the signing of a covenant between the Antichrist and Israel for a period of seven years. *"He will confirm a covenant with many for one 'seven' he will put an end to sacrifice and offering. And on a wing of the temple he will set up an abomination that causes desolation, until the end that is decreed is poured out on him."* This treaty will guarantee protection to Israel so that she may rebuild her temple and re-establish her ancient religious ritual of Judaism.

One day, there will appear on the horizon, a charismatic leader who through guile, persuasions, and diplomatic acumen that will be unparalleled in the history of the world, will convince even the most skeptical Israeli hard liner that the only way their safety can be assured is to put their trust in him. According to Dan. 2:38-44; 7:23-27, some think it is very possible he is alive today, waiting for "his" time to appear on the scene.

The internet now links together all but the remote areas of earth with instant communication capability. Just like the Babel builders of Genesis 11, people again are moving to create a world of their own design.

The Bible has forewarned us and history has taught us that a man made government that refuses to be guided by God's principles of morality, will inevitable degenerate and fall to tyranny within its own borders. The USA is rapidly becoming a nation of degenerate morality because of their constant refusal to be guided by God!

Mikhail Gorbachev and several politicians, futurologists, and New Agers met from September 20 through October 1, 1995, and took the world a giant step closer to global dictatorship. It was just a step toward a New Civilization, but it was one of the most significant steps forward in implementing the coming world government, which President Clinton referred to as the "global village."

The New Agers teach the same lies that Satan told Eve in the Garden of Eden. We find these lies that correspond to God's truth in Genesis 1:1, 4,

5, 6: (1) God's word cannot be trusted. (2) Man does not have to die. (3) Man can become a god. (4) Man can evolve through hidden knowledge.

It has been suggested that God is currently granting us a lull just before the prophesied end of time storm that will devastate a generation deserving God's wrath.

In the twentieth first century we are seeing a growing awareness that we are speeding toward a date with destiny. Many believe time is running out for this earth. This is especially true for those who have not accepted Christ as their Savior.

In Matthew 25:14-30 Matthew records Jesus' parable about the talents, which many think could be an indication that Christ would be gone for 2,000, 3,000 or more years. We have no way of knowing how long He will be gone. The only thing we know for sure is that Christ is coming back and we are instructed to *"watch"* and *"be ready,"* faithfully serving Him until His return. We must live our lives as though He could return today, but plan our work as if we have a hundred years to live. Man has the theory that because the Bible says that a day is as a 1,000 years with God, that there will be only 6,000 years before the Millennium. It is interesting to note that in the Book of Adam and Eve, it states that from the beginning of man to the death of Christ there would be a lapse of 5,500 years. This book is not canonized but this in itself does not necessarily make it wrong. In Psalm 90:4 it says 1,000 years is as 4 hours. So this theory is shot down.

The most serious announcement in Jesus' message was in Matthew 24:36 that no one is to set dates for His return.

The following are some of the "signs" of the events leading up to the second coming:

1—II Tim. 3:1-5 gives us the signs of society:

Lawlessness,   Boastful,
Violence,   Proud,

Rebellion,	Without Love,
Immorality,	Unforgiving,
Greed,	Slanderous,
Selfishness,	Without self-control,
Self Pleasure,	Having a form of godliness but denying its
Despair,	power.

2—Matt. 24:4-11; Mark 13:8; Luke 21:11; II Thess. 2:3; II Tim. 4:1-14 gives us the signs of the last days:

- Famine—people throughout the world are dying of starvation.
- Earthquakes—are happening each year.
- Plagues—we are inundated with new diseases and old diseases with different strains.
- Great signs in heaven.
- There will be False Christ's and false prophets—This is a daily occurrence.
- Apostasy in the professing church and wide spread heresies—this is getting worse.
- Movement toward one world religion—which is an ongoing thing today.
- Persecution of true believers—this is happening in other countries and is slowly creeping its way into the USA.
- Outbreak of demonic activity—we can see an increase of Satanic Churches and satanic worship today.

3—Gen. 15:18-21; Ex. 23:31; Num. 34:1-15; Ezek. 37:1-12; Zech. 12:1-14; Dan. 12:4; Matt. 24:6-12; Rev. 16-18 gives us the following signs:

- Arab hostility toward Israel and other nations.
- Re-gathering of Israel.
- Re-establishing the state of Israel with one leader.
- Wars and rumors of wars.
- Nations and kingdoms against one another.
- Reunification of Europe.
- Movement toward global economy.
- Movement toward a world government.

- Increase in knowledge.
- Rapid disintegration of society.
- "Birth pains," increasing in frequency and intensity.

Some of the signs in place today:

1. Israel became a sovereign state on May, 14, 1948.
2. Since the birth of Ishmael there is and always will be a constant conflict in the Middle East.
3. Weapons of mass destruction already exist.
4. Western powers are attempting to guarantee Israel's peace and security.
5. Many nations already have a global economy.
6. European nations are forming the European Union.
7. The potential of a world government is already in place.

The following is a list of a few things yet to be fulfilled:

1. Rapture of the Church.
2. Revival of the Roman Empire—a one-world government. This is an ongoing process.
3. Rise of the Antichrist—This could happen at any time. He could even be alive today.
4. Apostate world church—which we are seeing today.
5. Martyrdom of those who refuse to worship the Beast.
6. Israel has not regained its original territory.

Matt. 24:4-11; and Joel 2:28, 29 gives us hope for they tell us that there will be an:

- Outpouring of the Holy Spirit.
- Worldwide evangelism.
- Restoration of the Temple.
- Understanding of Bible Prophecy and as the "end times" approach, we will find that we will be able to understand more of God's Word.

IN REVELATION WE WILL FIND

1. **The Heavenly Throne**—surrounded by twenty-four elders, dressed in white and wearing crowns of gold.
2. **The Seven-Sealed Book**—the title deed to the forfeited inheritance of the earth lost by Adam when he fell. Only Christ through His death and Resurrection is worthy to open the book.
3. **The Vision of The Martyred Souls**—the persecution and death of the Christians and could also be a reference to the persecutions and death of the Tribulation Saints during the tribulation period.
4. **The Day of Wrath**—when the sun is darkened, the stars fall, the heavens are rolled up, mountains and islands are removed.
   A. *Lost Prayer*—kings, princes, generals, the rich, mighty, every slave and freeman hides in caves and among rocks of the mountains and call to the mountains and the rocks to fall on them and hide them from the wrath of God. (6:16).
   B. Four angels holding back evil until the Church of Christ grows strong.
   C. Sealing—consecrating the persons to God by showing the mark of God upon them—nothing could harm them.

When one reads and studies Revelation, they may first ask themselves what they believe about the timing of Jesus' return. Will He come before, during, or after the Tribulation, or does it really matter? Many don't even think about if Jesus is coming before the Tribulation, as many Christians know very little about the "end times."

The study of Revelation leaves us with many questions. As time progresses, and as more prophesied events in the Bible are being fulfilled, we will be able to understand more. We understand more today than our fathers did in their time, but our children will understand more than we do.

There are three basic teachings as to the return of our Lord and Savior.

I—**Amillennialists**—The Roman Catholic Church, the Greek Church, and a large portion of Protestantism hold to the Millennial View. The center of this view is usually traced back to St. Augustine (354-430). John Calvin and Martin Luther also held this view.

BELIEFS AND TEACHINGS

1. Christ's kingdom will transpire in the present age between the first and second coming.
2. The binding of Satan (Rev. 20:1-3) occurred at the first coming of Christ as a result of Christ's death and resurrection.
3. There will not be a 1,000-year reign of Christ on earth and there will be no earthly Kingdom of God.
4. When Christ returns to earth, He will take all believers (sheep) out, condemn all the unbelievers (goats) and eternity will begin right then. This, they believe is what is meant by the dividing of the sheep (believers), form the goats (unbelievers).

Some of the believers are: Augustine, Luther, The Church of Rome, Lutherans, Presbyterians, and the Methodists.

The future events according to Amillennialists:

1- A parallel development of both good and evil during this present age.
2- The second coming of Christ.
3- The general resurrection of all people.
4- A general judgment of all people.
5- Eternity.

II—**The Pre-millennial View**—This was the view of the early church. It was held by early church fathers such as Tertullian, Clement of Rome, Barnabas, Ignatius, Polycarp, Justin the Martyr, Peter, John, James, Paul, Irenaeus, Melito, Cyprian, Methodius, Nepos, Bohemian, Protestants, Waldensians, Wycliffites, Joseph Bede, Alford, Lange, Isaac Newbon, John Darby, Lightfood, and Westcotts. It gradually became the prevailing view.

Papias, one of the apostolic fathers, was a student of the apostle John. Papias believed in a literal one thousand year reign of Christ after his return to earth.

BELIEFS AND TEACHINGS

1. The second coming of Jesus Christ will occur before the millennial kingdom.
2. His return to earth will occur at the end of a literal seven-year period of terrible judgments called the Tribulation.
3. Maintain that the millennial kingdom will be a literal, physical, earthy kingdom of one thousand years, during which time Jesus will rule and reign over the earth from His throne in Jerusalem.

According to Premillennialists the following events will occur:

1- Increase in apostasy (this is happening today) as the church age draws to a close.
2- The rapture of the Church.
3- Seven year Tribulation period on earth.
4- The second coming of Christ to earth.
5- The campaign of Armageddon.
6- The millennial reign of Christ on earth.
7- The Great White Throne Judgment.
8- The creation of a new heaven and a new earth.
9- Eternity.

III—**The Postmillennial View**—They maintain that Jesus Christ will return to earth after the Millennium. The Millennium is the entire period of time between the first and second comings of Christ. Christ returns after the Millennium is completely over.

BELIEFS AND TEACHINGS

1. The Millennial Kingdom is not a literal thousand years but a golden age ushered in by the church's preaching of the gospel during this present age.

The future events according to the Postmillennial View:

1- Progressive improvement of conditions on earth as the end draws near, culminating in a golden age as the world is Christianized.
2- The second coming of Christ.
3- The general resurrection of all people.
4- A general judgment of all people.
5- Eternity.

Some believers are the Presbyterians, and Daniel Whitby.

All of these views believe that Jesus Christ is King of kings and Lord of lords, and will one day return to this world literally, physically, visibly, and gloriously as the Judge of all the earth.

There are ten key events in Bible Prophecy.

1- The rapture of the Church.
2- The judgment seat of Christ.
3- The marriage of the Lamb.
4- The Tribulation period.
5- The second coming of Christ.
6- The campaign of Armageddon.
7- The millennial kingdom.
8- The final revolt of Satan.
9- The Great White Throne Judgment.
10- The creation of the new heaven and the new earth.

There are several differences between Jesus coming at the Rapture and His second coming:

1. I Thess. 4:17-All believers will be translated to meet Christ in the air.
1. Zech. 14:4-At His second coming no translation will be seen.

2. I Thess. 4:17-Jesus will come as a thief and only the believers of the church will see Him.
2. Acts 1:11; Matt. 24:30-Every eye shall Him at His second coming.

3. I Thess. 4:13-17;—Believers will be taken from the earth and unbelievers will remain to go through the tribulation.
3. Matt. 24:37-39; Rev. 19:17-21-Unbelievers are taken and believers will be left to go through the millennium.

4. I Thess. 4:17-Christ will come for His saints and will take them to Heaven with Him.
4. I Thess. 3:13; II Thess. 2:10-12; Zech. 14:5; Rev. 19:7-Jesus will return with His saints.

5. I Thess. 1:10; Roman 13:11-14; I John 2:28-It will not be preceded by any event.
5. Matt. 24-It is preceded by specific signs included in the Tribulation.

6. I Thess. 5:9-10; Rev. 3:10-Jesus takes us from the wrath to come. He keeps us safe from the Tribulation.
6. Joel 2:1-11Matt. 3:11-12: 25:31-32, 46; Rev. 6-19; Jesus comes to judge the world.

7. I Thess. 4:18; Rev. 3:10-It is a source of comfort to believers.
7. Rev. 6:15-17; 9:11-It is a source of fear to man.

8. We find no recorded changes in nature mentioned in connection with the rapture.
8. Rev. 6; Isaiah 35-Many changes in nature are recorded.

9. I Cor. 15:51-In the OT it is a mystery, a truth hidden.
9. In the NT it is the subject of extended prophecy,

10. I Thess. 4:13-18-No reference or dealing with Satan. Instead his activity increases.
10. Rev. 20:1-3-Satan is bound for 1,000 years.

11. When the raptures occurs, the Mount of Olives is unchanged.
11. Zech. 14:4-5-When Jesus returns, the Mount of Olives is split, and forms a valley.

12. Rev. 19:7-10-We have the examination, rewards, and the wedding of the Bride.
12. Jesus' return to earth is followed by the wedding feast, and the church is seen already rewarded.

13. I Cor. 15:51-53-When the raptures occurs, believers will receive a glorified body.
13. Isaiah 65:20-25-Believers of the Tribulation go into the millennium with mortal bodies.

WHEN DOES THE RAPTURE OCCUR?

In all my 50 plus years of studying the Bible, I have found that in all the books about the Rapture, Revelation, the Second Coming of Christ, the commentaries, and all the pre-mid, amid, and post-mid theories I have read, everyone gave ample scripture to substantiate their views why they accepted either the pre, mid, or post views. We all must make our own determination according to what the scriptures have to say, as to our beliefs.

I Cor. 15:52 says, *"in a flash, in the twinkling of an eye, at the last trumpet will sound, the dead will be changed."* The last trumpet mentioned here is the last trumpet to be sounded before the Tribulation begins, not the last trumpet sounded in Rev.

When the Bible was speaking about Jesus coming as a thief in the night, it was talking about the rapture, not Jesus' coming after the tribulation period. Matt. 24:36 simply states that no man would know the day or the hour, but would know the general time.

Let us assume that the Antichrist is revealed on July 1, 2025. We know that 3 1/2 years later the Antichrist will declare himself God, Jan. 1, 2028. This would discount the mid-trib theory because Matt. 24:36 says that no would know the day or the hour. If the antichrist revealed himself on July 1, 2028, then we would know that Jesus would return seven years later, June 30, 2031.

The same reasoning is for the post-trib view. The antichrist is revealed July 1, 2025, and then we know that in seven years the day of His appearing would be at hand. From July 1, 2025 to June 30, 2031 would be seven years so we would know that Jesus would appear on June 30. We would know the day, and that Matthew says no one would know.

According to scripture, not counting all the scripture verses that indicate the "Rapture" will occur before the tribulation Period, Matthew 24:36

makes it very clear that the "Rapture" must occur before the Tribulation Period begins, because no one knows when the Rapture will occur.

We do know that the Tribulation Period starts after the Rapture occurs, but we do not know when the Rapture will. I have read several books where the writer will explain a verse in Revelation and claim that the Holy Spirit gave them the explanation for their interpretation of that verse. Then I would read another book and that writer would explain the same verse and say that the Holy Spirit gave them their interpretation. The Holy Spirit does inspire and enlighten us, but the only problem with these writers' so called 'spiritual enlightenment' is that they were different, indicating that the Holy Spirit gives different interpretations to different people. This is definitely not the case. For the Holy Spirit to do that would be lying. For the Holy Spirit to lie would be impossible.

Writers, ministers, etc., should be very wary in making such claims least we in making these statements, call the Holy Spirit a liar!

When we study the Bible, we find that there many questions about the "latter days" we do not understand. There are questions that seem to be unanswered even when commentaries of Revelation are read.

One of the questions we might ask is "Just what is the Tribulation?" When we study the Bible, we find the word 'Tribulation' mentioned several times. I have listed a few.

1. A time of God's special judgment poured out upon the earth. (Isaiah 10:5,6).
2. A time of unprecedented trouble. (Joel 2:2; Matt. 24:21).
3. A time of God's wrath or indignation and the vindication of God's Holiness. (Zeph. 1:15; I Thess. 1:10).
4. A day of utter darkness, gloom and extreme cloudiness. (Joel 2:2; Zeph. 1:15).
5. A day of destruction and global catastrophe. (Joel 1:15; 2:3; I Thess. 5:3).
6. A day of lawlessness, sin and demonic activity. (II Thess. 2:12).
7. A day of extreme deception and delusion caused by the removal of the Spirit indwelt church and its restraining influence, increase

of demonic. activity and the blinding judgment of God. (Dan. 8:24; II Thess. 2:6-12).

8. A time of death. (Rev. 6:3-11; 9:15).
9. A time of cold indifference and rebellion against God. (Rev. 6:14-17; 9:20).
10. A time of political, economical, religious and military nationalism. (Joel 3:2, 9-14; Rev. 13:17; 17).
11. A time of extreme Anti-Semitism. (Matt. 24:9, 13).
12. A time of unprecedented apostasy and blasphemy against God (II Thess. 2:3).
13. A time of martyrdom of all believers, both Jews and Gentiles. (Rev. 6:9).
14. A time of global and universal war, both angelic and human. (Joel 3:2).
15. A time of unprecedented evangelism. (Matt. 24:14).

SOME OF THE NAMES USED FOR THE TRIBULATION

1. Dan. 9:24-27; 12:1. Jacob's trouble, Daniel's 70th week, a time of trouble or distress.
2. Rev. 3:10; 6:17. Hour of testing which shall try the whole earth, the great Day, the one of His wrath.
3. Isa. 26:26, the Indignation.
4. Matt. 24:9, 21, 29: Mark 13:19, 24: Rev. 7:14. Tribulation and The Great Tribulation.
5. Joel 1:15; 2:1: The Day of the Lord.

Ezekiel prophesies in Chapter 37:1-14 that Israel would return to their land becoming a nation again. This became a reality in 1948.

Isaiah 31:5 states, *"Like birds hovering overhead, the Lord Almighty will shield Jerusalem; he will shield it and deliver it, he will pass over it and will rescue it."*

General Edmund Allenby, who was the commander of occupied Palestine for the British Empire in 1917, was ordered to take Jerusalem for the Jews.

Allenby started to comply but found he had a problem. The Turks were in possession of the city. To take the city by force meant risking initiation of hostilities that might so inflame the region that a massive conflict would result. Bloodshed could have raised the indignation of the whole world.

Allenby asked his government for advice and was told to use his own judgment. He again contacted his superiors, asking for advice, and this time he was told to pray. Allenby then ordered the commander of a fleet of airplanes to fly over Jerusalem. This action terrified the Turks so much that they surrendered the city without a shot being fired.

Ezekiel 38-39—The word of the Lord came to me: (2) "Son of man, set your face against Gog, of the land of Magog, the chief prince of Meshech and Tubal; prophesy against him (3) and say: 'This is what the Sovereign Lord says: I am against you O Gog, chief prince of Meshech and Tubal. (4) I will turn you around, put hooks in your jaws and bring you out with your whole army—your horses, your horsemen fully armed, and a great horde with large and small shields, all of them brandishing their swords. (5) Persia, Cush and Put will be with them, all with shields and helmets, (6) also Gomer with all its troops and Beth Togarmah from the far north with all its troops—the many nations with you.

(7) "'Get ready; be prepared, you and all the hordes gathered about you, and take command of them. (8) After many days you will be called to arms. In future years you will invade a land that has recovered from war, whose people were gathered from many nations to the mountains of Israel, which had long had been desolated. They had been brought out from the nations, and now all of them live in safety. (9) You and all your troops and the many nations with you will go up, advancing like a storm; you will be like a cloud covering the land.

(10) "'This is what the Sovereign Lord says: On that day thoughts will come into your mind and you will devise an evil scheme. (11) You will say, "I will invade a land of unwalled villages; I will attack a peaceful and unsuspecting people—all of the living without walls and without gates and bars. (12) I will plunder and loot and turn my hand against the resettled ruins and the people gathered from the nations, rich in livestock and goods, living at the center of the land." (13) Sheba and Dedan and the merchants of Tarshish

and all her villages will say to you, "Have you come to plunder? Have you gathered your hordes to loot, to carry off silver and gold, to take away livestock and goods and to seize much plunder?"

(14) Therefore, son of man, prophesy and say to Gog: 'This is what the Sovereign Lord says: In that day, when my people Israel are living in safety, will you take notice of it? (15) You will come from your place in the far north, you and many nations with you, all of them riding on horses, a great horde, and a mighty army. (16) You will advance against my people Israel like a cloud that covers the land. In days to come, O Gog, I will bring you against my land so that the nations may know me when I show myself holy through you before their eyes.(17) "'This is what the Sovereign Lord says: Are you not the one I spoke of in former days by my servants the prophets of Israel? At that time they prophesied for years that I would bring you against them.

(18) This is what will happen in that day: When Gog attacks the land of Israel, my hot anger will be aroused, declares the Sovereign Lord. (19) In my zeal and fiery wrath I declare that at that time there shall be a great earthquake in the land of Israel. (20) The fish of the sea, the birds of the air, the beast of the field, every creature that moves along the ground, and all the people on the face of the earth will tremble at my presence. The mountains will be overturned; the cliffs will fall to the ground. (21) I will summon a sword against Gog on all of my mountains, declares the Sovereign Lord. Every man's sword will be against his brother. (22) I will execute judgment upon him with plague and bloodshed; I will pour down torrents of rain, hailstones and burning sulfur on him and on his troops and on the many nations with him. (23) And so I will show my greatness and my holiness, and I will make myself known in the sight of many nations. Then they will know that I am the Lord.'

Ezekiel 39—*"Son of man. Prophesy against Gog and say: 'This is what the Sovereign Lord says: I am against you O Gog, chief prince of Meshech and Tubal. (2) I will turn you around and drag you along. I will bring you from the far north and send you against the mountains of Israel. (3) Then I will strike your bow from your left hand and make your arrows drop from your right hand. (4) On the mountains of Israel you will fall, you and all your troops and the nations with you. I will give you as food to all kinds of carrion birds and to the wild animals. (5) You will fall in the open field, for I have* spoken, declares the Sovereign Lord. (6) I will send fire on Magog and on those who live in safety in the coastlands, and they will know that I am the Lord.

(7) "'I will make known my holy name among my people Israel. I will no longer let my holy people be profaned, and the nations will know that I the Lord am the Holy One in Israel. (8) It is coming! It will surely take place, declared the Sovereign Lord. This is the day I have spoken of. (9)"'Then those who live in the towns of Israel will go out and use the weapons for fuel and burn them up—the small and large shields, the bows and arrows, the war clubs and spears. For seven years they will use them for fuel. (10) They will not need to gather wood from the fields or cut it from the forests, because they will use the weapons for fuel. And they will plunder those who plundered them and loot those who looted them, declares the Sovereign Lord.' (11) "'On that day I will give Gog a burial place in Israel, in the valley of those who travel east toward the Sea. It will block the way of travelers, because Gog and all his hordes will be buried there. So it will be called the Valley of Hamon Gog.

(12) "'For seven months the house of Israel will be burying them in order to cleanse the land. (13) All the people of the land will bury them, and the day I am glorified will be a memorable day for then, declares the Sovereign Lord (14) "'Men will be regularly employed to cleanse the land. Some will go throughout the land and, in addition to them; others will bury those that remain on the ground. At the end of the seven months they will begin their search. (15) As they go through the land and one of them sees a human bone, he will set up a marker beside it until the gravediggers have buried it in the Valley of Hamon Gog. (16) (Also a town called Hamonah will be there.) And so they will cleanse the land.' (17) "Son of man, this is what the Sovereign Lord says: Call out to every kind of bird and all the wild animals: 'Assemble and come together from all around to the sacrifice I am preparing for you, the great sacrifice on the mountains of Israel. There you will eat flesh and drink blood. (18) You will east flesh of mighty men and drink the blood of the princes of the earth as if they were rams and lambs, goats and bulls—all of them fattened animals from Bashan. (19) At the sacrifice I am preparing for you, you will eat fat till you are glutted and drink blood till you are drunk. (20) At my table you will eat your fill of horses and riders, mighty men and soldiers of every kind,' declares the Sovereign Lord. (21) "I will display my glory among the nations, and all the nations will see the punishment I inflict

and the hand I lay upon them. (22) From that day forward the house of Israel will know that I am the Lord their God. (23) And the nations will know that the people of Israel went into exile for their sin, because they were unfaithful to me. So I hid my face from them and handed them over to their enemies, and they all fell by the sword. (24) I dealt with them according to their uncleanness and their offenses, and I hid my face from them. (25) "Therefore this is what the Sovereign Lord says: I will now bring Jacob back from captivity and will have compassion on all the people of Israel, and I will be zealous for my holy name. (26) They will forget their shame and all the unfaithfulness they showed toward me when they lived in safety in their land with no one to make them afraid. (27) When I have brought them back from the nations and have gathered them from the countries of their enemies, I will show myself holy through them in the sight of many nations. (28) Then they will know that I am the Lord their God, for though I sent them into exile among the nations, I will gather them to their own land, not leaving any behind. (29) I will no longer hide my face from them, for I will pour out my Spirit on the house of Israel, declares the Sovereign Lord."

Nations that attacked Israel attacked them from the north, even though they may be from the east or the south.

The scripture says they will attack from the far north, not from the north as other nations have, which some say gives a good indication that it means Russia. Could very well be, but time will tell.

Some scholars, writers, give this as a definition of Ezek. 38, 39.

Gog, the Chief Prince (ruler) of Magog, Meshech, and Tubal,

ALONG WITH:

1. Persia (Iran).
2. Cush (Egypt, & Black African Nations).
3. Put (Libya, & Arabian Nations).
4. Gomer (Germany).
5. Beth Togarmah (Southern Russia).
6. Many other nations.

THEY WILL INVADE IN FUTURE YEARS:

1. A land that has recovered from war (Israel).
2. A land of unwalled villages.
3. Attack a peaceful & unsuspecting people.

THEIR GOAL:

Plunder and loot a nation rich in livestock and goods, who are living in the center of the land.

RESPONSE OF NATIONS:

Shedan, Dedan, and merchants of Tarshish will question their motives.

GOD'S RESPONSE:

A great earthquake will occur in Israel with the following results;

1. Fish of the sea
2. Birds of the air, and
3. Beast of the field will die.
4. Every creature that moves along the ground, and
5. all the people on earth will tremble.
6. Nations will be overturned.
7. Cliffs will fall to the ground.
8. Every man's sword will be against his brother.
9. There will be plague and bloodshed.
10. Torrents of rain, hailstones, and burning sulfur will fall.
11. Fire will fall on Magog and those who are in safety in the coastlands.
12. God's Greatness, & Holiness will be revealed.
13. Gog and his allies will fall on the mountains of Israel, and
14. they will fall in the open fields.

RESULTS:

1. It will take seven years to burn up the weapons.
2. Birds and animals will feast on the dead bodies.
3. It will take seven months to bury the dead.
4. After seven months they will search for any remains.

OTHERS THOUGHTS

Gog = ruler=Antichrist. He will rule over 3 nations, Rosh, Meshech, & Tubal.

Rosh=a title of leadership, because it does not appear in the Table of Nations in Gen. 10.

Josephus identifies the Magogites as Scythians who branched eastward & westward from the region north of the Black Sea.

Hitler acclaimed the title "The Third Reich." Rome was the First Reich and Kaiser Bismarck was the Second Reich.

From the following scripture, along with Rev. 20: 7-10, some find an indication on what will happen in the "latter days." Gog, the ruler of the land Magog, the chief prince of Meshech and Tubal, with their allies:

1. Persia (Iran). (Ezekiel 38:5), Russia reportedly needs Iran as an ally in order to move a large army across the Caucasus Mountains that borders Turkey, then the Elburg Mountains that border Iran. Even though Iran's terrain is less difficult to cross, transportation will be needed through both countries. This Russian force is called the "King of the North." Cush will be part of the "King of the South."
2. Egypt (Ethiopia, Cush—The Black African Nations). Cush was originally adjacent to an area near the Tigris and Euphrates Rivers. Gen. 2:13—Cushites were black people that migrated first to the Arabian Peninsula, later to the Red Sea, and then to the Southern area of Egypt. Many of the African nations will be united and allied with the Russians, Dan. 11: 36-45.

3. Put (Libya-Arabic African Nations). Put was the third son of Ham (Gen 10:6). The descendants of Put migrated to the land west of Egypt and became the source of the North African Arab Nations, such as Libya, Algeria, Tunisa, and Morocco, (Ezek. 38:5).

4. Gomer and all its hordes, (Germany, the Iron Curtain Countries). Gomer was the eldest son of Japheth and the father of Ashkinaz, Riphath, and Togarmah. They settled on the north of the Black Sea, and then spread out southward and westward to the extremities of Europe, (Ezek.38:6). This type of terrain exists between Israel and Russia.

5. Beth Togarmah (Southern Russia). Togarmah is part of the modern people of Southern Russia and probably are the origin of the Cossacks. The Cossacks, great lovers of horses, are reportedly producing the finest calvary in the world, actually predicted by Ezekiel and other prophets. The Red Chinese, during the Korean War, proved that in this rugged terrain, horses were still the fastest means of moving a large force into battle areas.

6. Many people with you will invade the land of unwalled villages (Israel). Israel will be a peaceful and unsuspecting people. Israel is at the present building a wall around their territory. It will one day come down.

The following are some of the reasons given why Russia will want to invade Israel:

1. Israel has a warm water entrance into the waterways of the world.
2. She has oil.
3. She has the mineral deposits of the Dead Sea, which is estimated to consist of two billion tons of potassium chloride (potash), twenty-two billion tons of magnesium chloride, 12 billion tons of sodium chloride, and six billion tons of calcium chloride.
4. Israel also contains cerium, cobalt, manganese and gold.

It was reported that during World War II, Russia sent England 50 thousand lead pencils with the imprint, "Gog of Magog."

Reportedly, Russia, fearful of Iran spreading the Islamic revolution throughout Central Asia was forced to sign a pact with Iran. This pact is a guarantee that Iran will have use of Russia's top nuclear and missile scientist, and Russia's commitment to fight alongside Iran against the west in the event of any future-armed interference against them.

When this Russian-Arab alliance attacks Israel, the prophet Ezekiel declared that God will intervene with supernatural earthquakes, hail, and pestilence to defeat the combined forces of Russia and the Arab armies. This could be the miracle of deliverance by the hand of God that may set the stage for Israel to build the third Temple as described in Daniel 9:24-27.

This great army, as they attack Israel, are met by the might of God. A great earthquake will strike Israel. Mountains will be overturned, cliffs will crumble and every wall will fall to the ground. Torrential rain, hailstones and burning sulfur will fall on the invading army. God will give the invading army as food to all kinds of carrion, birds and to the wild animals. (A prelude of what is to come during the Battle of Armageddon).

God will send fire on Magog and those who live in safety in the coastlands. (The U.S.A. and Great Britain)?

Ezekiel 38:13a says, *"Sheba and Dedan, and the merchants of Tarshish and all her villages."*

According to some scholars, the following is an interpretation of this verse:

1. Sheba is the name of an Arab people. Grandson of Cush settled in Yemen.
2. Dedan is a commercial people of Arabia, living in the area of Edom. Grandson of Cush.
3. Tarshish is England.
4. Her villages are the U. S., Canada, Australia, and New Zealand.

Gog is the ruler, the head of a great Northern Empire. Russia has, at present, ceased to be a united country. This does not mean that these countries will not reunite in their hatred of Israel and seek to destroy her.

Who is Gog and Magog? Ezekiel, Chapter 38 and 39 tell us that Russia is made up of Gog and Magog. In Gen. 10:2, the true Russians descended from Japheth, a son of Noah. The capital cities of Russia are named in the first verses of Ezekiel 38: *"Meshech"* is Moscow, the capital of Russia, and *"Tubal"* is the city of Tobolsk, chief city of Siberia. Referring to Gog and Magog, Ezekiel says, *"The chief prince of Meshech and Tubal."* Thus Russia is identified in Scripture as the land, the vast northern empire. Ezekiel goes further to tell us of Persia, Ethiopia, and many other nations coming under the leadership of Gog, *"like a cloud to cover the land."*

Reportedly Russia has placed enormous military supplies is Lebanon, Iraq, Libya and Egypt. They could be preparing, as some think, for the coming battle with Israel.

THE WAR WITH THE NORTH, According to Ezekiel:

1. Will attack a peaceful and unsuspecting nation, and will plunder and loot.
2. A great earthquake will occur causing
4. the fish of the sea,
5. the birds of the air,
6. the beasts of the field, every living creature,
7. and the people of the earth to tremble.
8. Mountains will overturn and cliffs will fall.
9. There will be plague and bloodshed,
10. torrents of rain, hailstones and burning sulfur.
11. God's greatness and holiness will be revealed.
12. Gog and his allies will fall on the mountains of Israel, and
13. they will fall in the open fields.
14. Their bodies will be food for the birds and animals.
15. Israel will use the weapons (shields, bows and arrows, war clubs and spears) as fuel for seven years.
16. Israel will bury the dead for seven months.

17. After seven months, search parties will go out and find the bones of the dead and mark them for the burial detail.

THE WAR WITH THE NORTH: According to Revelation:

1. Greatest earthquake since the creation of earth will occur along with
2. flashes of lightning, rumblings, and
3. peals of thunder.
4. The city (Jerusalem) will split into three parts, as will the
5. cities of the nations collapse.
6. Every island will disappear.
7. One hundred pound hailstones will fall to earth.

There is a big difference in these two events.

Others thoughts:

Russia's new weapons are said to be made from a new material named lignostone. This material is strong as steel, light, pliable, almost invisible to radar, burns at a very high temperature and can be used as an alternate fuel.

The following scenario is a loose interpretation of Daniel 11:40-45 showing what nations will go against Israel.

"At the time of the end the king of Egypt and the Muslim forces will engage in battle with the False Prophet in Israel; and Gog, leader of Russia, along with his army, will storm out against the False Prophet with chariots, Calvary, and a great fleet of ships. Gog, the Russian leader, will invade many countries and sweep through them like a flood."

"Gog, the Russian leader, will also invade Israel. Many countries will fall, but Edom, Moab, and the leader of the nation Jordan (Ammon) will be delivered from his hand. The Russian leader will extend his power over many of the surrounding countries, and Egypt will not escape."

"He will gain control of the treasures of gold and silver and all the riches of Egypt, with Libya, Tunisia, Algeria, Morocco, and Mauritania and put the Black Africans in submission. But reports from the Asians led by the Chinese and the west led by the Romans will alarm Gog, the Russian leader, and he will set out in a great rage to destroy and annihilate many. Gog will establish the Russian headquarters between the Mediterranean and Dead Seas of the Temple Mount. Yet Gog, the Russian Leader, will come to his end and no one will help him."

Napoleon is quoted as saying, "China is a sleeping giant and God pity the generation that wakes her up." It could be that America has awakened this giant. This was said about the United States as Japan sped her way to attack us. We were a giant then, but now? Our greatness has diminished because we have chosen to leave God out of our lives.

This great force will have 200 million troops. The breastplates of these troops and their horses will be fiery red, dark blue, and sulfur yellow. Some think it is possible that these horses are machines rather that horses. It is estimated that China has over 300 million armed and organized personnel.

The heads of these horses will resemble lion's heads and out of their mouths will come fire, smoke, and sulfur. These could possibly be projectiles or missiles.

The flag of China is red and yellow and many of China's army wears dark blue uniforms. China is commonly called the "yellow peril." A favorite Chinese symbol is fire-breathing dragons with large heads.

Ever since the fall of Satan, there has been war in heaven. Satan's domain has been heaven and earth. The Bible describes him as the God of this world and the prince of the power of the air.

Ezekiel 38:8, 16 tells us Russia will invade Israel in the "latter years." The latter years of Israel's history will not begin until right before or after the rapture of the church.

According to some, Russia will invade Israel,

1. At the end of this age, before the church is raptured?
2. At the beginning of the tribulation period?
3. At the beginning of the millennium?
4. In the middle of the tribulation period?

When will the rapture occur?
When will the "church" be removed?

The following years are a reference only. They are not a prediction of when these events will occur. No one knows except God.

Revelation 2:10 states that mankind will suffer persecution ten days (a day equals a year in accordance with Daniel's prophesy of seventy weeks, which meant seventy years).

2022—The Antichrist will make his appearance. He will come on the scene as a man with intelligence, charisma and seemly the ability to solve problems.

He will become prominent in the European Economy, working up in rank. The rapture could occur here.

2025—The Antichrist will become the Leader of the European Economy. His first act will be to sign a peace treaty with Israel, guaranteeing them peace and help in rebuilding the Temple.

Russia and her allies will invade Israel.

Judgments began to fall.

2028—Mid-Tribulation—Satan will enter heaven and make war with Michael the Archangel. Michael prevails. Satan and his followers are cast to earth. Satan will turn his rage against Israel. He will enter the temple and declare himself god.

The false prophet will make his appearance.

2031—The Second Coming.

Another scenario would be:

2022—Israel will have driven the Palestinians out of their country, especially the Gaza Strip or there is a real peace treaty drawn up between Palestine and Israel.

Israel is no longer at war, but at last they are a peaceful nation.

2024—Russia will attack Israel.

2025—The Antichrist will become the leader of the European Economy. His first act will be to sign a peace treaty Israel, guaranteeing them peace and help in rebuilding the Temple.

Judgments began to fall.

2028—Mid-Tribulation—Satan will enter heaven and make war with Michael the Archangel. Michael prevails. Satan and his followers are cast to earth. Satan will turn his rage against Israel. He will enter the temple and declare himself god.

The false prophet will make his appearance.

2031—The Second Coming.

INTRODUCTION

RONALD M. BARKER

APOKALYPSIS "*Revelation or discovery of what was concealed or hidden.*"

It is here said that this revelation, or discovery of hidden things, was given by God to Jesus Christ, then Christ gave it to His angel, (Gabriel), who showed it to John and John then sent it to the Churches.

In Revelation the Lamb is the center around which all else is gathered.

Revelation is a book of prophecy and a book of sevens:

> 1:12-20—Candlesticks, stars, angels, spirits.
> 4:1—Seals, trumpets.
> 4:5—Lamps.
> 5:6—Horns, eyes.
> 10:3, 4—Thunders.
> 12:1—Red Dragon with seven heads and seven crowns.
> 13:1—Leopard like beast with seven heads.
> 15, 16—Vials.
> 17:3, 7—A scarlet colored beast with seven heads.
> 17:10—Seven kings.

Jericho fell after seven priests, with seven trumpets, for seven days, marched around its walls and blew their trumpets seven times. It was on the seventh day that Naaman dipped in Jordan River seven times.

SEVEN BEATITUDES OF REVELATION

> 1- 1:3—Blessed is he that reads this prophecy.
> 2- 14:13—Blessed are the dead who die in the Lord.
> 3- 16:15—Blessed is he that watches for the Lord's coming.
> 4- 19:9—Blessed are those invited to the Lamb's Marriage Supper.
> 5- 20:6—Blessed is he that has part in the first resurrection.
> 6- 22:7—Blessed is he that keeps the words of this book.

7- 22:14—Blessed are they that wash their robes.

Some say we are now living between Revelation 3:7 and 3:20.

The Bible begins with seven days of creation and ends with a book of sevens about the ultimate destiny of creation. There are seven days in a week, seven notes in music and seven colors in the rainbow.

There are four sets of sevens that cover a very large section of the book:

(1) Seven messages to seven churches.
(2) Vision of seven seals.
(3) Vision of seven trumpets.
(4) Vision of seven vials.

The half of seven is used in the Old Testament to signify a time of tribulation.

Three is the numerical signature of God:

1. In Genesis, Abraham refers to the three angels as the judges of the earth.
2. God instituted three holy feasts during Moses' day and commanded him to build His altar three cubits high.
3. Three days were required after touching a dead body before one could begin the ritual of cleansing and purification.
4. Jesus was in the grave three days and three nights.

Numbers that are multiples or divisions of three were also signified in Jewish symbolism:

1. Solomon used three thousand, three hundred chief officers in building God's temple.
2. The temple was thirty cubits high, divided into three stories, built on three rows of pillars with a hall thirty cubits in circumference, that was supported by twelve bronze oxen, three facing north, three facing south, three facing west, three facing east, and held three thousand measures of water.

3. Zechariah paid thirty pieces of silver for a flock of sheep that was to be slaughtered. This was symbolic of Israel rejecting (betraying) God and the annulment of God's covenant with them.
4. Judas was paid thirty pieces of silver when he betrayed (rejected) Jesus as the Messiah.

Four is the numerical signature of nature or creation. Earth has four seasons, four corners and there are four winds.

Seven is the sacred number in scripture, while twelve is the number of the Covenant People. God dwells in the midst of His Covenant People, because He has a Covenant relationship with them.

SYMBOLISM OF THE NUMBER 7:

1. Nebuchadnezzar was insane for seven years.
2. There are seven petitions in the Lord's Prayer.
3. There are seven parables in Matthew 13.
4. There were seven loaves of bread fed to the multitude.
5. Jesus spoke seven times from the cross, and in Revelation
6. there are seven seals,
7. seven trumpets,
8. and seven bowls.

SYMBOLISM OF THE NUMBER 10:

1. Represents absolute perfection and development.
2. It is the number of the Ten Commandments.
3. Ten times ten or 100 represents God's flock.
4. Ten is also the number of worldly completion symbolizing perfect power.
5. The ten plagues of Egypt symbolized the complete pouring out of God's divine wrath.
6. Daniel 7:7, 24 tells us of the fourth beast who had ten horns.
7. The Red Dragon of the Apocalypse has ten horns, (Rev. 12:3),

8. as well as the First Beast or Antichrist (Rev. 13:1).

SYMBOLISM OF THE NUMBER 12:

1. Refers to the Kingdom of God.
2. Three, the signature of God, multiplied by four, is the signature of the world.
3. Twelve is the number of the Patriarchs,
4. the number of the Apostles, and
5. the tribes of Israel.
6. There were two times twelve courses of the priests,
7. four times twelve cities of the Levites, and
8. two times twelve is the number of the Elders.
9. The woman of Revelation 12:1 had a crown of twelve stars on her head, the New Jerusalem has twelve gates (21:14),
10. and the Tree of Life bears twelve different kinds of fruit (22:2).

SYMBOLISM OF THE NUMBER 40:

1. Forty was a mystical number to the Jews.
2. In Egypt when a person was embalmed, they were to be mourned forty days.
3. It rained forty days while Noah was in the Ark.
4. Moses waited forty days on Mt. Sinai for God to give him the commandments.
5. The Jews wandered in the wilderness forty years as punishment for rejecting the Promised Land.
6. The maximum number of lashings given out as punishment was forty.
7. Elijah fasted forty days before God revealed Himself.
8. Israel suffered under the Philistines forty years before they occupied the Promised Land.
9. King David reigned forty years over Israel.
10. Goliath persecuted Israel forty days before David killed him.
11. Jesus fasted forty days.

12. The Christian Jews mourned the death of their rejected Messiah forty years.

SYMBOLISM OF COLORS:

1. White symbolizes the color of innocence, purity, and righteousness, as well as spiritual age, maturity, and perfection.
2. Black denotes famine, distress, and suffering.
3. Blood red represents war, murder, and sacrificial death,
4. purple is the color of Royalty or voluptuous ease,
5. and pale yellow is the color of expiring life, and the kingdom of the dead (6:8).

These are only few of the symbolisms.

In Revelation we find there are 13 references to Genesis, 27 to Exodus, 79 to Isaiah, and 53 to Daniel.

There are twenty-seven different references to the activity of angels.

Listed below are some comparisons between Genesis and Revelation.

Gen. 1:10—*"And the gathering of the waters he called the sea."*
Rev. 21:1—*"And there was no more sea."*

Gen. 1:27,28—Describes the first Adam with his wife in the Garden of Eden.
Rev. 21:9—Describes the last Adam with his wife, the Church, in the City of God, reigning over the entire universe.

Gen. 1:5, 16—God creates the sun and moon, the day and night.
Rev. 22:5—*"There shall be no night there."* (21:23) *"And the city has no need of the sun, neither of the moon, to shine in it: for the glory of God did lighten it, and the Lamb is the light thereof."*

Gen. 3:22—The tree of life is denied to sinful man.

Rev. 22:2—*"yielded her fruit every month: and the leaves of the tree were for the healing of the nations."*

Gen. 3:17—God says, *"Cursed is the ground because of you."*
Rev. 22:3—Man will hear God say, *"And there shall be no more curse."*

Gen. 3:1—Satan appears to torment man for a while.
Rev. 20:10—Satan disappears, himself to be tormented forever.

Gen. 7:12—The old earth was punished through a flood.
Rev. 21:1—The new earth will be purified with fire.

Gen. 2:10—Man's early home was by a river.
Rev. 22:1—Man's eternal home will be by a river: *"And he showed me a pure river of water of life, clear as crystal, proceeding out of the throne of God and of the Lamb."*

Gen. 23:2—The Patriarch Abraham goes to weep for Sarah.
Rev. 21:4—The children of Abraham will have God himself wipe away all tears from their eyes.

Gen. 19—God destroys an earthly city.
Rev. 21:1—God presents a heavenly city, New Jerusalem, from the skies.

Gen. 50:1—Ends with a believer in Egypt, lying in a coffin.
Rev. 21:4—Ends with all believers in eternity, reigning forever.

The two beasts of Chapter 13, with their ten horns, which are ten kings, derive directly from the beast visions of Dan. 7, 8. The vision of the two olive trees and two candlesticks (chap. 11), is a reframing of a vision of Zechariah (Zech. 3-4). The time periods in the book of Revelation derive from Daniel, as time, times, and half a time (12:14), from Dan 12:7.

The word "rapture" is not found in the Bible, but is from "rapere," found in the expression "caught up" in the Latin translation of I Thess. 4:17. The Greek word is 'harpadzo'. We can say accurately that the English word rapture is not in our Bible. But to deny the Bible speaks of the rapture is foolish, just as we would be foolish to say that there are no grandfathers because the word 'grandfather' is not in the Bible. See more in Chpt. three.

EVENTS LEADING TO THE TRIBULATION PERIOD

1. The Jews will return to their land in unbelief (Isaiah 43:5-7).
2. The Rapture.
3. Russia with her allies will attack Israel and are defeated by God.

THE FIRST 3 ½ YEARS

1. The Antichrist will make his appearance (II Thess. 2:3). (The White Horse).
2. Israel will enter into a Covenant with Antichrist (Dan. 9:27).
3. The Temple will be rebuilt (Rev. 11:1, 2).
4. Testimony of the two witnesses (Rev. 11:3).
5. Sealing of the 144,000 Jews.

THE SECOND 3 ½ YEARS

1. Antichrist is revealed in his true character (Dan. 9:27).
2. The Red, Black and Pale horses make their appearance.
3. Antichrist kills the two witnesses (Rev. 11:7).
4. He stops the daily sacrifices (Dan. 9:27; 11:31; 12:11).
5. His image is set up for worship (Matt. 24:25; II Thess. 2:4; Rev. 13:14).
6. The Devil is cast to earth (Rev. 12:7-12).
7. Jerusalem is trodden down (Dan. 9:26; Rev. 11:2).
8. The judgments of the Tribulation (Jer. 30:7; Dan. 12:1; Matt. 24:21; Rev. 13:14, 17). The seals, trumpets and vials of Rev. 6-16.
9. Death for defiance of Antichrist (Rev. 13:116-17).
10. Armageddon (Rev. 16:14-1 17:14; Zech. 14:1-5).

Some think the seventieth week of Dan. 9:27 was accomplished when Christ died on the cross and 31/2 years later the church had taken hold with the Gentiles and Jews sharing the Word of Salvation. It should be noted that in the middle of the week when Christ gave His life for others, sacrifice and grain offerings did not cease.

EVENTS WHICH CONCLUDE AND IMMEDIATELY FOLLOW THE TRIBULATION.

1. Christ and His Glorified Saints return (Jude 14; Rev. 1:7; 19:11-16; II Thess. 1:7).
2. Israel delivered (Rev. 17:14; Zech. 12:9).
3. Beast and false prophet destroyed (Rev. 13:16, 17).
4. Satan bound (Rev. 20:2, 3).
5. Tribulation martyrs raised (Rev. 20:4).

CLIMAXED BY THE SECOND COMING OF CHRIST

1. God saves His own from divine wrath. In Jos. 6:25, He saved Rahab out of Jericho before the city was destroyed.
2. Lot was removed from Sodom before God's wrath was poured out on that city (Gen. 9:14-24).
3. Gen. 5:24 shows that Enoch was translated before the judgment of the flood.

John, unlike his fellow apostles Paul and Peter, escaped martyrdom under Nero's reign. Nero persecuted multitudes of Christians by throwing them to wild beasts or wrapped them in combustible clothing and burned them to death while he laughed at their pitiful cries.

Domitian came to power around 95 for a short but extremely cruel reign. During his reign, over 40,000 Christians were either tortured or slain. It was during his reign that John was exiled to Patmos.

CHAPTER 1

THE THINGS WHICH YOU HAVE SEEN

Genesis, the first book in the Bible is a book of beginnings. Revelation, the last book in the Bible, is a book of consummation. From Genesis, the beginning of mankind, and from the first sin by mankind, God has provided the Plan of Salvation. From Genesis through Revelation God provides us with a picture of man's failures and successes.

The message about the sovereignty of God is found in the book of Revelation. Our future is in the hands of God and throughout the Bible God reveals to us those things that will help us, but He conceals things that we do not need to know or cannot understand. God knows that we humans have our limitations and if God revealed to us the full picture of supernatural realities, we would be overwhelmed, and in our unglorified bodies could not comprehend what we saw.

V1-2-The revelation of Jesus Christ, which God gave Him, to show his servants things what soon must take place. He made it known by sending his angel to his servant John, (2) who testifies to everything he saw—that is, the word of God and the testimony of Jesus Christ.

The gospels unveiled Christ at His first coming in humiliation, and in Revelation He is revealed in His exaltation: (1) In blazing glory, vv7-20 (2) Over His church as Lord, chpts. 2, 3 (3) In His second coming, as He takes back the earth from Satan, and establishes His kingdom, chpts. 4-20 (4) He lights up the eternal state, chpts. 21-22.

This book is a revelation of Jesus Christ, which was revealed to Him by God. Jesus then revealed it to an angel who in return told John the Apostle. John then proceeds to write what he is instructed to write. Angelic revelation is one of the features marking Revelation as an apocalyptic work like Daniel and Ezekiel. John testifies to everything he sees.

There are some who say from God to Jesus to John. Most scholars I have read do not agree. In chapter 22 verse 16, Jesus says He sent His angel to testify to John.

Revelation explains in a deeper degree Jesus' discourse of things to come (Matt. 24, Mark 13, and Luke 21).

It was during Nero's reign that many of the apostles were martyred, but God who had other plans for John, let him escaped martyrdom. Nero persecuted a great multitude of Christians by wrapping them in combustible garments and burned them to death while he watched, or threw them to wild beasts.

In about 95, Domitian came to power. His term was short lived but his ruler-ship was extremely cruel. During his reign over 40,000 Christians were either tortured or slain. It was during his reign that John was exiled to Patmos.

There are some who have different thoughts about the author of Revelation:

1. It is unlikely that he was an apostle.
2. In 250, Dionysius, a great scholar who was the head of the Christian School at Alexandria, thought it was impossible that the author of the Fourth Gospel could be the same as the author of Revelation.
3. He was John the Elder.
4. The book was written in the 70's, during Nero's reign.

(3) Blessed is the one who reads the words of this prophecy, and blessed are those who hear it and take to heart what is written in it, because the time is near.

In ancient days, all reading was done out loud.

This "blessed" is the first of 7 beatitudes in Revelation. It means more than "happy." It describes the favorable circumstances God has put a person in.

Revelation is the only book in the Bible, which begins by promising a special blessing on those who read or study it (Rev. 1:3), and ends by promising a special curse on those who add or take away from it (Rev. 22:18-20). We know God's Word is being fulfilled and one day all of it will be fulfilled, maybe in our lifetime.

(4) John, to the seven churches in the providence of Asia: Grace and peace to you from him who is, and who was, and who is to come, and from the seven spirits before his throne,

It is interesting that Paul also wrote epistles to seven churches; Rome, Corinth, Galatia, Ephesus, Philippi, Colosse, and Thessalonica.

John was the sole survivor and representative of the apostles and eye witnesses of the Lord, therefore he needed no other identification except his name in order to be recognized by his readers.

Asia, modern Turkey, was a Roman Province on the western part of what is known as Asia Minor. Ephesus was its chief city, and Pergamum was its political capital.

The apostle, like the Jewish prophets, named himself in the messages that he receive from God to deliver to the seven churches in Asia.

The seven churches were located about 50 miles apart from each other, forming a circle in Asia and they were:

1. *Ephesus*—loveless church-no longer loved Christ as they once did.
2. *Smyrna*—persecuted church—no reproach—Bishop was Polycarp. Modern Ismir.
3. *Pergamum—(Pergamos)*—worldly church—called Satan's throne—offered incense to statue of Emperor. Now a mere tomb of its former greatness.
4. *Thyatira*—Paganized church—tolerated false prophetess referred to as Jezebel—Modern city of Akhisar.
5. *Sardis*—Lifeless church—had a name for spiritual life, Christ judged it spiritually dead. Destroyed by an earthquake and rebuilt. Now known as Sardo or Sart.

6. *Philadelphia*—Missionary church—no reproach—Their vigorous Missionary activities won many Jews of the city—Still a flourishing city.
7. *Laodicea*—Lukewarm church—Christ was on the outside asking to be let in to one of His own churches—Now deserted and uninhabited.

It is possible that John personally knew these local churches, and it is very probable that they were under his pastoral care at one time. The letters were admonitory, not just to these seven churches, but to all churches for all time. They were personal letters to those who had an ear to hear and would overcome. They were prophetic letters, disclosing seven phases of the spiritual history and condition of the church.

Grace is the Greek method of greeting; peace is the Hebrew form of greeting. Grace and peace are not our prerogative. Our possession of grace and peace is determined by our relationship with God.

There are some who think that the "seven spirits" could be: (1) a reference to Isaiah's prophecy, Isa. 11:2, concerning the seven-fold ministry of the Holy Spirit (2) a reference to the lampstands with 7 lamps (a menorah) in Zech. 4:1-10 (3) The seven angels before God's throne.

The seven spirits in Isaiah 11:2 are: (1) The Spirit of the Lord (2) The Spirit of wisdom (3) The Spirit of understanding (4)The Spirit of counsel (5) The Spirit of might (6) The Spirit of knowledge and (7) The Spirit of the fear of the Lord.

In Tobit 17:15 we find, "I am Raphael, one of the seven holy angels which present the prayers of the saints, and which go in and out before the glory of the Holy One."

Jonathan ben Uzziel's Targum on Gen. 11:7; "God said to the seven angels which stand before Him."

(5) and from Jesus Christ, who is the faithful witness, the firstborn from the dead, and the ruler of the kings of the earth. To him who loves us and has freed us from our sins by his blood,

This description of Jesus gives Him three titles:

1. The faithful witness.
2. The firstborn from the dead (He was faithful until death). The word used for firstborn does not mean the firstborn in sequence, but the first in preeminence.
3. The ruler of the kings of the earth.

Christ is the first one ever to have been resurrected in His glorified body. His resurrection guarantees us our ultimate resurrection, for we who believe will one day receive a glorified body.

Elijah, Elisha and Jesus raised people from the dead. These people however, died natural deaths later. They were not raised in a *"glorified body."*

Throughout our lives, in school or in life, we have found that there have been many great teachers. This will always be. These gifted people not only will enlighten us but they will challenge us to reach our potentials. Christ is called Rabbi (teacher), for He is the true teacher, His words are infallible and all His sayings will come to pass.

The statement He *"freed us from our sins,"* shows the attributes of Christ's shed blood on the cross for the redemption of one's soul, the remission and the purification from sin.

(6) and has made us to be a kingdom and priests, to serve his God and Father—to him be glory and power forever and ever! Amen.

Exodus 19:6, *"you will be for me a kingdom of priests and a holy nation. These are the words you are to speak to the Israelites."* Peter (I Peter 2:5, 9) quotes Exodus 19:6, which says that Christ made us to be a kingdom of priests. I Peter 2:5, 9, *"you also, like living stones, are being built into a spiritual house to be a holy priesthood, offering spiritual sacrifices acceptable to God through Jesus Christ' 'But you are a chosen people, a royal priesthood, a holy nation, a people belonging to God, that you may declare the praises of him who called you out of darkness into his wonderful light."*

God, through Christ, made for Himself a people who are to serve Him and obey His will. These obedient people are the church believers, His kingdom on earth waiting for the day of fulfillment.

Those who belong to God's kingdom have reached the highest position they can obtain here on earth and this is the position of priest.

We belong to God and are to glorify Him, for He alone deserves our glory. To God be the power, for He alone is omnipotent.

(7) Look, he is coming with the clouds, and every eye will see him, even those who pierced him, and all the peoples of the earth will mourn because of him. So shall it be! Amen.

During the incarnation, Christ's glory was veiled. John, James and Peter were the only ones who caught a glimpse of it at the transfiguration (Matt. 17:2). But at His second coming everyone will see Him, even those who nailed Him to the Cross. This indicates that those in hell (Hades) will see the events on earth play out. Those who nailed Him to the cross are dead, but they will see Him come back to earth. He shall return in the clouds, just as He went. It was thought impossible until now for everyone to see Him. Now we have satellites in orbit that can transmit from every corner of the globe to the television dish and cable receivers, which in return can transmit these events to our televisions.

Even without our modern means to telecommunicate, God could make everyone see His return. It is possible that we will all see Him in the air without the aid of television.

Jesus Himself said to Caiaphas, the high priest, recorded by Matthew in chapter 26:64; *"But I say to all of you: In the future you will see the Son of man sitting on the right hand of the Mighty One and coming on the clouds of heaven."* Caiaphas is now dead and, unless he had repented, according to Jesus' word, could be spending eternity in torment, and looking up to heaven sees Jesus, the one he rejected, sitting at the right hand of God.

There will be some people in hell that will mourn because they rejected Him, but it will be too late. Their rejection of Jesus has sealed their fate.

Dispensationalists teach that there will be a rapture of the church that will be in secret seven years before His appearing. This event (His appearing) is what they call the second phase of the second coming.

The first phase, the "rapture," is the catching up of all living believers and the raising up the bodies of those already dead and giving them glorified bodies.

Historical Premillennialists place the one return of Christ at the end of the Tribulation. They believe the church will endure the Tribulation.

Amillennialists and postmillennialists do not believe there will be a Tribulation preceding Christ's return, nor a literal millennium kingdom after it.

Postmillennialists teach that the church will grow progressively better in the present age until the end time when all will be saved. There is only one problem with this, I Tim. 4:1-4 says, *"The Spirit clearly says that in the later times some will abandon the faith and follow deceiving spirits and things taught by demons. Such teachings come through hypocritical liars, whose consciences have been seared as with a hot iron. They forbid people to marry and order them to abstain from certain foods, which God created to be received with thanksgiving by those who believe and who know the truth. For everything God created is good, and nothing is to be rejected if it is received with thanksgiving . . ."*

There are some who believe that when a person dies they go into a deep sleep.

If one is in a deep sleep, then how can they see Christ coming with the clouds? Christ told the thief in Luke 23:43, *"Jesus answered him, "I tell you the truth, today you will be with me in paradise."* Jesus told the thief that he would die that day and would be in paradise that very same day. No deep sleep, but immediate translation to paradise.

The question is asked, "Where is Paradise?" Christ, according to Scripture, after His death on the cross, descended into Hades, Ps. 16:8-11; Acts 2:24-27; Eph. 4:8-10; I Pet. 3:18-20, proclaiming His triumph over death and brought out those who were abiding in Paradise to His heavenly realm. Luke 23:42-43.

Hades was compromised of two parts, Paradise and Torments. Those who died believing in God went to Paradise, a place of peace and contentment. Those who rejected God went to Torments. The two were separated by a great chasm.

It was to Paradise that Christ took the repentive thief on the cross. He led "captivity captive." Those in Paradise were taken out and transported to the "Sea of Glass" directly beneath the throne of God (Rev. 4:6).

The now empty Paradise will be overtaken by the torments side, for hell continues to enlarge itself (Is. 5:14).

(8) "I am the Alpha and the Omega," says the Lord God, "who is and who was, and who is to come, the Almighty."

Alpha—Greek aleph—Omega—Greek tau. We take letters out of the alphabet and make words. Jesus is the Alpha and Omega. He is the A and Z, and all the letters in between. Jesus is the Word of God. He is living now. He was living in the beginning, and He is coming to earth again.

We find that nine of the ten occurrences of "Almighty" found in the NT are in Revelation: 1:8; 4:8; 11:17; 15:3; 16:7, 14; 19:6, 15; 21:22. The tenth occurrence is in 2 Cor. 6:18.

(9) I, John, your brother and companion in the suffering and kingdom and patient endurance that are ours in Jesus, was on the island of Patmos because of the word of God and the testimony of Jesus.

Jerome in his book, "Lives of Illustrious Men," wrote about John's banishment. "In the fourteenth year after Nero, Domitian raised a second persecution and John was banished to the Island of Patmos, where he wrote the Apocalypse (Revelation)."

John was banished to the Isle of Patmos (according to history from 95 to 96 AD during the final reign of Domitian's rule), for preaching the word of God, and for testifying of Jesus. Patmos is a rugged, volcanic island off the coast of Asia Minor (Turkey). The whole island is about 30 miles in circumference, lying in the Agean Sea. It is about 10 miles long and six miles wide. During the New Testament times, the island had a large administrative center, with at least three pagan temples (one each for Artemis, Apollo and Aphrodite), and also had a hippodrome for horse racing. It was governed by the proconsul of Ephesus. Here John worked in the mines suffering persecution and many hardships, but he still glorified Jesus.

Domitian had a brother named Titus whom he murdered. This was the same Titus who destroyed Jerusalem.

God used Domitian, Satan's servant, to persecute John and put him on Patmos so he could receive Revelation. Thus God allowed one man (Titus) to destroy His earthly city, and would use his brother (Domitian) to allow the heavenly New Jerusalem to first be described by man (John). God allows His servants to be persecuted so that they will be more receptive to His divine will.

Domitian, because of his excessive cruelty was executed. The Senate, after Domitian's execution annulled his acts, thus allowing John to return to Ephesus under the rein of Nerva and continue there until the time of the Emperor Trajan. John founded and built churches throughout Asia, and finally his body worn out by old age, died in the sixty eight year after our Lord's passion and was buried near the same city, ca 98.

Clement of Alexandria and Irenaeus affirm John's return from Patmos along with Eusebuis who not only affirms John's return from Patmos, but also dates his return immediately following the death of Domitian, which occurred in 96.

Victorinus, who wrote the first known commentary on Revelation, also said John worked as a prisoner in the mines of Patmos.

(10) On the Lord's Day I was in the Spirit, and I heard behind me a loud voice like a trumpet,

9

John, on the first day of the week Sunday, was supernaturally carried away in the spirit, when suddenly and unexpectedly he heard a loud voice that caught his undivided attention.

The first day of the week, is observed as the Christian Sabbath, because it was on Sunday that Jesus Christ arose from the dead, therefore it was called the Lord's Day.

After the resurrection of Christ, Christians began to celebrate communion on Sunday. It was a day of worship. There are those who still claim Saturday is the Sabbath and they claim that all of those who do not worship on Saturday are heathens and are doomed to eternal damnation. Does this mean that the Apostles were lost? I think not!! They were the ones who first instituted worshipping on Sunday. They were filled with the Holy Spirit and inspired by God.

In fact the two most important days initiating the birth of our Christian faith, the resurrection and the coming of the Holy Spirit at Pentecost, both occurred by God's providence on Sunday, not on the Saturday Sabbath!

The early writer Chrysostom wrote a commentary on Psalm 119 declaring that Sunday "was called the Lord's Day because the Lord rose from the dead on that day."

Justin Martyr, in his "Apology" says, "On Sunday we all hold our joint meetings; for the first day is that on which God, having removed darkness and chaos, made the world, and Jesus Christ our Savior rose from the dead. On the day before Saturday they crucified him, and on the day after Saturday which is Sunday, having appeared to his apostles and disciples, he taught these things."

It is interesting to note that Jews, who became Christians, worshiped on Saturday and then joined their Christians brothers in worshiping on Sunday. The commandment to worship on Saturday was given to Israel, and not to the Gentiles. Therefore we (those who are non Jewish) were not commanded to worship on Saturday. We were given direction from the Apostles and early Christians, to worship on Sunday.

We should keep in mind Romans 14 and Colossians 2, which show that we go to the Lord's House on what we call "the Lord's Day" as a testimony that we believe Jesus Christ rose bodily from the dead on the first day of the week.

I stated earlier that one thing we might consider is that the command to worship on Saturday was given to the Israelites only. This command was never given to the Gentiles, as most of us are. Those who would become proselytes (Gentiles accepting the God of the Israelites) also had to obey the law God had given to the Israelites. Basically, we Christians should worship God every day, but we set aside Sunday as a day of fellowship and worship.

(11) which said: "Write on a scroll what you see and send it to the seven churches: to Ephesus, Smyrna, Pergamum, Thyatira, Sardis, Philadelphia and Laodicea."

In Revelation John is commanded twelve times to write. He wrote on scrolls which were pieces of papyrus or vellum up to thirty feet long, rolled up and sealed with clay or wax. This is reminiscence of the tablets containing the Ten Commandments (written of both sides). The fibers of a papyrus run horizontally on the inside, which makes writing easier than on the reverse side, where the lines run vertically. He is instructed to carefully write down everything that is presented to him and he describes these heavenly visions in his own language and manner. Books, as we know them, did not come into being until about the second century AD.

In scripture, we find three ministries of Christ; His intercession, His intervention, and His inspection.

The Holy Spirit is made up of three personalities, ministering, convicting and restraining. The ministering spirit reveals God and the convicting spirit convicts us of our sins. The restraining spirit restrains evil.

As long as the Church Age remains on earth, the Holy Spirit will remain on earth, however, when the Church is caught up to meet Jesus in the air, the Holy Spirit will go with the Church (I Thess. 2:7). The Holy Spirit does not cease His convicting ministry when the church is removed, but

His restraining ministry ceases. I Cor. 6:19 states that our bodies house the Holy Spirit. When we accept Christ as our savior the Holy Spirit abides in us.

(12) I turned around to see the voice that was speaking to me. And when I turned I saw seven golden lampstands,

1. *Seven Candlesticks (lampstands)*—The seven Churches.
2. *Seven Stars*—The seven angels (pastors) of the Churches.
3. *The Seven Churches—(candlestick, not the light, but the bearer of the light.)*

The Seven candlesticks represented the seven churches, in which the light of God was continually shining and the love of God continually burning. Christ is continually present and His activity among His people on earth is ceaseless.

These seven churches, some believe, represent the seven basic divisions of church history.

(13A) and among the lampstands was someone "like a son of man"

John says this was one *"like a son of man."* Daniel 7:13 says, *"one like a son of man came up to the 'Ancient of Days,' (God) and was given an everlasting dominion where everyone would serve Him."* This would indicate 'like a son of man' was referring to Jesus because Jesus was the Son of God, but in the physical body He was a Son of Man. John was in reverent awe as he described Jesus' clothing as those of a priest and judge, a long robe secured with a golden sash. He is a priest for those who accept Him, and a judge to those who reject Him.

(13B) dressed in a robe reaching down to his feet and with a golden sash around his chest.

This is a description of the High Priest, and even in heaven we find the emblem of both regal and sacerdotal dignity. Jesus clothed in His priestly attire in the garment of priest and judge is reigning in Heaven.

The Son of Man is standing in the middle of the churches. Remove Christ and the church is simply a dead church, void of life.

(14) His head and hair were white like wool, as white as snow, and his eyes were like blazing fire.

The attributes of his hair was not only an emblem of His antiquity and purity, but also was the evidence of His glory. The whiteness or splendor of His head and hair undoubtedly proceeded from the rays of light and glory. His all seeing eyes penetrate to the very depths of our souls.

(15) His feet were like bronze glowing in the furnace, and his voice was like the sound of rushing waters.

Brass is consider the most durable of all metallic substances or compounds and here is an emblem of Jesus' stability and permanence, Ezek. 43:2. Brass in the Word of God stands for judgment, Micah 4:13.

(16) In his right hand he held seven stars, and out of his mouth came a sharp double-edged sword. His face was like the sun shining in all its brilliance.

The stars were afterwards interpreted as representing the seven angels, messengers, or bishops of the seven churches. Their being in the right hand of Christ shows that they're under His special care and are protected by His power.

The sharp two-edged sword was like the Thracian sword. The sword in 6:4; 13:10, 14 was a small sword. The Word of God is living and active and sharper than any two-edged sword and pierces to the depths of our soul and spirit. The sword symbolizes divine judgment.

Jesus is the sun to the Church. His ministers are the stars. We, the ministers of Christ, are reflectors of His light. The Church consists of all born again individual believers, and is a bearer of light in a dark, sinful world. The church is here, like individual believers, to reflect the light of Jesus, who is the light of the world. We, the light of the world are like candles. Each candle will disperse some darkness, but when several candles come together, darkness is dispelled to a greater degree. We are a greater beacon together than when we are by ourselves.

TEN CHARACTERISTICS OF CHRIST ENVISIONED BY JOHN:

(1) "... *one like a Son of man"* indicates that this person was a man like person. The "Son of man" is used of the Messiah in all four gospels and also in Daniel 7:13.

(2) "... *dressed in a robe reaching down to his feet."* This was typical of the long robes the high priests wore as they ministered in the Holy Place in the Temple.

(3) "... *with a golden sash around his chest"* refers to a symbol of strength and authority common in the ancient world. The average man wore a short tunic of loose fitting clothes. Only those in authority wore a girdle or sash.

(4) "*his head and hair were white like wool"* reminds us of the vision of Daniel 7:9—where Christ came up to the "ancient of days," and conveys the thought of antiquity The whiteness represents the righteousness of God, who is from everlasting to everlasting.

(5) "... *His eyes were like blazing fire."* The Greek rendering is literally "His eyes shot fire."

(6) "... *his feet were like bronze."* The bronze represents judgment. The brazen altar of the tabernacle was brass, and where sin was judged.

(7) "... *his voice like the sound of rushing waters."* In the last days all voices will be stilled by the deafening, overpowering voice of the Son of God.

(8) "*in his right hand he held seven stars."* These are the pastors of the churches. Some say they are special assigned angels working for us.

(9) "... *out of his mouth came a sharp double-edged sword."* Ephesians 6 refer to the Word of God as "the sword of the Spirit." Hebrews 4:12 tells us that the Word of God is "sharper than any two edged sword."

(10) "... *his face was like the sun."* This speaks of the divine nature of God. Matthew 17:2 tells us that at the Mount of Transfiguration, Christ "was transfigured before them, and his face did shine as the sun, and his raiment was as white as the light."

(17) When I saw him, I fell at his feet as though dead. Then he placed his right hand on me and said: "Do not be afraid. I am the First and the Last.

The appearance of the Lord in all of His glory had the same effect on Daniel and Ezekiel. The glorious splendor of such majesty was more than the apostle could bear, and he fell down deprived of his senses, but the touch of our Lord's right hand gave him strength and assurance.

"The first and last" speaks of Christ's eternity. He is before all things and after all things are through, He will still be in control.

V18-19—I am the Living One; I was dead, and behold I am alive forever and ever! And I hold the keys of death and Hades. (19) "Write, therefore, what you have seen, what is now and what will take place later.

Jesus says He is the Living One and He gave His life on the cross for mankind, and being raised from the dead, He has conquered death. Jesus is the resurrection and the life and holds the key of authority and power over life, death, and the grave. All Jesus has to do is speak and the dead will appear.

In the Garden of Gethsemane, God sent an angel to strengthen the Lord (Luke 22:43). And after Jesus had conquered death, hell and the grave, the angels appeared both outside and inside His tomb (Matt. 28:2-7, John 20:11-13). When Jesus hung on the cross, there were no angels!

The ancient church, as mentioned earlier, believed that when Jesus died on the cross, He descended into Hades where He unlocked the doors and brought out Abraham and all of God's faithful people who had lived and died in the generations before.

History relates the account of Julian the apostate, a nephew of the Roman Caesar Constantine. Julian was reared in a Christian home. But in his youth he renounced his faith and embraced paganism. When he became Emperor in 361, he sought to blot out Christianity. In the days of his cruel reign, one of his friends said to a humble Christian, "And our Jesus—what is your carpenter of Nazareth doing now?"

The Spirit filled believer quietly replied, "He is building a coffin for your emperor!" In 363, after a reign of only two years, Julian fighting against the Persian army was severely wounded in battle. One of the most famous incidents of history then followed. As they carried the Emperor off the field and as he lay dying, he lifted up his dimming eyes to heaven and, with a bloody gasp, cried out," O Galilean, thou hast conquered at last!"

Jesus also assures John that, *"I hold the keys of death and Hades."* There are five keys mentioned in the New Testament and Jesus carried all of them!

Matt. 16:19 — Keys to the kingdom of Heaven.

Luke 11:52 — Keys of knowledge.

Rev. 1:18 — Keys of death (Hades). Hades was known in Greek originally as the name of the pagan god of the underworld. By the first century it meant "the place of the dead."

Rev. 3:7 — Keys to the throne.

Rev. 9:1; 20:1 — Keys to the bottomless pit (the Abyss).

Jesus has the key to Hades and death for He is the resurrection and life.

(20) The mystery of the seven stars that you saw in my right hand and of the seven golden lampstands is this: The seven stars are the angels of the seven churches, and the seven lampstands are the seven churches.

The seven churches are represented by the seven lampstands and the seven churches' angels (pastors, elders) are called stars.

CHAPTER 2

THE THINGS WHICH ARE.
EPHESUS-LOVELESS CHURCH.
THE APOSTOLIC CHURCH, A.D. 30-100

(1A) "To the angel of the church in Ephesus write:

It has been suggested that Christ addressed the Ephesians first because they were the first church on the postal route. These seven churches represented the spiritual condition of all churches of all time.

Ephesus was known as a "free city," a title conferred upon cities because of their services to Rome. These "free cities" were allowed to self govern themselves and were exempt from having Roman soldiers garrisoned in their city.

Ephesus also known as the "Vanity Fair of Asia," was a city of Ionia located in the western part of Asia Minor, directly south of the Black Sea, and was a city for all classes of people, a home for the rich, poor, cultured, and the uncultured. It was the central gathering place for false religious superstition cults and was located at the mouth of the Cayster River, on the shore of the Agean Sea, about fifty miles south of Smyrna. Ephesus was a metropolis and commercial city with an excellent harbor and a large banking center, and had a population of about 225,000.

Its Temple of Diana was one of the Seven Wonders of the World. It was 418 feet by 240 feet, and had over 100 external columns about 56 feet tall of which 36 were hand carved. It was built over a marsh on an artificial foundation of skins and charcoal so that earthquakes would not affect it. The doors were of cypress wood, the columns and walls were of Parian marble, and the staircase was carved out of one vine from Cyprus. The temple served as the bank of Asia and was the depository of vast sums of money. It housed an art gallery, which held their masterpieces of art.

Behind a purple curtain was the lewd and crude image of Diana, the goddess of fertility. She had many breasts and carried a club in one hand and a trident in the other.

The impact of the gospel on Ephesus was so great that four great pillars were placed at the entrance to the harbor, and upon them was the emblem of the cross. One monument each was dedicated to Matthew, Mark, Luke and John. Only one pillar stands there today, still bearing the symbol of the cross. Legend has it that John buried Mary (the mother of Jesus) there.

The Basilica of St. John, which is located on Ephesus' highest point, is built over the traditional burial spot of the apostle John.

Ephesus was also the home of Aquilla and Priscilla, who were dedicated Christians, and who had labored for a long time in this city of idolatry.

Of the seven churches mentioned in chapters 2 and 3, this is the only one where reference is made to the apostles. This would bear out the thought that the message of Christ to the church at Ephesus was directed not only to one local church, but also to the church of the first century, usually called "the early church" or the "apostolic church." This covered the period of the time from the day of Pentecost around 30 to 100.

Ephesus is considered by Bible scholars to have been one of the finest and largest churches of New Testament times. The apostle Paul started the church at Ephesus on his second missionary journey, and lived there for thirty years. Three of Paul's epistles related to Ephesus: Ephesians, I and II Timothy.

Timothy was also involved at Ephesus. Paul ministered at Ephesus, and then after he had left, Timothy became the superintendent of the congregation. Timothy, reportedly, after the death of Paul, spent most of his time here and suffered martyrdom under Domitian. This was the same persecution that sent John to the Isle of Patmos.

The Ephesians were losing their zeal for Christ. They no longer loved Him as they once did. They were warned to repent, or else their

Candlestick would be removed, and sadly, it was. Ephesus first became a small village, and then later it became deserted and remains so today.

Between 1869-1874, Ephesus was excavated by J.T. Wood and by the British Museum in 1904-1905. Among their findings were; A Temple of Diana, the ruins of the Theater in which the great riot was held (Acts 19:29), the remains of a Roman Bath that was constructed of marble, consisting of many rooms, (steam rooms, cold rooms, lounge rooms) giving evidence as to the luxury of the city.

They also found a temple, which contained a statue of Domitian, the Emperor who called himself "God," who had banished John to the Isle of Patmos.

Ephesus' harbor on the eastern shore of the Aegean Sea, by the 300's, had been silted up from the flow of the Cayster River so that today the site is an uninhabited ruin several miles inland.

(1B) These are the words of him who holds the seven stars in his right hand and walks among the seven golden lampstands:

Jesus holds the seven (pastors) in His right hand and walks among the golden lampstands (churches).

The Hebrew word for "angel" notes office, not nature. Angels are messengers or "ministering spirits" to the heirs of salvation. The seven lampstands signify that the church is complete before God, and one day it will be presented to the Lamb without blemish (Eph. 5:26-30).

These angels (pastors) were to relate to their respective congregations what John had written to their church. Some say they were prophets through whom the message was to be delivered to the congregation. As angels in their "holy" form would not communicate with the church, then sound reasoning would deduce that they were indeed pastors who were to read the letter received from John to their congregation.

Scripture does give us reason to believe that each church has its own guardian angel. It could be that John gave the message to the churches' angels who in return inspired the pastor, but this doesn't seem probable.

Commendation

(2) I know your deeds, your hard work and your perseverance. I know that you cannot tolerate wicked men, that you have tested those who claim to be apostles but are not, and have found them false.

These Ephesian Christians labored hard and were patient. Jesus knew the deeds of each of them. There were some who claimed to be apostles, but after being put to the test, they were found to be liars.

To be put to the test was a necessity for correct doctrine and dependable advice, and was widely recognized in the early church.

(3) You have persevered and have endured hardships for my name, and have not grown weary.

To persevere is to patiently endure difficulties without giving up.

For over 40 years since its founding, this church had remained faithful to the Word and Jesus.

Ignatius, who was the bishop of Antioch in the second century, commended Ephesus for its loyalty to the truth that had prevented any false sect from gaining a hearing among its members.

Condemnation

(4) Yet I hold this against you: You have forsaken your first love.

They had not only lost their *"fire"* for God, but through the years their zeal for God had also cooled. They had forgotten the love they had when they were first brought to the knowledge of truth and how through their faith in Jesus Christ, they were found justified. Many today can look back in their lives and remember when they first became Christians and the zeal they had for proclaiming the Gospel, but through the years this had cooled.

Counsel

(5) Remember the height from which you have fallen! Repent and do the things you did at first. If you do not repent, I will come to you and remove your lampstand from its place.

They were told to remember the heights they had obtained before they fell. They were to repent, humble themselves before God and return to the zeal, and love they previously had for spreading the gospel of salvation to mankind.

They were to return to when they were once obedient, had denied themselves, and to the fervor of their prayers when they prayed privately. They were to return to their former zeal and diligence, and if they did not repent, Christ would remove their lampstand, which symbolized their removal from Christ's Church. Their removal symbolized immediate judgment.

When our spiritual love has cooled so does our love for God, and then it is replaced by the love for the things of the world, which results in compromise and spiritual corruption, and this is followed by a departure from the faith and loss of effective spiritual testimony.

(6) But you have this in your favor: You hate the practices of the Nicolaitans, which I also hate.

The Nicolaitans were a sect of the Gnostics. They taught doctrines and followed practices that were impure. Licentiousness was one of their doctrines. It is thought that they were followers of Nicolas of Antioch, who was one of the seven deacons. Tradition has it that Nicolas strayed from his teaching and began to teach that Christian freedom and the insignificance of the physical body permitted believers to engage in sexual immorality and other offenses without consequences. This is not the teaching of the Bible.

The word "Nicolaitans" comes from two Greek words: niko, meaning "to conquer, or overthrow'" and laos, meaning "the people or the laity."

There are those who think that this was the beginning of the priestly order in the church, which even to this day is not only practiced by the Roman Catholic Church but by other denominations as well.

I Peter 5:2,3—Be shepherds of God's flock that is under your care, serving as overseers—not because you must, but because you are willing, as God wants you to be; not greedy for money, but eager to serve; (3) not lording it over those entrusted to you, but being examples to the flock.

God never intended his church to be divided into priests and laity. All Christians are priests. No man has a right to be "Lord over God's heritage."

Ephesus continued and was later the scene of a major church council, but after the first century both the city and the church declined. The immediate area has been uninhabited since the fourteenth century.

Challenge

(7) He who has an ear, let him hear what the Spirit says to the churches. To him who overcomes, I will give the right to eat from the tree of life, which is in the paradise of God."

We all should pay attention to what the Holy Spirit says to the churches.

The Holy Spirit plays several roles, mentioned earlier, including:

1. Revealing God and His purposes.
2. Convicting us of our sins.
3. Restraining evil.

The Spirit of God was at work revealing the future of these churches. Everyone should pay attention (be attuned) to the Spirit's revelation of God's plan for the future and His expectations of His people.

Hear What The Spirit Says was an expression of the Lord Jesus Christ, which appears in many of His parables (e.g. Matt. 13). The implication is that there are three kinds of individuals:

1. Those without ears. Those who are not attuned to the Holy Spirit.
2. Those that are dull of hearing. Not all born again Christians are willing to hear the Spirit of God.
3. Those spiritually minded Christians. Those who are willing to hear what the Spirit says to the churches.

In scripture hearing means two things:

1. Hear what God says. Pay attention!!
2. Put what you hear into practice. Do it!!

Eternal Life For Overcomers

Only "overcomers" will eat the fruit from the tree of life. Who is an overcomer? 1 John 5:4, 5 gives the following answer. *"For everyone born of God overcomes the world. This is the victory that overcomes the world, even our faith. Who is it that overcomes the world? Only he who believes that Jesus is the Son of God."*

We might ask, "How exactly are we to understand the promises to those who overcome?"

There are four prevailing views:

1. *The loss of salvation*—The promises are written to believers to encourage them to overcome or else they will lose their salvation.
2. *The ultimate triumph of faith or the perseverance of the saint's view*—All genuine believers who persevere and overcome the world by living godly and obedient lives. Overcoming equals faith or obedience, which proves a person's genuine salvation.
3. *All believers' view*—All believers become overcomers the instant they put their faith and trust in Jesus and accept Him as their Lord.

4. *The rewards view*—The overcomer's passages are promises of rewards given to believers to encourage them to be faithful by overcoming the trials and temptations of life through their faith in Jesus Christ.

SMYRNA
THE PERSECUTED CHURCH, A.D. 100-312

Smyrna had been a Greek Colony as far back as 1,000 BC. Around 600 BC it was invaded by the Lydeans and destroyed. It lay barren for 400 years and around 200 BC Lysimachus had it rebuilt with streets that were broad, straight, sweeping and beautifully paved. Cicero referred to Smyrna as one of Rome's most faithful and ancient ally.

Now also called Ismir, it is the largest and richest city in Asia Minor. Ismir or Smyrna is situated about 183 miles southwest of Constantinople, on the shore of the Aegean Sea. The city sloping to the sea, housed a large amphitheatre along the sides of the hill, which could seat more than 20,000 people. It was considered then to be the most beautiful city in Asia, and is the traditional birthplace of Homer, the author of "Lliad and the Odyssey."

Early in this period, a translation of the Bible in Syriac, known as the "Peshito Manuscripts," became the official Scriptures of the Eastern Churches, and later translations into Arabic, Persian and Armenian were taken from the Syriac translation.

There is no word of fault, but only loving comfort. Jesus reminded them that He had already suffered what they were about to suffer, and that they too, like Him, would live forever.

Polycarp, a convert and pupil of John, was appointed Bishop of Smyrna by John. In 155 Polycarp was burned at the stake in Samaria because he would not renounce his faith in Christ. Even the Jews carried wood to fuel the fire! The Roman proconsul promised him, "Swear by Caesar and I will release thee. Revile Christ." The serene Polycarp replied as he was led to the stake to be burned, "Eighty and six years have I served him and He never did me wrong: how can I revile my King and my Savior?" As the flames rose around him they offered him freedom if he would reject Christ. He died victoriously with these words on his lips, "I am a Christian." Tradition has it that as the flames raged higher, Polycarp was lifted out of the flames by a pillar of smoke and without being harmed by the flames was taken to Heaven.

The church in Smyrna was a wealthy city, and severely persecuted. Smyrna had little time for Christians. The city itself, founded about three centuries before Christ, was a well-planned accomplishment of Alexander the Great. It was called "the ornament of Asia," because of its beauty and splendor.

Apollonius of Tyana referred to Smyrna as the "crown of porticoes," a circle of beautiful public buildings that ringed the summit of Mount Pagos like a diadem.

Smyrna is still a flourishing city with a population of approximately 200,000 people.

Some champions during this period would include:

1. *Justin Martyr (100-167), early defender of Christianity, died for Christ in Rome.*
2. *Irenaeus (130-200), was a pupil of Polycarp (John's disciple).*
3. *Tertullian (160-220), was the Bishop of Carthage and a defender of Christianity.*
4. *Eusebius (264-340), was the founder of church history. He was the court theologian to Constantine and theological heir to Origen.*

(8) "To the angel of the church in Smyrna write: These are the words of him who is the First and the Last, who died and came to life again.

Jesus is everlasting. All things come from Him, and all things must return to Him.

Smyrna means "myrrh," a substance used for anointing and for anointing a dead body for aromatic purposes. It is said, even though the Christians were experiencing the bitterness of suffering, their faithful testimony was like myrrh or sweet perfume to God.

Commendation

(9) *I know your afflictions and your poverty—yet you are rich! I know the slander of those who say they are Jews and are not, but are a synagogue of Satan.*

He knew their:

1. Afflictions,
2. Poverty, and the
3. Slandering of the Christians by the so called Jews.

True wealth cannot be measured in material terms. Those of us who are under persecution and poverty are rich if we hold fast to our faith in Christ.

These persecuted Christians even though they had lost all of their earthly possessions, still remained rich in their faith and were heirs of the Kingdom of Christ. There were Jews there who professed Judaism. They had a synagogue, and professed to the worship of God, but theirs was a false religion for their god was Satan. There are Gentiles and some Jews who today profess Christianity. They go to church and assemble together, and go through the motions, but in reality they do not know God.

Condemnation

None!

Counsel

(10) *Do not be afraid of what you are about to suffer. I tell you, the devil will put some of you in prison to test you, and you will suffer persecution for ten days. Be faithful, even to the point of death, and I will give you the crown of life.*

God punishes the disobedient, and even those who are faithful often face tests such as persecution and immorality. All believers who are faithful until death are promised a crown of life.

"Be faithful," be firm, hold fast to your faith, confess Christ to the very last of all your trials and tribulations, and you shall have a crown of life.

The crown of life may be contrasted to the other crowns promised to a child of God:

1. The *Crown of Righteousness* for a godly life (II Tim. 4:8).
2. The *Crown of Glory* for faithfulness (I Peter 5:4).
3. The *Crown of Gold,* the evidence of our redemption (Rev. 4:4).
4. The *Crown of Rejoicing* (I Thess. 2:14).
5. The *Incorruptible Crown* (I Cor. 9:25).

When trials and temptations come in my life, and many have, I am reminded of Job. The angels appeared before God to present themselves and Satan also came and stood before God's Holy presence. God asked Satan where he came from and Satan's reply was, *"from roaming through the earth and going back and forth in it."* God began to brag on Job, stating that there was no one on earth like him. Satan told God that the only reason Job was faithful was because He had built a hedge around Job. Satan tells God that if He would remove the hedge, Job would deny Him. God told Satan to go ahead and do what he wanted but he could not kill Job. Satan tried his best, but God's faith in Job proved to be well based. Job did not deny God.

I like to think that all of the trials in life that God allows to befall upon us are His way of showing His faith in us.

There is no power except that which comes from God. God allows Satan to test us so that we may be strengthened.

God, who controls all of the circumstances of life, will not permit Satan to persecute the Smyrna Church for long. Jesus promised that they would have tribulation for only ten days. Ten days of what? Are these literal days? Are they symbolic days? Ten days meaning a limited time? Ten years of Roman persecution?

There are no known historical records that show that the Smyrna Christians endured these days.

Some scholars believe what Jesus predicted in verse 10, *"You shall have tribulation ten days,"* refers to a short time while others believe it referred to the fact that this church age saw these as the ten periods of persecution under Roman emperors.

Nero	54-68 Paul beheaded and Peter crucified.
Domitian	81-96 John exiled. Thousands of believers killed
Trajan	98-117 Ignatius burned at the stake. Simeon, half brother of Jesus, Bishop of Jerusalem, was crucified when he was 120 years old.
Marcus Aurelius	161-180 Justin Martyr beheaded.
Severus	193-211 Had Origen's father, Leonidas, a theologian, killed.
Maximinius (Thracian)	235-238 Commanded that all Christian leaders were to be killed.
Decius	249-251 Determined to exterminate Christians.
Valerian	253-260 Killed Cyprian, Bishop of Carthage.
Aurelian	270-275 Persecuted Christians.
Diocletian	284-305 Searched caves for believers for ten years just to kill them.

Pius who ruled from 137-161, killed Polycarp, John's disciple.

This would make 11 periods. Perhaps Jesus was referring to ten years of tribulation or persecutions. Daniel mentions ten days and if we use the day for a year teachings, then it would mean ten years. If we interpret the ten days as ten years then we could see the rapture occur three years before the start of the Tribulation. This would allow the Antichrist to sign a peace treaty with Israel, and then Russia, as some think, would attack Israel. This would also allow the weapons of war to be burned during seven years (as mentioned in Ezekiel 39:9) and not allow an overflow into the Millennium.

Some thought that the next pope would be the Antichrist, but this hasn't happened.

Diocletian is considered the worst emperor in Rome's history and the greatest antagonist of the Christian faith. He led a violent attempt to destroy the Bible from the face of the earth. It was under the leadership of Diocletian that many Roman cities had public burning of the sacred Scriptures.

During this period of persecution some Christians were covered with tar and set on fire to serve as torches. Some were boiled in oil and burned at the stake, as they were under Nero. One church historian has estimated that during this period, five million Christians were martyred for the testimony of Jesus Christ.

It is believed that Diocletian's own wife and daughter accepted Christ. Imagine how sad it would be if Diocletian never accepted Christ as his Lord and Savior, and in hell he would lift his eyes up to Heaven and see his wife and daughter in Paradise basking in the light and love of the One he persecuted! How sad!

Challenge

(11) He who has an ear, let him hear what the Spirit says to the churches. He who overcomes will not be hurt at all by the second death.

Churches are local bodies of churches (individuals) and each church body determines their individual directions, but all come under the Lordship of Christ. Each church or congregation must be obedient to the Word of the Spirit and the teachings of the Scriptures.

We, who hold fast to God and obey His commandments, will be able to conquer our adversaries, and we will not be separated from God.

The Bible teaches that there are two deaths. The first death is physical, the second eternal (spiritual). If we were born once, we die twice. If we were born twice, we die once.

PERGAMUM-THE WORLDLY CHURCH.
THE INDULGED CHURCH, A.D. 312-606
THE CHURCH OF COMPROMISE

Pergamos-A town of Mysia, the name literally means "citadel," situated on the Caicus River, was the capital of the ancient Greek Kingdom of Pergamos until 133 BC when the last of the Pergamenian kings, Attalus III of the Attalids dynasty, bequeathed his kingdom to Rome. It was famous in those days for its library, which contained, according to Plutarch, 200,000 volumes. The library was later given by Mark Anthony to Cleopatra. It was here that the membranac pergameniac, (Pergamenmian) skins were invented; from which we derive our word "parchment." This parchment or vellum, is made by smoothing and polishing the skin of animals. Pergamum, the capital city of Asia until the close of the first century was built on a conical hill one thousand feet above the surrounding countryside, which created a natural fortress.

Two of the most prominent religious systems of the city were the worship of Bacchus (the god of revelry) and the worship of Asclepius (the god of healing). Symbolized by the serpent, the Caduceus is the symbol of the medical profession today. There were four idolatrous cults, Zeus, Dionysus, Asclepius and Athena at its center. In this city stood one of the ancient wonders of the world, a massive and famous altar to Zeus, the greatest of the Greek gods. It was 120 feet by 112 feet in size. Around the walls ran the great frieze, 400 feet long and 7 feet high, depicting the battle of the gods against the giants who attempted to storm Olympus. Now a small village called Bergama is located below its ruins, showing that a city known for its greatness, is now a mere tomb.

Satan has a kingdom, and Babylon has from the earliest times been considered the capital of this kingdom. When Babylon was destroyed, Satan is said to have moved his capital to Pergamum.

After Diocletian's unsuccessful attack on the church, Constantine succeeded him as emperor of Rome.

Roman history tells us that Constantine contended for the throne with Maxentius after the death of Galerius. Both Roman history and church tradition indicate that Constantine, already attracted by Christianity, allegedly saw a vision of a fiery cross in the sky and heard a voice saying "In this sign conquer!" He decreed that Christianity was the religion of Rome. Professing to be a Christian, he made his army march through the river in order that they may be baptized. He removed the Eagle from the Roman Standard and replaced it with the Cross.

There is a coin in the British Museum in London, stamped during days of Constantine, which depicts the emblems of Christians on one side and on the other side the emblems of heathen gods are depicted.

One thing Constantine was credited with was that he ordered Eusebius, the Bishop of Rome, to supervise the production of fifty copies of the Holy Scriptures to be used by the churches. Some of these manuscripts are said to comprise our oldest existing copies of God's Word.

(12) To the angel of the church in Pergamum write: These are the words of him who has the sharp, double-edged sword.

Jesus' word pierces like a sharp, double-edge sword, and it cuts every way, convicting us of our sins. Jesus has the sword with two edges, because He is the Savior of sinners and the Judge of the quick (living) and the dead.

Commendation

(13) I know where you live—where Satan has his throne. Yet you remain true to my name. You did not renounce your faith in me, even in the days of Antipas, my faithful witness, who was put to death in your city—where Satan lives.

He knew:

1- Where they lived.
2- Their faithfulness.

Pergamum (Pergamos in KJV), became the site of the first temple of the Caesar-cult, which was erected to Rome and Augustus in 29 B.C. A second shrine was later dedicated to Trajan. The worship of Asklepios and Zeus was also predominant. Pergamum was a seat of Emperor Worship, where incense was offered before the statue of the "Divine Emperor." The Emperor declared himself to be God and Christians who refused to offer incense were often put to death. It was a notorious center of heathenism and wickedness because it was a city of Balaamite and Nicolaitan teachings. It was called "Satan's Throne."

The people of Pergamum lived where Satan had his throne, where he reigned as king and was universally obeyed. The Jews believed that where God's Law was not studied Satan was free to dwell there, but he was obliged to leave the place where a synagogue or academy was established.

Antipas—Church tradition tells us that this martyr was brought before a statue of Caesar and told to swear that Caesar was God, but Antipas boldly proclaimed that Jesus alone was the Lord, and that there was no other God but He. The Roman official exclaimed. "Antipas, don't you know that the whole world is against you?" to which Antipas replied, "Then Antipas is against the whole world!" Antipas was put inside a brass bull, which was heated with fire until he was roasted to death.

Condemnation

V14,15—Nevertheless, I have a few things against you: You have people there who hold to the teaching of Balaam, who taught Balak to entice the Israelites to sin by eating food sacrificed to idols, and by committing sexual immorality. (15) Likewise you also have those who hold to the teaching of the Nicolaitans.

1. Some held to the teaching of Balaam.
2. Some held to the teaching of Nicholas.

3. Some who committed fornication and held to eating things offered to idols. This was done to honor those idols. They associated with idolaters in the heathen temples and participated in their religious festivals.

THE DOCTRINE OF BALAAM

Balaam (Num. 22), in his greed tried for money to prophesy a curse against Israel but God would not allow it. Balaam showed Balak that he could cause a stumbling block before the children of Israel by getting them to eat things sacrificed unto idols, and by committing fornication. At Balaam's suggestion, the Israelites intermarried with the Moabites, contrary to the will of God.

THE DOCTRINE OF THE NICOLAITANES

To set up a distinct class of men called clergymen and the denial of the common priesthood of all believers.

The followers of Balaam, the Nicolaitans and the Gnostics were probably all the same kind of people.

God told us to separate ourselves from evildoers.

Some think Nicholas started the Nicolaitanes.

Counsel

(16) Repent therefore! Otherwise, I will soon come to you and will fight against them with the sword of my mouth.

He calls for them to repent thus giving them a chance to save their souls. Their failure to repent would allow God's judgment to fall upon them. This judgment is one we choose when we fail to accept Jesus as our Lord and Savior.

Challenge

(17) He who has an ear, let him hear what the Spirit says to the churches. To him who overcomes, I will give some of the hidden manna. I will also give him a white stone with a new name written on it, known only to him who receives it.

During the Israelites wandering in the wilderness, God provided for them manna to eat and they put some in the Ark of the Covenant (Ex. 16).

The overcomer would receive hidden manna and a white stone with a new name written on it.

The "manna" of the Old Testament was the bread of life. The "manna" of the New Testament is Jesus Son of God.

There are several traditions concerning the present location of the Ark of the Covenant:

1. Jeremiah had taken the Ark of the Covenant, containing a golden pot of manna with him when he fled Egypt before the Babylonians destroyed Jerusalem. It was believed by some that at the initiation of the kingdom age, Jeremiah would return, bringing with him the Ark of the Covenant and would serve a feast of manna that had been hidden for centuries.
2. King Josiah had hidden the Ark of the Covenant, containing the tablets of stone, Aaron's rod, the holy anointing oil and the pot of manna when the Chaldeans took Jerusalem, and that these should all be restored in the days of the Messiah. Jesus is the Ark, oil, Rod, testimony and the manna
3. Solomon married the Queen of Sheba and she gave birth to a son and they called him Menelik. Prince Menelik grew up to look a lot like his father.

Menelik lived with Solomon and while being educated by the priests of the Temple, became a strong believer in God, and because it was too far for him to travel so he could worship at the temple in Jerusalem, he was given a replica of the Ark to take with him to Ethiopia.

Prince Menelik was deeply concerned with the growing apostasy of Israel and the fact that his father was allowing idols to be placed in the temple to please his pagan wives.

Solomon gave Menelik a farewell dinner, and after the priests were filled with wine, Menelik and his loyal associates switched arks, left the replica in its place, and took with them the true Ark of the Covenant. Many people believe that this ark is now in some church along the northern boundary of present day Ethiopia near Aduwa or Aksum, but, if it is there, it is so well guarded by the priests that no one can confirm or deny the legend.

It is interesting to note that I Kings 8:9 says that when Solomon finished the temple, and when the Ark of the Covenant was brought in, it only contained the two tablets of stone Moses had put in it at Mt. Horeb.

The White Stone

During the time in which John wrote, a white stone was used in social life and judicial customs. The legend of this custom goes back to the trial of Orestes, the son of Agamemnon, king of Mycenae, in the Areopagus, the ancient supreme court of Athens. Orestes' mother, Clytemnestra, and her lover, Aegistheus, killed his father and Orestes took it upon himself to avenge his father's murder. Orestes stood before the Athenian judges and awaited his fate. As the votes were clearly divided, Pallas Athene, who favored him, threw in a white stone (the Calculus Minervae) and thus got him acquitted. On a painted Greek vase, Greek heroes, painted by the Greek painter Duris, fifth century BC, are seen voting as to who should receive the weapons of the dead Achilles; Athena, standing behind the altar on which the stones are placed, decides in favor of Odysseus. In the social customs, a white stone noted days of great festivals and a black stone noted days of calamity. If a host had a special person whom he greatly appreciated, the guest was given a white stone with a name or a message written on it. On the judicial side it seems that in ancient times a white stone meant acquittal. For example, if the court had tried a man, the jurors cast their vote on his guilt or innocence by laying down a white stone, signifying that they acquitted him of the crime, a black stone if he was found guilty.

It is suggested here that we will receive a white stone (symbol of acquittal) with a new heavenly name written on it, given to us by Jesus our King. This new name will be a sign of a unique relationship with God. This would indicate an important change in a believer's status, just as Abram became Abraham, and Jacob became Israel. Maybe our new name will be a name characterizing our deeds on earth.

The Following Pagan Practices Introduced Into The Churches (AD)

> *300-Prayers for the dead, and making sign of the cross.*
> *375-Worship of saints and angels.*
> *394-Mass first instituted.*
> *431-Worship of Mary began.*
> *500-Priests began dressing differently than laymen.*
> *526-Extreme unction, (anointing with oil).*
> *593-Doctrine of purgatory introduced.*
> *600-Worship services conducted in Latin, and prayers directed to Mary.*

Around 312, the Roman Catholic Church practices became more and more Roman and less Christian. Today the Roman Catholic Church finds it hard to trace its beginning beyond 312. Until that time the Church was an independent collection of local churches, working together whenever possible, but not dominated by central authority.

The Chaldean tau, which was the elevation of a large 'T' on the end of a pole, was changed to the sign of the cross. The rosary, which comes from pagan origin, was introduced. Celibacy of priests and nuns, which has no scriptural verification, but finds a counterpart in the vestal virgins of paganism, was conceived.

The condemnation of Christ given to the church of Pergamum reveals that, although their theological doctrine was correct, their practical doctrines were radically evil.

THYATIRA—THE PAGANIZED CHURCH.
606 TO THE TRIBULATION
(THE DARK AGES)

The city of Thyatira was probably founded by Seleucus Nicator who ruled after the death of Alexander, some three hundred years before Christ. There is not total agreement as to who the founder was. It was a wealthy city in Macedonia, noted in the ancient world for its outstanding color dyes. It has been said that the road from Thyatira to Pergamos was one of the most beautiful in the entire world.

Thyatira was a commercial center mixed with pagan religions, and was guilty of tolerating the false prophetess Jezebel, even though it was a church of works. This woman is so designated because she was a copy of Ahab's wicked wife who introduced depraved Phoenician cults into Israel. Its local god was called Tyrimnus and he appeared on the coins on horseback armed with a battle-axe and club. Thyatira possessed a fortune telling shrine, presided over by a female oracle called the Sambathe. The modern city of Akhissar marks the site of ancient Thyatira (Turkey). It now has a population of about 30,000 people.

Thyatira means "continual sacrifice," and some think could be a general reference to the Roman Catholic Church.

The first Christian mentioned in Thyatira was a woman by the name of Lydia (Acts 16:14).

In the papacy the word "pope" means "father." In the beginning it was applied to all Western bishops, but around 500 it began to be restricted to the bishop of Rome. The idea that the Roman bishop should have authority over all the church was a slow growth because it was bitterly opposed at every step.

The popes of Rome, who appointed themselves Lords of Christendom, were replacing God's Lordship here on earth. In doing so, they put the following practices in place:

1. They put themselves between man and God, eliminating Christ's mediator-ship, claiming that man could only approach God through them.
2. It was heresy for a Christian to read the Bible for himself, and
3. the punishment for heresy was death.

It was by order of the Popes, through subservient governments, over a period of 500 years, that unnumbered multitudes of Christians were tortured and murdered for the 'heresy' of reading the Bible. Thus, God's Word was driven out of circulation, and became an unknown book. Martin Luther, in nailing his thesis, started the reformation, and restored the Bible to the people.

Some heroes of this time included:

John Wycliffe (1320-1384). He was the first to translate the entire Bible into English.

John Huss (1369-1415), was a fearless preacher who honored the Bible above the church. He was burned at the stake by the pope.

William Tyndale (1484-1536), in 1525 printed (Wycliffe had written) the first copy of the New Testament in English.

Erasmus (1466-1536), was a great student of the Greek New Testament.

Some believe that Rome is revealed in the Bible as the headquarters of the Mystery Babylon religion of the last days.

In 1564, the Roman Catholic Council of Trent declared that Rome believes that the truth concerning salvation, etc. is determined solely by the popes and church councils, not the Bible as the Word of God. Cardinal D'Allen declared "The Reformation was a Protestant revolt disrupting the unity of the church. Union will take place when the rebels accept the authority of the Pope and abandon the authority of Scripture. Rome can accept nothing short of this." The Council of Trent, though not surprising, has never been rescinded.

Rome has laid claim that it has never changed, but history informs us that there have been several changes since 1190.

Let me say that even though Catholicism has set itself on a plane equal with God, contrary to the Bible, there are many Christian Catholics.

(18) To the angel of the church in Thyatira write: These are the words of the Son of God, whose eyes are like blazing fire and whose feet are like burnished bronze.

Thyatira was located halfway between Pergamos and Sardis. Today it is known as Akhisar and was founded by Seleucus I (311-280 BC) as a military post.

The statement *"eyes like blazing fire"* and *"feet like burnished bronze"* shows that Christ is looking through His eyes with piercing judgment on the Church of Thyatira because she has permitted the false teaching to creep into her congregation.

Commendation

(19) I know your deeds, your love and faith, your service and perseverance, and that you are now doing more than you did at first.

They began slowly, but as they grew in their knowledge of the Lord, so did their deeds grow.

Christ noted five commendations:

1. Deeds—Our deeds reveal our spiritual condition.
2. Love—This was a church of love.
3. Faith—This is the foundation of works and love.
4. Service—They were doing service for the Lord.
5. Perseverance—They had shown their endurance.
6. Last works—what we have done in the latter part of our lives.

The omniscient God not only knew the depths of their love, faith, service and perseverance, but He also knows ours. There is absolutely nothing that we say, do, or think, that God doesn't know about!

Condemnation

V20-21—Nevertheless, I have this against you: You tolerate that woman Jezebel, who calls herself a prophetess. By her teaching she misleads my servants into sexual immorality and the eating of food sacrificed to idols. (21) I have given her time to repent of her immorality, but she is unwilling.

1. Thyatira was condemned for permitting a false teacher to lead astray God's servants into sexual immorality,
2. For eating food that had been sacrificed to idols, and
3. for not repenting when she had the opportunity.

The church in Thyatira, perhaps the least significant of the seven, was active in services and charities. They relied upon God's promises and were vigorous in their endeavors, but they lacked the proper zeal for the maintenance of godly discipline, and doctrine. Their indulgence in sin led the church toward idolatry.

A woman was the first to sin and the false prophet who first enticed the members of this church to sin was a woman.

This woman, *"Jezebel,"* was thought by some to be the wife of the Bishop of the church. Through her teachings she instituted her will, setting aside the true prophets of God with her lies, and had entirely taken possession of the church for her own impurities just as her namesake of old. She was creating confusion and turmoil in the church which is not allowed by any gender. She was not only teaching immorality and idolatry, but she was totally unrepentant.

This "Jezebel" had introduced the abominations of Astarte worship and burned sacrifices and poured drink offerings to her. The congregation at Thyatira not only accepted her teachings but also allowed her to be a fellow pastor, with which the Lord was greatly displeased.

The New Testament clearly warns those who do not repent will face chastisement from God.

Their Punishment:

V22-23—So I will cast her on a bed of suffering, and I will make those who commit adultery with her suffer intensely, unless they repent of her ways. (23) I will strike her children dead. Then all the churches will know that I am he who searches hearts and minds, and I will repay each of you according to your deeds.

"I will cast her on a bed of suffering." This could be literally or figuratively. This sick bed may not be a literal illness, but a reference to a direct judgment from God. Her *"children"* could be a reference to her followers or her natural offspring. This could also be a reference of God's judgment on her for committing adultery. Today's judgment could be aids and other sexual transmitted diseases.

Perhaps since she used a luxurious bed to commit her immorality, and the reclining couch at the idol feast to eat things offered to false gods, He was to give her a bed in hell where she would live forever.

Jeremiah in Chapter 44:17-18 said Ashtaroth was called the "Queen of Heaven," and was the goddess Jezebel caused Israel to worship. In the middle Ages the church introduced the worship of Mary as the "Queen of Heaven."

Jesus threatened to "kill" her children with death. Some say this referred to the plagues, including the Black Death, which began in 1347, and decimated the European population in the middle Ages. Again this could be death caused by aids and sexually transmitted diseases or some new strain.

Works do not save, but they do give evidence of salvation. Judgment based on works is taught by Jesus (Matt. 16:27), and Paul (Rom. 2:6) as well as John in Revelation. We are judged by our works in order that we may be rewarded our crowns.

Counsel

(24) Now I say to the rest of you in Thyatira, to you who do not hold to her teaching and have not learned Satan's so-called deep secrets (I will not impose any other burden on you): (25) Only hold on to what you have until I come.

There was a remnant that was still true to God, regardless of the false teachings of others.

Some think Satan's deep secrets could be a reference to a Gnostic sect known as the Ophites who worshipped the serpent. They boasted of a superior spiritual perception. They taught that their doctrines as the depths of God, but here Christ called it the depths of Satan. Those who have been faithful are encouraged to hold on. This is even true today. We must let our faith in God sustain us.

In the first century mysterious religions and cults were plentiful. A person's reward for joining a cult was the receiving of "deep secrets" or "special wisdom."

Challenge

V26-29—To him who overcomes and does my will to the end, I will give authority over the nations. (27) He will rule them with an iron scepter; he will dash them to pieces like pottery, just as I have received authority from my Father. (28) I will also give him the morning star. (29) He who has an ear, let him hear what the Spirit says to the churches.

What is the morning star? There are those who say it is the planet Venus, which during certain times of the year is the last bright heavenly body to fade at dawn. Caesar's legions carried the sign of Venus on their standards as a symbol of conquest.

Those who will do God's will and endures to the end will rule with Him when He comes again.

CHAPTER 3

SARDIS—THE LIFELESS CHURCH.
THE DEAD CHURCH, 1520 TO THE TRIBULATION

The city of Sardis was the capital of King Croesus, (560-546 BC), a very wealthy monarch of ancient times. Sardis' textile and jewelry industries made it a wealthy city. Sardis means "escaping ones" or those who "come out." Sardis is credited with being the first to mint coins. She was known for her burial mounds, raised like a thousand hills on the skyline some seven miles from the city. Sardis stood high above the Valley of Hemus, situated on a natural acropolis rising 1,500 feet above the valley floor, surrounded by deep cliffs that were almost impossible to scale. This made it an ideal fortress, and because of this, they became overconfident, and added to this was their failure to watch, and in 214 BC, armies of Antiochus the Great (III) captured the city by scaling the cliffs under the cover of darkness, bringing about the fall of Sardis. In 546 BC the Persian King Cyrus ended the rule of Croesus by the same method.

The magnificent Temple of Artemis dating from the fourth century BC was one of its points of interest and still exists as an important ruin. The remains of a Christian Church building, which have been discovered immediately adjacent to the temple, testifies to the witnessing of Christians to a wicked and pagan city noted for its loose living. They worshiped the mother goddess, Cybele.

Sardis, a town once renowned, was destroyed by an earthquake, during the reign of Tiberius. It is now called Sart or Sardo.

The tragedy of the reformation Churches was that it earned for them the condemnation by the Lord of being "dead" was two-fold:

1. They became state churches. Luther, seeking approval of the political leaders eventually led the Lutheran Church to become the state church of Germany.

2. The reformation Churches did not notably change many teachings and customs of the Roman Church. Infant baptism was continued in spite of the fact that there is no scriptural verification for it. Sprinkling was also continued, and ritualism, including some elements of the sacraments, was continued.

Church historians agree that the Sardis Church Period began when Martin Luther nailed his 95 Thesis to the door of the church in Wittenberg, Germany. This reformation period, as it was known, came to a standstill, thus allowing complacency to set in, and then the church tried to live on its reputation but failed miserably.

The most prominent person from the church at Sardis known to history is Melito, who served as bishop of Sardis in the late second century. He also wrote the earliest known commentary on passages from Revelation.

Aesop, the famous author, also came from Sardis.

Commendation

None. He found their deeds empty, without any meaning.

Condemnation

(1) To the angel of the church in Sardis write: These are the words of him who holds the seven spirits of God and the seven stars. I know your deeds; you have a reputation of being alive, but you are dead.

Jesus' words to the church of Sardis were very critical. He knew their deeds. He knew that they had a reputation of being alive, their doing good deeds were only for the acknowledgement of man. They put on a great front and fooled the people into thinking they were righteous people, but God knew their heart. They lacked the Holy Spirit in their lives and they did not have the life of God in their souls, nor had they walked consistently and steadily before God and therefore He judged them dead, and there is nothing worse than a dead church. There are many souls traveling in this world of darkness seeking hope. They enter into a church, hoping to find this hope only to find upon entering that it is completely dead. Their hope also dies. Churches are dead because the individuals are spiritually dead.

Counsel

V2-3—Wake up! Strengthen what remains and is about to die, for I have not found your deeds complete in the sight of my God. (3) Remember, therefore, what you have received and heard; obey it and repent. But if you do not wake up, I will come like a thief, and you will not know at what time I will come to you.

Sardis was given the following warnings:

1. It was called upon to *"awake, to strengthen, what remains."*
2. To remember what it had received and heard, obey it and repent.
3. Failure to do so would mean the Lord would come when they least expected it and they would not receive blessings but judgments.

Like many church members today, the people of Sardis were constantly starting something but never finishing it.

Challenge

V4-6—Yet you have a few people in Sardis who have not soiled their clothes. They will walk with me, dressed in white, for they are worthy. (5) He who overcomes will, like them, be dressed in white. I will never blot out his name from the book of life, but will acknowledge his name before my Father and his angels. (6) He who has an ear, let him hear what the Spirit says to the churches.

God always has a remnant of faithful followers. There are always some who keep their first love by following and obeying God. Elijah thought that he was the only one left alive that believed in God, but he was informed that there were 7,000 people who still followed and obeyed God.

Perhaps the church at Sardis was being sustained, like America, by the righteousness of a few, but eventually, unless there is repentance, judgment will fall.

The few true believers in Sardis, the *"overcomers"* are those *"who have not soiled their garments."* Soiled garments refer to the sins of men in immorality, apostasy and idolatry.

There are at least four reasons why one's name is blotted out of the Book of Life:

1. For sinning against God (Exodus 32:33);
2. For not being an overcomer, which is synonymous with being born again or putting one's trust in Jesus the Christ (I John 5:1-4);
3. For taking away from the words of the prophesy of Revelation (22:19).
4. Rejecting Jesus as the Son of God.

Those who were true to Christ were given three promises:

1. They would be dressed in white.
2. They would not have their names blotted out of the Book of Life.
3. They would be acknowledged by Christ before God.

The story is told that years ago, when America established relief camps to help Armenian refugees, there was a certain young girl who came for medical assistance. As she waited outside the tent, her dark eyes betrayed the tremendous pain that racked her body. Someone asked her, "Have you been hurt?" To which she replied, "I am bearing the cross. I bear on my body the cross of Jesus Christ. Now I know how He suffered." The relief workers did not understand what the young girl meant, but when the nurse who assisted her in the medical tent helped the young girl slip off her dress, she saw that a cross had been branded on her shoulder with a hot iron. The wound was swollen and burning with infection. The girl explained, "Every day they would say to me, "Mohammed or Christ?" When I said "Christ" on the last day, they branded my shoulder with this cross. Now as long as I live, I will bear this cross, and someday when I see Jesus I will be glad."

What would we do if we were faced with the same decision?

We must hold fast and be overcomers and live a holy life. When we do we will live our lives with:

1. Glorification (Rom. 8:17, 18),
2. justification (Rom. 5:16-18), and
3. sanctification (1 Thess. 4:3, 4).

PHILADELPHIA-THE MISSIONARY CHURCH.
THE CHURCH CHRIST LOVED
1750 TO THE RAPTURE

King Attalus II-Philadelphus founded a Lydian city in 140 BC, and because of the great love Attalus II had for his brother Eumenes who was king of Pergamum, it was named Philadelphia and was known as "the city of brotherly love." It is now known now as Allah Shair (Alasehir).

Philadelphia renowned for its fine wine, was built as a center of Greek culture around 200 BC. Philadelphia, subject to earthquakes, was struck by one in the year 17, (the same earthquake that destroyed Sardis) and was totally destroyed. Philadelphia was soon rebuilt by Tiberius Caesar, and still remains, and even though it is threatened by severe earthquakes that could be destructive, you still can find a group of Christians meeting there on a regular basis.

Commendation

V7-8—"To the angel of the church in Philadelphia write: These are the words of him who is holy and true, who holds the key of David. What he opens no one can shut, and what he shuts no one can open. (8) I know your deeds. See, I have placed before you an open door that no one can shut. I know that you have little strength, yet you have kept my word and have not denied my name.

Isaiah 22:22, *"I will place on his shoulder the key to the house of David; what he opens no one can shut, and what he shuts no one can open."* (This was said about Eliakim, son of Hilkiah).

This letter like that one to Smyrna, contains no word of condemnation.

Philadelphia's vigorous missionary activities won many Jews of the city, causing a violent opposition of the local Jewish populace who claimed to be the people of God, but their actions proved them to actually be of Satan's synagogue.

Condemnation

None!

Counsel

V9-11—I will make those who are of the synagogue of Satan, who claim to be Jews though they are not, but are liars—I will make them come and fall down at your feet and acknowledge that I have loved you. (10) Since you have kept my commandment to endure patiently, I will also keep you from the hour of trial that is going to come upon the whole world to test those who live on the earth. (11) I am coming soon. Hold on to what you have, so that no one will take your crown.

Jesus said He would keep those who kept His commandments from the tribulation that would engulf the world. The expression, *"I will also keep you from,"* means to "protect someone from something" Prov. 7:5; Jn. 17:15. The hour of trial (another name for the Tribulation) coming to the whole world refers to the tribulation. Jesus says He will keep us from these trials. This doesn't mean we won't face trials in life, for everyone must face trials and tribulations in life. He said He would keep us from going through the "great tribulation."

This promise is indicative that the church, of which the Philadelphian church, some say, was representative, will be glorified and taken (raptured) to heaven before the Great Tribulation begins. The promise is to all who belong to Christ "because you have kept (obeyed) My Commandments."

One passage speaks of Christ's coming in the air and in secret, like a thief coming in the night. Another part of the scripture describes Christ's coming in power and majesty to the earth, with every eye seeing Him.

In Chapter 2 and 3 we find that scripture repeat seven times, *"He who has an ear let him hear what the Spirit says to the churches,"* while in Chapter 3 we read, *"If anyone has an ear, let him hear."* Here we have the same warning but no mention of the church. There are those who take this to mean that the church has been removed. They feel it seems unthinkable that God would leave out mentioning the church if it was still on earth during these terrible judgments. The church will be as in the days of Noah and Sodom and Gomorrah. We do see here and other scripture that before God's judgment fell, He removed His people. The church was not mentioned as being in heaven either. Maybe we are trying to put words into Scripture! I firmly believe, according to Scripture, that the "rapture" will occur before the Tribulation, but I am not convinced that this is what Scripture is saying here.

Challenge

V12-13—Him who overcomes I will make a pillar in the temple of my God. Never again will he leave it. I will write on him the name of my God and the name of the city of my God, the new Jerusalem, which is coming down out of heaven from my God; and I will also write on him my new name. (13) He who has an ear, let him hear what the Spirit says to the churches.

Archaeological digs from many ancient sites have yielded evidence of the custom of writing upon pillars of a temple. At Palmyra a whole street had been adorned with writings on its pillars.

This tradition is carried on today, but now it is writing names on bricks. When a memorial is erected to honor those who have died during a war, those who donate to the memorial have their names etched in a brick and then the brick is laid in a sidewalk or some other structure. Several towns in the United States practice this, but one that comes to mind is

Nashville, Indiana. They have given one side of their courtyard to be a memorial to those who have died in the wars and those who have donated to the memorial have their names etched in bricks and they have been laid around the memorial on the ground and in the sidewalk.

The promise relates to Christ's advent for His own, (Jn. 14:1-3: I Thess. 4:13-17; I Cor. 15:51-52) and the rewards of Christians, here called overcomers. Believers will be clearly identified as God's own possession with the name of God and the New Jerusalem and Christ's new name on them.

There are four things promised to an overcomer:

1. He will make him a pillar in the temple.
2. He will write on him the name of his God.
3. He will write on him the name of the City of God. See pg 55
4. He will write on him the new name of Jesus. See pg 55

"Pillar" is a figure of speech meaning we shall be strong and steadfast like a pillar, probably an allusion to the two pillars in the Temple, Jachin and Boaz.

In Matthew 13 we find 7 parables. Some think they refer to the following:

1. Parable of the sower—Ephesian church, the age of missionary. There will be a sowing of the Gospel throughout the world, with a variety of responses.
2. Parable of tares and wheat—Church at Smyrna. The first seeds of evil were sown among the true wheat, which resulted in the age of persecution.
3. Parable of the Mustard Seed—Pergamos. The abnormal, unnatural growth of the nominal church.
4. Parable of the Leaven—Thyatira. The leaven of evil doctrines and practices are introduced with its superstitions and paganism. Leaven always symbolizes evil, not good.
5. Parable of the Treasure—Sardis. The reformation church with its discoveries of hidden truths and treasure.
6. Parable of the Pearl of great price—Philadelphia. The true church of Jesus. God will gather to Himself a special people.

7. Parable of the Drag Net—Laodicea. The final denial of Christ, followed by the second coming of Christ. God will end the age with judgment.

LAODICEA, "THE LUKEWARM CHURCH." THE APOSTATE CHURCH OR THE PEOPLE'S CHURCH 1900 TO THE TRIBULATION

Commendation

None

It was the wealthiest city in Phrygia during Roman times. The members of this church in the proud and wealthy city of Laodicea received no commendation.

Laodicea was a city known for its medical center, racetrack, and three lavish theaters. Christ was on the outside asking entry into one of His own churches. It is quite true of many churches of the present time.

Antiochus Theos built this town of Phrygia on the Lycus River about 261-246 BC, located at what is known as the "Gate of Phrygia," and named it after his wife Laodice. Great camel caravans came down through the Gate of Phrygia and through Laodicea from the Oriental East. Antiochus later divorced her to marry Bernice. Laodice who considered her divorce a betrayal by her husband, avenged herself by killing him.

Mohammed invaders later destroyed Laodicea. It is now deserted and uninhabited; its ruins are covered with a growth that some say looks like wild oats. Its ruins lay now near modern day Denizli.

Epaphras worked here (Col. 2:1; 4:12-16).

Condemnation

V14—"To the angel of the church in Laodicea write: These are the word of the Amen, the faithful and true witness, the ruler of God's creation.

Christ is here called *"the amen, the faithful and true witness, the ruler of God's creation,"* which denotes His sovereignty over all of God's creation.

This city's wealth was so great that in the year 60, when it was almost completely destroyed by an earthquake, its citizens refused Rome's aid and rebuilt the city at their own expense.

Cicero is said to have held court here, and in 51 BC he stopped here and cashed drafts.

V15-17—I know your deeds, that you are neither cold nor hot. I wish you were either one or the other! (16) So, because you are lukewarm—neither hot nor cold—I am about to spit you out of my mouth. (17) You say, 'I am rich; I have acquired wealth and do not need a thing.' But you do not realize that you are wretched, pitiful, poor, blind, and naked.

Laodicea was an industrial center known for the production of fine black wool, its Phrygian powder (used to treat eye diseases), and its hot mineral springs made it a medical center as well. These features are used in the letter to illustrate the Laodicean church's true spiritual condition; for Christ calls its lukewarm profession, as He does all churches that practice lukewarmness, nauseating, and utterly deceptive of its true spiritual condition.

Historians and scholars have said the hills around Laodicea "have a very funny color." The people took the clay from the hills, added spikenard, and made salve for the eyes and ears. The salve was shipped all over the Roman Empire. According to chemical analysis of the clay, there were no healing properties present. The power of advertisement!!

The Bible gives us three possible temperatures of the heart:

1. The burning heart (Luke 24:32).
2. The cold heart (Matt. 24:12).
3. The lukewarm heart (Rev. 3:16).

The Phrygian Mountains have an abundance of snow on their peaks. The Laodiceans built an aqueduct to bring the cold water down from the mountains. When it left the mountains it was ice cold, but by the time it got to the city it was lukewarm.

Down in the valley where the Lycus River joins the Maeander River there are hot springs. These springs are so hot that steam is produced. When the hot water was taken to Laodicea, because of the length of the trip, it was no longer hot but lukewarm. The Turkish Government has now capped these hot springs and are using them today.

The Laodiceans knew exactly what Jesus meant when He said, *"you are neither hot nor cold."*

There is an inscription on the cathedral in Lubeck, Germany, which is true even today:

> Thus speaketh Christ our lord to us;
> Ye call Me Master and obey Me not,
> Ye call Me Light and see Me not,
> Ye call me Way and walk Me not,
> Ye call Me Life and choose Me not,
> Ye call Me Wise and follow Me not,
> Ye call Me Fair and love Me not,
> Ye call Me Rich and ask Me not,
> Ye call Me Eternal and seek Me not,
> Ye call Me Noble and serve Me not,
> Ye call Me gracious and trust Me not,
> Ye call Me Might and honor Me not,
> Ye call Me Just and fear Me not,
> If I condemn you, blame Me not.

Counsel

V18-20—I counsel you to buy from me gold refined in the fire, so you can become rich; and white clothes to wear, so you can cover your shameful nakedness; and salve to put on your eyes, so you can see. (19) Those whom I love I rebuke and discipline. So be earnest, and repent. (20) Here I am! I stand at the door and knock. If anyone hears my voice and opens the door, I will come in and eat with him, and he with me.

Christ advises the church *"to buy from me gold refined in the fire."* Once gold is mined, it is placed into a red-hot furnace to be purified. The impurities are drawn out and the residue (pure gold) is left. When God puts us in His furnace of testing, it is to refine our faith. The gold we buy from Him is spiritual treasures.

The true wealth of mankind is Jesus our Savior. We can receive from Him our *"white raiment"* of a regenerated and satisfied life because He cleanses our hearts. We receive true spiritual insight and knowledge from the *"eye salve"* of faith.

Christ loves those in Laodicea, even though they are lukewarm, and promises them chastisement. They are told to repent of their unbelief, compromising and their disloyalty, but they, like so many today, lacked spiritual insight. No one is saved against his will. The invitation is extended to all and each of us must choose to open the door.

The lack of spiritual perception, devotion, and faith in God manifested in the lukewarm state is revealed in the desire of material wealth instead of spiritual wealth. We cannot serve man and God at the same time. We must choose one. By not choosing God, we choose man.

Those who accept Jesus as their Savior will open their lives to Him and will invite Him to be their honored guest.

Challenge

V21-22—To him who overcomes, I will give the right to sit with me on my throne, just as I overcame and sat down with my Father on his throne. (22) He who has an ear, let him hear what the Spirit says to the churches.

Christ, having been removed by the church appears on the outside knocking on the doors of individual hearts, waiting for them to receive Him and to enter into fellowship with Him. The overcomer is promised the right to sit with Christ on his own throne in the coming kingdom which is only one of the many promises made to overcomers in the letters to the seven churches.

OVERCOMERS ARE ALSO PROMISED:

1. The privilege of eating from the tree of life (2:7).
2. The crown of life (2:10).
3. Protection from the second death (2:11).
4. The hidden manna (2:17).
5. A white stone with a new name written on it (2:17).
6. Authority to rule the nations (2:26, 27).
7. The morning star (2:28).
8. White garments, symbolizing purity and holiness (3:5).
9. The honor of having Christ confess their names before God the Father and the Holy Angels in Heaven (3:12).
10. To be a pillar in God's Temple (3:12).
11. To have written on them the name of God, of the New Jerusalem and of Christ (3:12).

Some think the rapture takes place after the third chapter when the Church Age has been removed. The overcomers have been translated to meet the Lord in the air.

The rapture of the Church, when it occurs, will remove the Bride of Christ to Heaven. Those left behind will find themselves facing the difficult and dreadful times in the Bible known as the Great Tribulation.

It will be a time of wars more dreadful than any history has known, or will know causing conflict, suffering and death.

There exist today, many thoughts on the rapture which leads to confusion. There are some who think there will not be a rapture, because, they say, the word rapture is not in the Bible. This is correct to a point. It is true that the word rapture is not in the English Translation. It is an English version of a word that appears in the Latin Translations. Most of the New Testament was written in Greek, which was translated into Latin and then into English. St. Jerome, in 405, completed most of the Latin translation. His translation was later translated into English. Several verses in the Latin version contain the word "rapere" or one of its derivations. It means 'caught up', or taken by force.

There are several examples of the "Rapture."

1. Gen. 5:24, Heb. 11:5—Enoch
2. II Kings 2:11—Elijah
3. Acts 1:9—Jesus
4. Acts 1:39—Philip
5. II Cor. 12:1-4—Paul
6. Rev. 11:3-12—Two Witnesses

I have read many commentaries on the rapture, Christ's second coming, the end times, and Revelation. The one thing the writers had in common is that the church would be removed when the rapture occurred.

The church is made up of individual believers. When one accepts Christ as their Lord and Savior, he/she becomes the church, housing the Holy Spirit of God.

We should clarify the above statement for those who might become confused when we say the church will be removed. If the church is removed with the rapture, then how can anyone be saved? Since one who accepts Christ as their Lord becomes a Church of Christ, then if Revelation tells us that 144,000 Israelites receive the seal of God, becoming 144,000 individual Churches of Christ, then we cannot say that the church, per se, is removed from the earth.

The "church" is made up of individual believers who will never be removed until the end of earth as we know it. The "church" will never be removed for there will be those who will accept Christ in the Millennium. The Church Age will be removed. The present Church Age is all believers who have accepted Christ as their Lord and Savior and who are living when the "rapture" occurs.

The word Church (ekklesia) refers to those who profess to believe in Christ in this present age.

Those in the Old Testament who acknowledged God as their only God were known as the Old Testament Saints. When Christ died on Calvary and was resurrected, all believers who accepted Him as Lord and Savior became Christians or the Church. This was or is known as the Church Age. The Holy Spirit is still at work during the Tribulation Period for a multitude of people are saved. The Holy Spirit's restraining power is removed, but not the saving power. During the Tribulation Period, those who accept Christ as their Savior will still be individual churches, but they will be known as the Tribulation Saints.

This body of believers is distinctly different from the body of all believers of every age and does not include the saints of the Old Testament or Israel, or the saints who will be on earth after this church age is raptured.

CHAPTER 4

PART 3—CHAPTER 4-22—
"THE THINGS WHICH TAKE PLACE AFTER THIS."

V1—After this I looked, and there before me was a door standing open in heaven. And the voice I had first heard speaking to me like a trumpet said, "Come up here, and I will show you what must take place after this."

Chapter 4 and 5 gives us the source of the visions and judgments which are to follow. The setting is in Heaven before God's Throne.

Some see Chapters 4 and 5 as an interlude before the appearance of the first rider on the white horse in Chapter 6. Some say this rider is the victorious Roman Army on its way to Jerusalem in 67.

The Tribulation will not necessarily follow the "rapture" of the church. Time will elapse. How much time, we do not know. After the "rapture," there will be mass confusion. People will be trying to figure out what has happened to the people who had disappeared. Governments will try to come up with a plausible answer. Even some government leaders will have disappeared. They will search for the missing people, but to no avail.

There will be some who will remember what they had learned in church and loved ones and will begin to figure it out.

It will take time for the Antichrist to woo and beguile the government.

John, some say, is here representing true believers, and is invited to come up immediately and is caught up in the spirit and taken to Heaven.

AN OPEN DOOR IN HEAVEN—*"After this,"* refers to the Church Age represented by the seven churches in Chpt. 2 and 3. The scene is changed from earth to heaven as the trumpet call of Christ summons John to heaven.

It's been said that somewhere, high in the heavens, out in the universe, a *"throne is set,"* which is the throne of God.

The Bible teaches us that there are three heavens:

1. The first, the atmospheric heaven where *"the prince of the power of the air"* dwells, will one day be destroyed.
2. The second heaven is the stellar heaven, known to us as the universe.
3. The third heaven, into which John was caught up in verse 1, is the heaven of God. Could this be the *"empty place"* referred to by Job in 26:7? It was once thought that the heavens were filled with stars wherever the telescope could reach, and it seemed that behind the North Star there was an empty place. For that reason it has been suggested that this could be the third heaven, the heaven of God, where His *"throne is set."* This *"empty place,"* also known as "the black hole" is no longer an empty place or a black hole. Recently a satellite that had been sent up by NASA sent back pictures revealing that this black hole or empty place is neither. The pictures reveal that there is another galaxy that was not visible until now.

There are at least five things told about Heaven in Revelation. Heaven is;

1. the full and complete expression of God's kingdom.
2. where rewards are offered for those who overcome in this life.
3. God's judgment seat, where He pronounces judgment.
4. full of God's presence and glory, both which will overwhelm us.
5. a place of worship and praise, because of God's holiness and His awesome power.

There are those who seem to think that Saturn is Heaven. They say that around Saturn are the four Seraphim: Jupiter, Uranus, Neptune, and Pluto. The four terrestrial planets, Mercury, Venus, Earth, and Mars are the heavenly fliers called Cherubim in Ezekiel. They claim that their concentric orbits are the wheels within wheels Ezekiel saw in his visions of the heavens. Ezekiel saw one of the wheels upon earth, so earth, they reasoned, is one of the four Cherubim. According to this theory, planets speak!

Both Seraphim and Cherubim are personified and depicted as having powers of speech. Of the Cherubim, Ezekiel said, *"I heard the noise of their wings, like the noise of great waters, as the voice of the Almighty, the voice of speech, as the noise of a host."* The Seraphim say, *"Come and see"* as the seals are broken in Rev. 6. There are nine planets at present. The four inner planets are called Cherubim. The four outer planets that surround the throne are called Seraphim. Saturn makes nine.

They also say that the flaming sword that was put in the Garden of Eden to guard the Tree of Life was also a planet that can be seen with the naked eye. This is a very interesting concept, but scripture gives no indication of this being true.

V2-4—At once I was in the Spirit, and there before me was a throne in heaven with someone sitting on it. (3) And the one who sat there had the appearance of jasper and carnelian. A rainbow, resembling an emerald, encircled the throne. (4) Surrounding the throne were twenty-four other thrones, and seated on them were twenty-four elders. They were dressed in white and had crowns of gold on their heads.

John's spirit leaves earth and arrives in heaven where he sees his friend and Savior, Jesus, occupying the throne of God until His second advent. John's body could not enter because it had not been glorified. The Spirit had been cleansed and purified by the righteousness of Jesus the Christ.

Precious gems symbolizes God's glory. Here Jesus is described as a jasper and a carnelian stone. The jasper was clear as crystal and the carnelian was blood red. The jasper and the carnelian (sardine, Sardius) are also mentioned in a list of precious stones set in the breast-plate of the High Priest (Ex. 28:17-20).

However, here the order of stones is reversed. John sees Jesus first as the jasper and as the carnelian second.

In the Old Testament they looked forward to the day when the Lamb would come. They looked forward to the cross, therefore they saw the blood-red stone first. They looked beyond that and saw the jasper, the clear white stone representing His power and His rule at His second coming to set up His kingdom. John was now on the other side of Calvary and the rapture, and was looking back. John, saw first of all the clear jasper stone and then the red stone, the cross and sacrifice.

The rainbow was God's covenant with Noah promising him that He would not destroy the earth again with a flood. The Noahic rainbow was semi-circle. The throne was encircled (complete) with a rainbow, symbolizing the absolute sovereignty of God, the unbroken power, love, and mercy of God. The rainbow was emerald, a color pleasing to the eye.

God's covenant with man is complete through our acceptance of His Son as our Lord and Savior.

V4—Daniel in chapter 7:9 saw these thrones being set up with the "ancient of days" the only one sitting on a throne, the rest were empty. John sees these thrones occupied with twenty-four elders.

One tradition identifies the twenty-four elders as representing both Israel and the Church. The representation of Israel is by the twelve patriarchs, and the Church by the twelve apostles, but Matthew 19:28 says the twelve apostles will sit on twelve thrones and will judge the twelve tribes of Israel.

Titus 1:5 says, *"For this reason I left you in Crete, that you should set in order the things that are lacking, and appoint elders in every city as I commanded you—."*

There were thousands of priest in Israel's day under David and Solomon, but they could not all minister at the same time. Accordingly they were divided into twenty-four orders, each of which was represented by a priest.

The number twenty-four occurs six times in the OT. In every case, it is associated with the priests of Israel, who represented all of Israel. It could be that one day the twenty-four elders will represent all believers from Pentecost to the Rapture, or all elders from the beginning of time.

The apostles will sit on separate thrones not depicted in Revelation.

There are Seven acts of the elders:

1. They sit on thrones (4:4).
2. They worship God (4:9).
3. They cast their crowns before God (4:10).
4. They fall prostrate before God (4:10).
5. They give John the revelation (5:5).
6. They sing and play harps (5:8-10).
7. They act as priests (5:8).

There are different trains of thoughts, some are:

1. Represent either Israel or the Old Testament Saints, the church or both.
2. Angelic beings or representing Old Testament priestly orders.
3. Special class or order of angels.
4. Represents the church age believers and the complete body of Christ. All believers, Gentile and Jews from the day of Pentecost until the rapture of the church.
5. Represents the 24 patriarchs listed in the line of the promised seed: Adam, Seth, Enos, Cainan, Mahalaleel, Jared, Enoch, Methuselah, Lamech, Noah, Shem, Arphaxad, Salah, Eber, Peleg, Reu, Serug, Nahor, Terah, Abraham, Isaac, Jacob, Judah, and Pharez.

(5) From the throne came flashes of lightning, rumblings and peals of thunder. Before the throne, seven lamps were blazing. These are the seven spirits of God.

The lightning and thundering John hears are indicative of the awful storm of the great tribulation, which is about to unleash its fury.

Some believe one of the reasons the church age has been raptured at this point is because the seven lamps of fire which were the seven churches on earth are now before the throne in heaven.

The seven spirits (Isa. 11:2) are: (1) The Spirit of the Lord, (2) Wisdom, (3) Understanding, (4) Counsel, (5) Might, (6) Knowledge, (7) Fear of the Lord.

V6-8—Also before the throne there was what looked like a sea of glass, clear as crystal. In the center, around the throne, were four living creatures, and they were covered with eyes, in front and in back. (7) The first living creature was like a lion, the second was like an ox, the third had a face like a man, the fourth was like a flying eagle. (8) Each of the four living creatures had six wings and was covered with eyes all around, even under his wings. Day and night they never stop saying: "Holy, holy, holy is the Lord God Almighty, who was, and is, and is to come."

The Greek word for beast is *zoa*, which means "a living creature."

There is no sea in heaven (21:1), but the crystal pavement that serves as the floor of God's throne stretches out like a great, glistening sea. This "sea of glass," directly beneath the Throne of God, were those saints in Paradise was taken out by Christ and transported beneath the Throne of God. "Paradise" was taken from within the earth to Heaven.

These four living creatures are seraphim, described by Isaiah in his vision of the throne of God (Isa. 6:1-3).

In Daniel 7:17 the four beasts are as follows:

1. Lion—Babylon
2. Bear—Medo-Persia
3. Leopard—Greece
4. Beast not named—Roman Empire

We find that each Gospel portrays Jesus differently:

1. Matthew presents the Lord Jesus as King.
2. Mark presents Jesus as servant.
3. Luke presents Jesus as the Son of Man.
4. In the Gospel of John, the eagle communicates the deity of Christ.

The creature being full of eyes is representative of God's omniscience and omnipresence.

There are different thoughts on what these 4 living creatures represent:

1. Lion-King of Beast; Lion, tribe of Judah-Jesus, King of the Jews; power.
2. Ox-Beast of burden; Jesus as servant; faithfulness.
3. Man-human-Jesus, Son of Man; intelligence.
4. Eagle-rules the skies-Jesus, God; sovereignty.

The four quarters of the Zodiac;

1. Leo—Lion.
2. Taurus—Bull or Calf.
3. Scorpio—Eagle.
4. Aquarius—Man.

Or they represent:

1. This represents the attributes of man.
2. This represents the four aspects of nature; wild beasts, domesticated animals, human beings, and flying creatures.
3. They are the cherubim of the Old Testament.

These eyes mean that the creatures see all things and are watchful protectors of God's throne. Some think these are not literal creatures but are symbolic.

V9-11 Whenever the living creatures give glory, honor and thanks to him who sits on the throne and who lives for ever and ever, (10) the twenty-four elders fall down before him who sits on the throne, and worship him who lives for ever and ever. They lay their crowns before the throne and say: (11) "You are worthy, our Lord and God, to receive glory and honor and power, for you created all things, and by your will they were created and have their being."

The twenty-four elders fall prostrate before the throne showing their humility and lay their victors crowns before God, declaring that God is worthy of all glory, honor, and power because He created all things.

CHAPTER 5

THE SCENE OF CHAPTER 5 IS SET IN HEAVEN.

V1-4—Then I saw in the right hand of him who sat on the throne a scroll with writing on both sides and sealed with seven seals. (2) And I saw a mighty angel proclaiming in a loud voice, "Who is worthy to break the seals and open the scroll?" (3) But no one in heaven or on earth or under the earth could open the scroll or even look inside it. (4) I wept and wept because no one was found who was worthy to open the scroll or look inside.

History informs us that under Roman law all legal documents pertaining to life and death were to be sealed seven times. The scroll (ancient book) written on the front, the back and *"sealed with seven seals"* indicated the completeness and the legality of the sealing until someone would appear who was legally qualified to open the tightly closed legal document. It is apparent that the scroll not only contained the record of God's judgments, but also of His mercies. Therefore it seems plausible that this is not the title deed to the earth, but the title deed to the universe containing God's judgments on both the earth and the heavens.

The wills of Emperor Vespasian and Caesar Augustus were sealed with 7 seals. The person would write awhile, roll the parchment up to conceal the words he had written, and seal the document, then continue writing on the parchment, stopping at various intervals, seal the scroll, then write again until he had used up the parchment. The scroll was rolled up on a spindle as it was written.

The scroll would be read a section at a time, after each seal was opened.

The fibers of a papyrus scroll run horizontally on the inside, which makes writing easier than on the reverse side, where the lines run vertically.

This legal document, guaranteeing the dispossession of Satan and wicked men from the earth, (Eph. 1:13-14, Rom. 8:22-23), provided by Christ's atoning death, is seen lying upon the opened right hand of the One sitting on the throne (God the Father).

The big question, "Who is able to open the scroll?" No one in heaven, on the earth or under the earth was able to open it. The angelic beings were not able to open it because the inheritance was lost by a human being, not by them. Adam's descendants could not open it because they were all sinners. The devil or his demons could not open it because they rebelled against God.

Adam did not lose ownership of earth when he sinned, for it was not his to lose. He did lose access to the Garden of Eden, and he lost the dominion entrusted to him. God, who owns the deed to earth, will only relinquish His ownership to His son, Jesus.

There are some who think that:

1. The scroll with its seven seals is the sentence handed down by God (as Judge) against Jerusalem for its part in the shedding of the righteous blood of martyrs.
2. The redemptive plan of God and seen as God's Last Will and Testament.
3. This is actually the legal title deed of the earth.
4. This scroll sealed seven times contains the secret of the future.
5. God's judgment scroll.

V5, 6—Then one of the elders said to me, "Do not weep! See, the Lion of the tribe of Judah, the Root of David, has triumphed. He is able to open the scroll and its seven seals. (6) Then I saw a Lamb, looking as if it had been slain, standing in the center of the throne, encircled by the four living creatures and the elders. He had seven horns and seven eyes, which are the seven spirits of God sent out into all the earth.

Genesis 3 tells us that thorns are first mentioned in connection with the curse of God upon the earth and upon vegetation. It is fitting that Christ, at Calvary, not only took upon Himself our sins, but wore a Crown of Thorns, signifying that He took upon Himself this curse of Genesis 3 to deliver us from the bondage of sin.

Who is worthy to open the book-5-10—Jesus alone is worthy because:

(1) He is from the royal tribe, the *"Lion of the tribe of Judah." "Lion" is a* Lion's whelp and promised the right to rule "until Shiloh comes."

(2) He is human *"the root of David,"* the offspring of David.

(3) As the God man, He has "overcome" to open the scroll,

(4) He is the *"slain"* Lamb. Pictured as the sacrifice for sin (Isa. 53:7; John 1:29), and as a mighty conqueror (17:14). Revelation uses a special word for "lamb" (29 times in Rev. and only once elsewhere in the NT John 21:15).

(5) He is divine. He has the seven spirits of God.

Jesus is our kinsmen redeemer in that He came as a man (John 1:10 "God became flesh," "lived as a man," John 1:14, and in Romans 5:15 "He dies as a man"). He was fully man and fully God, born of a virgin and conceived of the Holy Ghost. Christ holds the title deed to this earth and He alone has absolute sovereignty over the affairs of this world.

Jesus was often called the "son of man," which referred to His entitlement not only to the earth, but to the whole world. He is also called the "son of David," which revealed His right to the throne. He was also called the "son of Abraham," which revealed His title to the land of Israel and all of the royal grants given to Abraham. He is also called the "Son of God," because He was the heir to all things.

"He had seven horns." The horn is the symbol of power and of government, and seven (the number of completion or perfection) shows us that Christ's power and government are perfect. As prophesied in Isaiah 11, He will be victorious over all His enemies and He will rule in perfect righteousness and justice.

The death of Christ is the basis of the redemption not only of sinners, but also of the earth (Romans 8:18-22).

V7-10—He came and took the scroll from the right hand of him who sat on the throne. (8) And when he had taken it, the four living creatures and the twenty-four elders fell down before the Lamb. Each one had a harp and they were holding golden bowls full of incense, which are the prayers of the saints. (9) And they sang a new song: "You are worthy to take the scroll and to open its seals, because you were slain, and with your blood you purchased men for God from every tribe and language and people and nation. (10) You have made them to be a kingdom and priests to serve our God, and they will reign on the earth."

Jesus, the only one who was worthy, stepped forward and took the book (scroll) sealed with seven seals (containing the redemptive terms for the earth), out of the right hand of God who was sitting upon the throne. Christ shed His blood and paid the redemptive price, which enabled Him to do what no other could do. When Jesus took the scroll, all of the elders and living creatures fell at His feet and began to worship Him.

Priests stood twice daily before the inner veil of the temple and burned incense so that the smoke would carry to the Holy of Holies and be swept into the nostrils of God.

THE REDEMPTIVED ACTS:

1. Jesus redeemed our souls at Calvary (I Peter 18:23).
2. He will redeem our bodies at the rapture (I John 3:1-2).
3. He will redeem the earth and all creation during the time of the removal of the seven seals from the scroll (Romans 8:18-23).

Today we offer up our prayers consisting of confession, intercession, and worship. When we humble ourselves before God Almighty and offer up the confessions of our sins, we are occupied only with our sins. When we intercede for others, we are then occupied with human needs, others' and ours. When we worship God we are occupied with Him alone. The day will soon come when all prayers will be emptied of their need of confession, and then there shall be only praise and worship.

We see the worship of the heavenly bodies

V11-12—Then I looked and heard the voice of many angels, numbering thousands upon thousands, and ten thousand times ten thousand. They encircled the throne and the living creatures and the elders. (12) In a loud voice they sang: "Worthy is the Lamb, who was slain, to receive power and wealth and wisdom and strength and honor and glory and praise."

WE SEE THE UNIVERSAL WORSHIP OF THE LAMB.

V13-14—Then I heard every creature in heaven and on earth and under the earth and on the sea, and all that is in them singing: "To him who sits on the throne and to the Lamb be praise and honor and glory and power, for ever and ever!" (14) The four living creatures said, "Amen," and the elders fell down and worshiped.

These verses tell us of Christ's rights to the kingdom and glory and is climaxed by His taking the seven sealed book to claim possession of the earth, evokes the praise and worship of myriads (thousands and thousands) of angels who are the living creatures and redeemed humanity in heaven. Their great theme song is "worthy is the Lamb."

Participation of God's creation-13-14—All of God's creation praises the Lamb. All creation worships the Lamb, and again the four living creatures and the twenty-four elders fall down and worship God.

CHAPTER 6

This chapter sets forth the first of the three chronological judgments:

1. The seals,
2. trumpets, and
3. bowls.

The seal judgments, some say, cover approximately the first twenty-one months of the Tribulation, still others say it is the last 3 ½ years instead.

We shift from future events in Heaven to future events on the earth. Rev. 2:10 speaks of *"ten days of repentance."* Since the seventieth week (or the Tribulation Period) corresponds to seven years (one day of the seventieth week equals one year of the Tribulation Period), it could be reasonable to assume that the ten days of awe would correspond to ten years. This period of time would give all people, Gentiles and Jews, an opportunity to grieve, mourn, repent and accept Jesus as Messiah before the Second Coming occurs and their fate is sealed forever. If people have ten years to repent, then it is therefore reasonable to believe that the Rapture could possibly occur three years before the Tribulation Period begins. It will also allow three years for the Antichrist to come on the scene and begin his rise to power before the Tribulation Period begins.

Some scholars believe that there will be three and one half years instead of three. Daniel gives us an indication that there will be more than three years. Whether it is three or three and one half, no one knows for sure. When these years start is not known.

The Lamb had:

1. Power, authority and the physical strength to do what He wanted.
2. He had wealth, wisdom, and all the riches of God.
3. He had the honor, rewards, glory, and was in the image of God.
4. He had the praise of all creatures because He alone was worthy.

There are seven Jewish Feast days;

1. Passover-Jesus crucified on.
2. Unleavened bread-Jesus in the grave-second feast day.
3. First fruits-Jesus arose on third feast day.
4. Pentecost-Church began on fourth feast day.
5. Trumpets-Church could possibly be raptured on the fifth feast day.
6. Day of atonement-Second coming could possibly occur on the sixth day and the tribulation will end.
7. Tabernacle-Millennium could begin on seventh feast day.

V1, 2—I watched as the Lamb opened the first of the seven seals. Then I heard one of the four living creatures say in a voice like thunder, "Come!" (2) I looked, and there before me was a white horse! Its rider held a bow, and was given a crown, and he rode out as a conqueror bent on conquest.

There are several interpretations of the rider on the white horse:

1. Its rider is a conquering king. This may symbolize Christ setting out to conquer the world. Near the end of the book, 19:11, another white horse appears whose rider is plainly stated to be Christ. They may be the same; the one starting, the other finishing his conquest.
2. This horseman may symbolize, not Christ, but the world power under which Christ was starting His work. The statement at the end of the Seven Seals and Seven Trumpets, 11:15, "The Kingdom of the World is become the Kingdom of our Lord and His Christ," may imply that the "Kingdom of the World" was in the saddle at the start.
3. This horseman may symbolize the beginning of the reign of Anti-Christ at the time of the end, or possibly, both, the World Power under which Christ started His work and the final World Power under which He will finish it.
4. Victorinus, a bishop of New Vienna wrote, "Therefore the white horse is the Holy Spirit sent into the world." For the Lord says, "This Gospel shall be preached throughout the world for a testimony to all nations, and then shall come the end."

There are several reasons why this rider cannot be Christ:

1. This event occurs too early in the Tribulation. Christ, at this time is in heaven rewarding His bride while at the same time He is pouring out wrath from the throne mentioned in chapter 4:2. When Christ comes on a white horse, it is at the end and the culmination of the Tribulation. We see that Rev. 6:16 views the Lamb as still in heaven. He is the one opening the seals.
2. Another reason that supports that the white horse rider is not Christ is the parallelism with the other three horses. Each of the riders is an instrument of evil and judgment on the earth's inhabitants. Christ is the Lamb who opens the seals, allowing the riders to go forth and would not be one of the riders.
3. Here the judgments of the entire Tribulation as yet to unfold. In Rev. 19, Christ's coming puts an end to the Tribulation.

I believe that the Antichrist is the rider on the white horse. This is "the little horn," and that "willful king" that has been prophesied for many years. One interesting characteristic of his coming is that he has a bow in his hand, which is symbolic of aggressive warfare, but no arrow, indicating that he will conquer by diplomacy rather than war. Ushering in a false peace, he will be the superman who promises to solve all the problems of the world.

Psalms 45 and Revelation 19:11 show us that this rider is not the Lord.

When we look at Chapter 5 we see that Christ was the only one found worthy to open the sealed scroll. He would not open the scroll and then put a crown on His head, go and complete His task and then come back and deal out the following seals. Scripture tell us that the Lamb opened the scroll and then gave the commands to the riders, thus this confirms that Christ was not the rider on this white horse.

This rider on this white horse begins the terrible events, while the rider on the white horse in Chapter 19 ends these events.

I read one book where the author made the comment that Revelation was not in chronological order. Could be. When we look at the rider on the white horse as being the Antichrist, then we realize that there could be a lapse of three and one half years before the rider on the red horse appears.

The seven-year tribulation starts when the Antichrist signs a peace treaty with Israel. Along with this peace treaty, I believe that the Antichrist will promise the Israelites that he will help them rebuild the temple. This will assure him (the Antichrist) that Israel will sign the peace treaty.

This rider on the white horse must bring peace, because the rider on the red horse takes away peace.

If the red horse takes away peace, then it is very possible that he does not make his appearance until three and one half years later when the Antichrist desecrates the temple and begins his reign of terror. The other judgments will fall and throughout the judgments the other riders will ride the two horses, famine and death, as they occur during the last three and one half years.

The pre-tribulation theory looks at events that took place in the Old Testament.

- As long as Noah was on the earth, God did not send the flood. As soon as he was on the ark and out of harm's way, the rains fell.
- Sodom and Gomorrah were not destroyed until Lot and his family, were out of the cities and out of harm's way.

Many scholars feel as long as the church is in the world God will not send these terrible judgments on the earth.

V3, 4—When the Lamb opened the second seal, I heard the second living creature say, "Come!" (4) Then another horse came out, a fiery red one. Its rider was given power to take peace from the earth and to make men slay each other. To him was given a large sword.

The second seal—The red horse—Civil War—Symbol of War. He has the ability to *"take peace from the earth, and to make men slay each other."* It is possible that the Antichrist will come on the scene ten years before the millennium. He will emerge as one who has answers for every problem and will charm the people with his knowledge and begin to win them over. After three and one half years he will become the leader of the nations. This charismatic leader will then sign a peace treaty with Israel. This is also evidence of the fact that a great sword is given to him. Obviously, in the Antichrist's takeover of the world, some dissatisfied nations will have waited too long to make their play to avoid his domination, so they will revolt.

If Russia is the King of the North as depicted in Ezekiel 38 and 39, then this could fit strongly in the promotion of war and the removal of peace.

This could also fit in with Ezekiel 38 and 39 that say it will take them seven years to burn the weapons of war. It would seem highly unlikely that they would burn the weapons during the Millennium, although possible.

V5, 6—When the Lamb opened the third seal, I heard the third living creature say, "Come!" I looked, and there before me was a black horse! Its rider was holding a pair of scales in his hand. (6) Then I heard what sounded like a voice among the four living creatures, saying, "A quart of wheat for a day's wages, and three quarts of barley for a day's wages, and do not damage the oil and the wine!"

The third seal-The black horse-Famine (result of war.) Scales— means that food would be scarce, and sold by weight—A *Penny*—is not equivalent to our penny. It was at that time an ordinary day's wage. A *measure* of wheat was about a quart. A quart was barely enough for one person for one day.

The olive trees and the grapevine may not be affected by this outbreak of war because these were not harvested until after the harvest of the wheat.

You could buy 15 to 20 measures for a penny—*"Do not damage the oil and the wine"* may indicate as some think, a situation where rulers had plenty while the common people were in want as a result of the prolonged wars of the second seal.

One measure, found in Carvoran, England, belonged to the reign of Domitian, is marked with the date and a line showing a capacity of sixteen sextarii, equaling one modius or "measure." [A modius was equal to a bushel.]

The horseman is to declare a measure of wheat for a denarius, and three measures of barley, usually consumed in time of need and normally fed to horses or donkeys, for a denarius. This measure is the choinix, about the equivalent to a quart. One choinix of grain was sufficient for one day, but the pay for a day's work was only one denarius and it was a famine price to have to pay a whole day's wages for one measure of wheat.

Barley was three times as cheap as wheat, even in time of famine.

There are many Christians that live on farms. When these Christians are caught up, "raptured," then there will be very few left to grow the food necessary to feed the multitude of people.

During the primitive conditions of production, a drought and a failure of crops in one part of the world would affect the rest of the world.

Some scholars associate this rider with Russia and communism. Ezekiel foretold of a rise of a dictator from the far north, Russia, who would go forth and attack Israel in the last days.

V7, 8—When the Lamb opened the fourth seal, I heard a voice of the fourth living creature say, "Come!" (8) I looked, and there before me was a pale horse! Its rider was named Death, and Hades was following close behind him. They were given power over a fourth of the earth to kill by sword, famine and plague, and by the wild beasts of the earth.

To the ancient Greeks, Hades was the god of the underworld.

The fourth seal brings the Pale Horse. The end results of war and famine are death. This rider on the pale horse is given the power to kill a fourth of the earth. He will have four instruments of destruction at his disposal:

1. The sword=war, and bloodshed.
2. Famine=starvation.
3. Plague=diseases.
4. Wild beasts=the animals of earth.

The last weapon (wild beasts) could be a wakeup call to those who worship Mother Nature and place more value on the life of animals than unborn babies. The Biblical word for pale is "chloros" meaning pale green like chlorophyll. The horse is the color of spoiled meat and rotting flesh.

One fourth of the world's population will be killed. It is estimated that only 2% of the world's population will be taken during the rapture.

In Genesis 9:2 God told Adam that He would put the fear of man in the animals so man would be protected from them. Undoubtedly He removed this protection for during 200 to 300AD the Roman Empire, in its century of Civil War, suffered colossal loss in its population by an enormous increase of wild animals. The fear of man will be removed during the Tribulation.

Death has a threefold meaning:

1. Physical death—refers to the death of the body.
2. Spiritual death—is separation from and rebellion against God.
3. Eternal death—eternal separation from God (the spirit is eternal).

In ancient times there was little knowledge of bacteriology and hygiene, and the lack of this knowledge resulted in terrible outbreaks of epidemic diseases, which periodically ravaged the Roman World.

Tribulation not worldwide???—

1. The first four seals apply to a fourth part of the earth.
2. The martyrdom of the saints in Rev. 6:9-11 is primarily inside the Roman Empire Territory where the great whore of Rev. 17 dominates the 10 kings.
3. The 144,000 Jews of Rev.7:1-8 are sealed from the Nation of Israel in Palestine.

4. The Great Tribulation Saints of Rev. 7:9-17 are martyred only in that part of the earth where the Tribulation will be in the Old Roman Empire Territory.
5. The first, second, third, and fourth trumpets are over only a third part of the earth.
6. The sixth trumpet causes only a third part of men to be killed.
7. Jerusalem and Israel are the ones affected in the trouble of Rev. 11:1-13.
8. The Antichrist's rule will be over only the ten kingdoms of the Old Roman Empire.

V9-11—When he opened the fifth seal, I saw under the altar the souls of those who had been slain because of the word of God and the testimony they had maintained. (10) They called out in a loud voice, "How long, Sovereign Lord, holy and true, until you judge the inhabitants of the earth and avenge our blood?" (11) Then each of them was given a white robe, and they were told to wait a little longer, until the number of their fellow servants and brothers who were to be killed as they had been was completed.

The fifth seal-A vision of the souls of Martyrs—There had been many thousands of martyrs from the persecution of Nero and Domitian. There will be unnumbered thousands more yet to be martyred. There were, according to some, 10 imperial persecutions of the church from Nero in 64 through Diocletian's rule in 305 (See Chapter 2). There are many beings clothed in white in Revelation. The martyrs during the Great Tribulation are clothed with white robes, a badge of honor reserved just for them.

Some think that these visions may also be a prophetic hint of the papal persecutions of the middle ages and perhaps also of the persecutions of the tribulation period of the last days.

The fifth seal parallels Matthew 24:9-14 and undoubtedly occurs during the last half of the Tribulation. Matthew 24:4-8 refers to the first half of the Tribulation, the beginning of birth pangs, and verses 9-28 refer to the last half of the Tribulation.

One early Christian wrote: "The blood of the martyrs is the seed of the Church." This would allow non-Christians to see the faith and courage of martyrs and then decide to convert, causing the Church to grow.

Following the rapture, multitudes will accept Jesus as their Lord. These multitudes are referred to as the Tribulation Saints.

Jewish thought held that God rules the world according to a predetermined time schedule (2 Esdras 4:35-37) and the end awaits the death of a certain number of the righteous (1 Enoch 47:4).

V12-17—I watched as he opened the sixth seal. There was a great earthquake. The sun turned black like sackcloth made of goat hair, the whole moon turned blood red, (13) and the stars in the sky fell to earth, as late figs drop from a fig tree when shaken by a strong wind. (14) The sky receded like a scroll, rolling up, and every mountain and island was removed from its place. (15) Then the kings of the earth, the princes, the generals, the rich, the mighty, and every slave and every free man hid in caves and among the rocks of the mountains. (16) They called to the mountains and the rocks, "Fall on us and hide us from the face of him who sits on the throne and from the wrath of the Lamb! (17) For the great day of their wrath has come, and who can stand?"

The sixth seal—The day of wrath has come—When the sixth seal is removed the earth:

1. Will go into upheaval and convulsion. V12
2. The sun will turn dark, black as sackcloth, (made of goat hair and was black as soot). V12
3. The moon will turn blood red, V12
4. The stars will fall. V13
5. The heavens will roll up. V14
6. The mountains and islands will be removed. V14
7. Kings, princes, generals, the rich and poor and the mighty of the earth will be frightened. This may be a preliminary hint for in some respects the descriptions are similar to the description of the Battle of Armageddon, 16:12-21. VV15-17.

The word for star can refer to either a star or meteor. In verse 13 it could be that meteors are intended. When meteors first strike the atmosphere of the earth they glow with a fiery red color.

The earth has been struck by a number of objects smaller than the Apollo asteroids. A meteorite weighing two million tons, or 300 feet across struck Arizona and created a crater 4,200 feet across and 600 feet deep. (I saw this crater through a window of an airplane 30,000 feet up in the air. It was huge, even from that height). Siberia was struck by a meteorite or comet in 1908 and 1,000 square miles of land was devastated. The shock was felt as far away as Europe while trees up to twenty miles from the site were blown over.

Meteors are small bodies of iron ranging in size from small particles of dust to 38 tons.

Some think that the Apostle John was describing an earthquake set off by many nuclear explosions.

During a nuclear blast, the wind is displaced (pushed out) for several miles, creating a vacuum at the center of the blast site. Suddenly the wind rushes violently back into the vacuum. The sky rolls up on itself!

John's description of the sun becoming black as sackcloth and the moon becoming like blood perfectly describes the phenomena that would result from the massive amounts of dust and debris blown into the sky by multiple nuclear blasts. A cobalt bomb is made by placing a shield of cobalt 59 metal around a hydrogen bomb. Because of its fallout scientist have dubbed it "the dirty bomb."

Reportedly, according to one writer, Russia is in possession of weapons called 'fractional orbital bombs.' It consists of a dozen or more nuclear tipped missiles, which can be fired simultaneously from an orbiting platform. They can strike several cities at the same time. And according to the same writer Russia is supposedly secretly developing biological weapons of mass destruction including a "super plague" for which the west has no antidote.

Many of us remember when a comet hit Jupiter and caused such a array of splendor, we were informed that the G fragment that smashed into Jupiter caused a fireball 5 miles in diameter that had a temperature greater than the sun, at least 14,000 degrees Fahrenheit, about 4,073 degrees hotter than the sun. The fireball expanded within one and a half minutes to hundreds of miles across. The energy released by the impacts on Jupiter had a force of over 20 million megatons. This makes us aware of the fact that meteors indeed can hit the earth, as they have in the past, causing extensive damage.

In Matt. 24:29, 30 Jesus used similar language, in speaking of the time of His coming again:

"Immediately after the distress of those days" 'the sun will be darkened, and the moon will not give its light; the stars will fall from the sky, and the heavenly bodies will be shaken.' "At that time the sign of the Son of Man will appear in the sky, and all the nations of the earth will mourn. They will see the Son of Man coming on the clouds of the sky, with power and great glory."

Chapters 17 & 29 of Isaiah say that Damascus would be turned into a ruinous heap and the Mountains of Lebanon would be on fire. He said Egypt would turn to utter waste and desolation for forty years. If these are the result of atomic or nuclear weapons will it happen during the Tribulation? It is possible.

In reading the preceding verses, it sounds like there could be not only nuclear war, but also meteors falling from the sky.

CHAPTER 7

Chapter 6 closes with the sixth seal but the seventh seal is not opened until chapter 8.

Between the sixth and seventh seal judgments, God calls a divine time-out. During this pause, two significant events take place:

1. The conversion and call of the 144,000.
2. The conversion of the great multitude from every nation (Gentiles and Jews.)

V1-2—After this I saw four angels standing at the four corners of the earth, holding back the four winds of the earth to prevent any wind from blowing on the land or on the sea or on any tree. (2) Then I saw another angel coming up from the east, having the seal of the living God. He called out in a loud voice to the four angels who had been given power to harm the land and the sea:

The angels were holding the winds from the North, South, East and West so no harm could come to the land or the sea until the 144,000 were sealed.

Could it be that during this time of Revelation and the Bible, the earth was considered flat, hence "four corners."

There are three categories of angels:

1- There are the angels of God who remained faithful when Lucifer (Satan) rejected God and led a rebellion against Him.
2- There are the angels who followed Lucifer in the rebellion but are still free to work against God's purpose. These are fallen unbound angels and are usually referred to as demons.
3- This group are fallen angels who are bound and imprisoned. Genesis 6:2 gives us the indication that these are a particularly unclean group who so overstepped their authority that God cast

them into a place called "the abyss" to wait the final execution of their sentence.

This angel in verse two appears to be an angel of a higher order, and *"coming up from the east."*

The seal is the name of the Lord stamped on the forehead of Jesus' followers. Its primary purpose is to protect God's people from the coming judgments. In Ezek. 9:4, the mark is the Hebrew letter TAW; made like the x or +.

(3) "Do not harm the land or the sea or the trees until we put a seal on the foreheads of the servants of our God."

In Ezekiel 9:4 God told an angel to put a mark on those who were sorrowful of the sins of Israel. Their lives were spared. This mark of God upon them showed that they were under His immediate protection and that no harm would come to them. In the East and West it was custom to stamp with a hot iron the name of the owner upon the forehead or shoulder of his slave. During the siege of Jerusalem, not one Christian died. They had left the city and escaped to Pella.

A person might be a "secret" believer today, but during the Tribulation God's men will really be "marked men."

(4) Then I heard the number of those who were sealed: 144,000 from all the tribes of Israel.

In the number 144,000, are included all the Jews converted to Christianity, 12,000 out of each of the twelve tribes. These 144,000 are just the beginning of converts during the tribulation.

V5-8—From the tribe of Judah 12,000 were sealed, from the tribe of Reuben 12,000, from the tribe of Gad, 12,000, (6) from the tribe of Asher 12,000, from the tribe of Naphtali 12,000, from the tribe of Manasseh 12,000, (7) from the tribe of Simeon 12,000, from the tribe of Levi 12,000, from the tribe of Issachar 12,000, (8) from the tribe of Zebulun 12,000, from the tribe of Joseph 12,000, from the tribe of Benjamin 12,000.

There are three things we notice in the above verses:

1. The tribe of Levi is mentioned here even though they had no inheritance in Israel; but they belonged to the spiritual priesthood.
2. The tribe of Dan and the tribe of Ephraim are omitted even though they did have an inheritance.
3. The tribe of Joseph is here added in the place of Ephraim. Ephraim and Dan, who were the principal promoters of idolatry, are left out in this enumeration.

There are various interpretations of these verses. Some are:

1. Many scholars believe that the tribe of Dan is missing because the Jewish Antichrist (the false prophet), will come from it. This certainly seems to be the meaning of the ancient prophesies that Jacob gave about the tribes of Israel in the last days. In Genesis 49:17 we find, *"Dan will be a serpent by the roadside, a viper along the path that bites the horse's heels so that its rider tumbles backwards."*
2. There are those who believe that the Antichrist will be from Rome. Daniel 9:26b (The prince who is to come) indicates he will be a Roman for it says that his people shall destroy the city and sanctuary. Destroyed by the Romans in 70. The Antichrist a Roman or a Jew? See chapter 13.
3. There are some who think the Antichrist will be a homosexual.
4. There are those who believe this is symbolic of the entire church.
5. There are still others who believe it is a symbolic number representing the full number of Jewish Christians who escaped Jerusalem before its destruction.
6. This has no application to the church because the church has been translated "raptured." The vision states clearly that the 144,000 are from the twelve tribes of Israel.

There are a few theologians who believe the 144,000 is symbolic and expresses a multitude marked by perfection (12X12X1,000), (12 squared times 10 cubed).

(9) After this I looked and there before me was a great multitude that no one could count, from every nation, tribe, people and language, standing before the throne and in front of the Lamb. They were wearing white robes, and were holding palm branches in their hands.

144,000 evangelists leading a "great multitude," that no one could count, to the saving Grace of our Lord Jesus Christ!

According to the above verse the entire world is represented.

(10) And they cried out in a loud voice: "Salvation belongs to our God, who sits on the throne, and to the Lamb."

God alone is the author of salvation of man. When we love Jesus, we will praise Him! Christians find that praising Him will be a natural thing. Man cannot forgive us our sins or give us salvation. Only God and God alone can do this.

V11-12—All the angels were standing around the throne and around the elders and the four living creatures. They fell down on their faces before the throne and worshipped God, (12) saying: "Amen! Praise and glory and wisdom and thanks and honor and power and strength be to our God for ever and ever, Amen!"

The angels, elders and the four living creatures fall prostrate to worship God, giving Him their praises of gratitude.

There are seven different praises given to God and the Lamb:

1. Praise.
2. Glory.
3. Wisdom.
4. Thanks.
5. Honor.
6. Prayer.
7. Strength.

V13,14—Then one of the elders asked me, "These in white robes—who are they, and where did they come from?" (14) I answered, "Sir, you know." And he said, "These are they who have come out of the great tribulation; they have washed their robes and made them white in the blood of the Lamb.

The blood is the life and life belongs to God, and the blood (life) must be sacrificed to God. Many will be saved during the tribulation, and many of those who accept Christ during the last three and a half years will be martyrs.

(15) Therefore, "they are before the throne of God and serve him day and night in his temple; and he who sits on the throne will spread his tent over them.

All 16 references to the temple in Rev. use this word to designate the inner shrine where God dwells, rather than the larger precincts.

Being washed in the blood of the Lamb gives them immediate admission to the presence of God. They serve Him without ceasing for they are filled with the spirit of prayer, faith, love and obedience. God lives in His own church (the heart of every true believer).

(16) Never again will they hunger; never again will they thirst. The sun will not beat upon them, nor any scorching heat.

They will no longer be hungry or thirsty. These martyrs apparently had to face life without much food or water because they would not take the mark of the beast. No longer will they be subjected to the heat of the sun, for God will be their light.

(17) For the Lamb at the center of the throne will be their shepherd; he will lead them to springs of living water. And God will wipe away every tear from their eyes."

Jesus shall give to them "living water," and they shall never thirst. We will not be able to remember unpleasant things. God will remove our capacity to remember unpleasant things.

CHAPTER 8

Chapter 6 described the opening of the first six seals, but ended before reaching the seventh seal. Chapter 7 covered the sealing of the 144,000 but likewise failed to mention the seventh seal. It is not until Chapter 8 that we learn about the seventh seal.

The Tribulation Period carries several names: The Seventieth Weeks of Daniel, the Time of Jacob's Trouble, and the Day of the Lord's Vengeance.

V1—When he opened the seventh seal, there was silence in heaven for about half an hour.

Heaven has been filled with the sound of praises, and hymns for several thousand years but now there is silence. This silence is the lull before the storm! Jesus' revelations to John and the heavenly hosts concerning the terrible judgments which are about to fall upon the earth, leave all the heavenly hosts standing in breathless wonder and awe.

In the Bible, silence often comes before or with God's judgments, Hab. 2:20; Zech. 2:13. This dramatic pause signifies that the judgment to come is going to be as dramatic.

V2-6—And I saw the seven angels who stand before God, and to them were given seven trumpets. (3) Another angel, who had a golden censer, came and stood at the altar. He was given much incense to offer, with the prayers of all the saints, on the golden altar before the throne. (4) The smoke of the incense, together with the prayers of the saints, went up before God from the angel's hand. (5) Then the angel took the censer, filled it with fire from the altar, and hurled it on the earth; and there came peals of thunder, rumblings, flashes of lightning and an earthquake. (6) Then the seven angels who had the seven trumpets prepared to sound them.

These seven angels are special angels. Not all angels are said to stand before God. Gabriel stood before God (Luke 1:19). Tobit 12:15 tells us there are seven archangels representing the full power of God in judicial judgment. Other sources tell us their names were: Uriel, Raphael, Michael, Sariel, Gabriel, Remiel and Pravuil.

A censer is thought to be a ladle or shovel-like container used to carrying live coals of fire on which incense was to be burned. Censers came in different sizes and styles. The censer in the tabernacle was made of bronze (Ex. 27:3), while in the Temple they were made of gold (I Kgs. 7:50).

The tabernacle was filled with the sweet aroma of incense (Ex. 30:7-10), as it was burned morning and evening, just as heaven is filled with the sweet aroma of incense.

In preparation of the coming events an angel offers incense. This incense and the prayers of all the saints, was offered up together and laid on the golden altar. Another angel steps up to the altar, fills his censer with the fire and hurls it down to earth. This censer once filled with prayers now becomes a censer filled with God's judgments.

We should always have a prayer on our lips and in our hearts. Times of danger should be times of preparation and of great expectation. All our hopes and fears should put prayer on our lips and hearts constantly. I Thess. 5:17 says, *"Pray without ceasing"* (KJV).

Trumpets are used to call soldiers to war, in worship, for the convocation, to proclaim festivals such as the year of Jubilee, the Feast of the Tabernacles, and for judgments.

FIRST TRUMPET

(7) The first angel sounded his trumpet, and there came hail and fire mixed with blood, and it was hurled down upon the earth. A third of the earth was burned up, a third of the trees were burned up, and all the green grass was burned up.

The 'Four Winds of the Lamb's Wrath' were held back when the elect were sealed, now the sounding of the four trumpets announces their release.

Was the blood of the victims mingled with hail and fire (lightning), or was it mingled before hitting the earth?

In Gen. 1:11 we find that plant life was the first to be created on earth, and here it is the first to be destroyed.

"All the green grass burned up" was in the third part, not all of the earth, as Chapter 9:4 says the grass is not to be harmed, so if all the grass was burned up, then there would be no need to say "do not harm the grass."

God sends down fire and hail mixed with the blood of all His martyred ones upon the earth, just as He did on Sodom and Gomorrah (Gen. 19).

To John, not knowing what ICBM's were, could the holocaust he witnessed that looked like hail and fire, mixed with blood raining down from the atmosphere, possibly be an ICBM?

This devastation could be a massive nuclear attack much larger than the first one described in the sixth seal of Chapter 6. The sounding of the trumpet brings:

1. Hail and fire mixed with blood.
2. Blazing meteorite or missiles?? Both??
3. Great Star.
4. One third of the sun and moon darkened.
5. Zechariah 14:12 says, *"This is the plague with which the Lord will strike all the nations that fought against Jerusalem: Their flesh will rot while they are still standing on their feet, their eyes will rot in their sockets, and their tongues will rot in their mouths."*

When there is a nuclear detonation in the atmosphere, it can send a shock-wave of compressed atmosphere that travels about one-half mile in two seconds. This causes enormous over-pressure. Here the first shock wave meets a reactive reflection. Thermal radiation also occurs, and humans and animals within a radius of twelve miles from ground zero (where the bomb detonated) can be cremated. Buildings will also suffer extensive damage from the explosion and fire.

When a nuclear detonation occurs, the humidity in the air is instantly compressed into water and driven straight up into the freezing temperatures of the upper stratosphere. It is then instantly frozen and falls back to earth as giant chunks of ice.

It has been reported that in 1921, in Chek Shoe, Yunnen, China, fire and hail mingled with blood fell all over the countryside.

2 Peter 3:10—*But the day of the Lord will come like a thief. The heavens will disappear with a roar; the elements will be destroyed by fire, and the earth and everything in it will be laid bare.* Peter describes in accurate terms the untying of the atom and the resulting rushing fiery destruction which follows it, which describes a nuclear explosion.

Why only one third? It has been said it was because the Jews killed the Son, one third of the Trinity.

SECOND TRUMPET

V8-9—The second angel sounded his trumpet, and something like a huge mountain, all ablaze, was thrown into the sea. A third of the sea turned into blood, (9) a third of the living creatures in the sea died, and a third of the ships were destroyed.

This reminds us when God turned Egypt's water into blood (Ex. 7:19). John said it was *"something like a huge mountain, all ablaze."* This could refer to a meteoric mass from the sky falling headlong into the sea, probably the Mediterranean Sea. The result is to turn a third part of the sea into a blood red color and bring about the death of a third part of the life in the sea. Death may be caused by the chemical reaction in the water, such as radioactivity following atomic explosion.

This could also be a colossal H-bomb. A hydrogen bomb exploded in the ocean would look like a huge flaming mountain smashing into the sea.

There would be a massive reduction of the world's food supply. A giant missile falling to the earth could look like a mountain falling.

The terms "mountain of fire" or "falling star" comes close to a description of nuclear "fireballs." All those who depend upon the sea for jobs, food, defense, or the transporting of cargo will suffer.

A third of the sea turning to blood is a miracle within a miracle. Just think of a vast sea where only 1/3 becomes blood and the other two thirds is as clear as can be. It was just as there was a wall separating 1/3 from the other two thirds. There was no "bleeding" of the bloody water into the clear water.

What caused 1/3 of the ships to be destroyed? Perhaps a tsunami created by the meteorite, bomb, or whatever it was that fell into the water.

THIRD TRUMPET

V10-11—The third angel sounded his trumpet, and a great star, blazing like a torch, fell from the sky on a third of the rivers and on the springs of water (11) the name of the star is Wormwood. A third of the waters turned bitter, and many people died from the waters that had become bitter.

The third trumpet is a fulfillment of Jer. 9:13-15.

"Wormwood" is a perennial herb, extremely bitter, used in the manufacture of absinthe, which is used in France as a beverage. This bitter herb causes drunkenness and eventually death. Wormwood is also associated with another poison called "gall." This substance was used to produce a stupefying drink offered to Jesus on the cross (Ps. 69:21; Matt. 27:34), which He refused.

Asteroids are strong chunks of broken planets. Comets are chunks of frozen gas. When a comet approaches earth, it comes in tail first, for the tail of a comet always points directly away from the sun. Doing so, it appears to burn like a torch as described in Revelation.

This could also be another thermo-nuclear weapon with chemicals.

According to a former Soviet Scientist, as mentioned before, Russia has developed an extremely deadly biological weapon, including a strain of bacteria that could produce a "super plague" capable of wiping out tens of thousands of people within a week.

There are some who think this star could refer to a meteor containing stifling and bitter gases, which fall on the Alps or some freshwater source.

FOURTH TRUMPET

(12) The fourth angel sounded his trumpet, and a third of the sun was struck, a third of the moon, and a third of the stars, so that a third of them turned dark. A third of the day was without light, and also a third of the night.

It was on the fourth day of creation God said, *"Let there be light and there was light."* Now God will diminish the light one third. Actually, day and night will seem to be reversed, for there will be sixteen hours of darkness and eight hours of daylight.

The loss of solar heat could cause a drop in earth's temperature and upset earth's climatology and meteorology. Scientist found in the 80's evidence that the sun is remarkably shrinking in size. This could also be true of stars.

This light reduction could also be a result from the tremendous pollution in the air left from nuclear explosions.

(13) As I watched, I heard an eagle that was flying in midair call out in a loud voice: "Woe! Woe! Woe to the inhabitants of the earth, because of the trumpet blasts about to be sounded by the other three angels!"

How many animals speak in the Bible??? 3—(1) serpent, Gen.—(2) donkey, Num. 22—(3) and here the eagle.

The eagle sounds the alarm by uttering a threefold woe to earth's inhabitants who repeatedly ignored the first four trumpets. God does not want anyone to perish.

CHAPTER 9

The first woe (fifth trumpet) and the second woe (sixth trumpet) cover five months each. These woes (trumpets) are different than the previous judgments because they predict an increase in the destructive powers to be unleashed upon men. Woe is a prophetic pronouncement of doom.

FIFTH TRUMPET-The First Woe

V1-2—The fifth angel sounded his trumpet, and I saw a star that had fallen from the sky to the earth. The star was given the key to the shaft of the Abyss. (2) When he opened the Abyss, smoke rose from it like the smoke from a gigantic furnace. The sun and sky were darkened by the smoke from the Abyss.

The key to the abyss was given to the *"star that had fallen"* referring to an angel. Upon opening the abyss, a great smoke will arise which will darkened the sun and the sky. The power of hell will be released.

The abyss is the intermediate place of punishment for the fallen angels, demons, the beast, the false prophet and Satan. Some believe Romans 10:7 indicates that Christ descended into the spirit world between His death and resurrection. It is here that Satan himself is confined for a thousand years during the reign of Christ.

There are three different theories as to who the star is:

1. Some think he is Christ, but Christ did not fall from Heaven.
2. Some think Satan,
3. and others a fallen angel.

Perhaps this angel was not a "fallen" angel but one that "fell" or descended from heaven to earth and was given the power and authority to open the abyss and to execute on creatures the effects of death that give him his name.

Rev. 1:18 tell us that Christ has the keys to Heaven and Hell.

It is possible that Christ gives the keys to Satan who then in return opens the bottomless pit, but Satan is nowhere connected with the Abyss until he is cast into it, Rev. 20:1-3. Satan walks up and down the earth and accuses the saints before God in heaven, (Job 1:1; I Peter 5; Rev. 12).

Whether it is Christ, another angel or Satan is not important. What is important is that Christ allows the bottomless pit to be open and this unleashes a judgment that is unparalleled in its torment. The "Locusts" of Revelation 9:3 are said to be possessed by hell's worse demons, fallen angels so ferocious that God has kept them bound since the days of Noah (II Peter 2:4, 5). Their leader is apparently a demon of almost the power and authority of Satan himself.

V3-6-And out of the smoke locusts came down upon the earth and were given power like that of scorpions of the earth. (4) They were told not to harm the grass of the earth or any plant or tree, but only those people who did not have the seal of God on their foreheads. (5) They were not given power to kill them, but only to torture them for five months. And the agony they suffered was like that of the sting of a scorpion when it strikes a man. (6) During those days men will seek death, but will not find it; they will long to die, but death will elude them.

These 'locusts' were told not to harm:

1. the grass of the earth,
2. any plant, or
3. any tree.

They were told only to harm those who did not have the seal of God on their foreheads.

This plague will last for five months, which is the normal life span of a locust from birth, through the larva stage, and then death. This also coincides with the length of the growing season in Israel, from April to September. See Job 3:21; *to those who long for death that does not come, who search for it more than for hidden treasure,* Jer. 8:3; *Wherever I banish them, all the survivors of this evil nation will prefer death to life, declares the LORD Almighty.'*

In 1889, it was reported that a swarm of locust had appeared over the Red Sea covering 2,000 square miles. In 1951-52 the worst locust plague struck the Middle East, where in Iran, Iraq, Jordan and Saudi Arabia every green and growing thing was devoured across thousands of square miles.

The venom of the scorpion affects the veins and nervous system. The pain and discomfort usually last for several days. God's punishment on the world will be so severe, and the pain so great that people will desire death over life.

Is John describing mobilized ballistic missile launchers as some have suggested? This could very well be a picture of modern warfare, or are these demons the fallen (sons of God) in Genesis 6?

V7-12—The locusts looked like horses prepared for battle. On their heads they wore something like crowns of gold, and their faces resembled human faces. (8) Their hair was like women's hair, and their teeth were like lion's teeth. (9) They had breastplates like breastplates of iron, and the sound of their wings was like the thundering of many horses and chariots rushing into battle. (10) They had tails and sting like scorpions, and in their tails they had power to torment people for five months. (11) They had as king over them the angel of the Abyss, whose name in Hebrew is Abaddon, and in Greek, Apollyon. (12) The first woe is past; two other woes are yet to come.

In Joel 2:2-11—*² a day of darkness and gloom, a day of clouds and blackness. Like dawn spreading across the mountains a large and mighty army comes, such as never was of old nor ever will be in ages to come. ³ Before them fire devours, behind them a flame blazes. Before them the land is like the garden of Eden, behind them, a desert waste—nothing escapes them. ⁴ They have the appearance of horses; they gallop along like cavalry. ⁵ With a noise like that of chariots they leap over the mountaintops, like a crackling fire consuming stubble, like a mighty army drawn up for battle.⁶ At the sight of them, nations are in anguish; every face turns pale. ⁷ They charge like warriors; they scale walls like soldiers. They all march in line, not swerving from their course.* *8 They do not jostle each other; each marches straight ahead. They plunge through defenses without breaking ranks. 9 They rush upon the city; they run along the wall. They climb into the houses; like thieves they enter through the windows. 10 Before them the earth shakes, the sky trembles, the sun and moon are darkened, and the stars no longer shine. 11 The LORD thunders at the head of his army; his forces are beyond number, and mighty are those who obey his command. The day of the LORD is great; it is dreadful. Who can endure it?*

Job 39:20—*Do you make him leap like a locust, striking terror with his proud snorting?*

There are those who believe these "locust" resemble the Cobra helicopters. The "sting" from its tail is "nerve gas." Some say the general shape looks similar to that of a locust. The whirling blades of a helicopter could appear to be women's hair.

It has been reported that in Italy and some other foreign countries locusts are called "little horses" because some of them resemble a horse.

Whatever they are, humans, helicopters, locusts or demons, they are not allowed to hurt those who have the seal of God on their foreheads.

It is thought that God showed His mercy by allowing people to be tormented five months in an effort to bring them to accept Christ as their savior, and by doing so avoid the torment of the damned for eternity. This would be possible only if the people are remorseful and repentant of their sins and then must ask Christ to forgive them of their sins before they can receive salvation. Satan believes in God, but is not repentant.

These locusts are not ordinary locust, for:

1. They eat no grass, vegetables, or trees,
2. have a king, and
3. are not stifled by the smoke nor are they burned by the fire of the abyss.
4. They are not confined to the infernal regions, but

5. they are spiritual, intelligent beings,
6. and have power to torment men.
7. They look like horses prepared for battle, and
8. wear a crown of gold on their heads.
9. Their hair is like a woman's hair.
10. Their teeth are like those of a lion.
11. Their breastplates are like iron.
12. Their wings make the sound of many horses and chariots.
13. Their tails have the sting of a scorpion and
14. Have the power to torment people for five months.
15. Their king is Abaddon, the angel over the Abyss.

Those who do not know the Lord Jesus Christ as Savior will come under demonic possession and affliction. What is true in that hour is also true today, for there is no deliverance neither from the power of Satan, or from his affliction apart from Salvation in Christ.

SIXTH TRUMPET-The Second Woe

V13-16—The sixth angel sounded his trumpet, and I heard a voice coming from the horns of the golden altar that is before God. (14) It said to the sixth angel who had the trumpet, "Release the four angels who are bound at the great river Euphrates." (15) And the four angels who had been kept ready for this very hour and day and month and year were released to kill a third of mankind. (16) The number of the mounted troops was two hundred million. I heard their number.

It is thought that the 6th trumpet marks the mid-point of the Tribulation, but some think Chapter 12 marks the mid-point.

The Book of Enoch describes some angels as "the Angels of Punishment."

The sixth angel is given two commandments:

1. Blow the trumpet.
2. Release the four angels bound at the Euphrates River.

There are several events that have taken place near the Garden of Eden:

1. Cain murdered Abel.
2. The building of the Tower of Babel (the first great revolt against God).
3. It was in this area Noah built an ark, and
4. the flood began.
5. Babylon was built in this area and here is
6. where government and world religion began.
7. The first ruler set up his kingdom at Babylon.
8. Abraham came from Ur.

The wicked sins of Babylon have been astrology, idolatry, and worship of demons, witchcraft, and various other sins.

The Romans, Babylonians, and Greeks always considered the Euphrates River the boundary line between the East and the West. Rome's power and the power of the Parthia were divided by the Euphrates. It was not until the second century that Rome conquered the lands beyond the Euphrates.

These four angels being bound at the Euphrates River and their confinement at the Euphrates could be because they are very powerful servants of Satan. The angels' function is to slay the third part of men and that they have been prepared to fulfill this purpose at the given hour. The releasing of the four fallen angels will cause the loss of one third of earth's population. We find a few hundred million will leave in the rapture. One fourth of those left on earth will die when the fourth seal is opened. Many others will die from war, famine, natural disasters, and poisoned water. One third of the remainder will die when the four angels are released.

V17-21—The horses and rider I saw in my vision looked like this: Their breastplates were fiery red, dark blue, and yellow as sulfur. The heads of the horses resembled the heads of lions, and out of their mouths came fire, smoke and sulfur. (18) A third of mankind was killed by the three plagues of fire, smoke and sulfur that came out of their mouths. (19) The power of the horses was in their mouths and in their tails; for their tails were like snakes, having heads with which they inflict injury. (20) The rest of mankind that were not killed by these plagues still did not repent of the work of their hands; they did not stop worshiping demons, and idols of gold, silver, bronze, stone and wood—idols that cannot see or hear or walk. (21) Nor did they repent of their murders, their magic arts, their sexual immorality or their thefts.

Scientist are now trying to create an EMP (electronic magnetic pulse). Once it is released, it will kill all electrical devises. Perhaps this is why Daniel & John saw horses. Once the "EMP" is released there will be no cars, trucks, planes, trains, lights, or heat. We would be set back to the 19th century.

Magic according to Isaiah 47:12-15 often involved drugs and the casting of spells on people. This kind of magic touches the evil spiritual forces, which are in opposition to God.

There are a couple of possibilities:

1. Many more will turn to drugs when they are stung or bitten by these "locusts." It could be that the sting from the "tail" is biological warfare. People will resort to anything that will deaden the pain or lift them out of their troubles at that time.
2. That these are not to be taken as humans, for horsemen do not wear *"breastplates were fiery red, dark blue and yellow as sulfur."* This could be a description of unnatural, demon like evil spirits.

Verses 20 & 21 lists the six sins that are not only prominent now but will also be prominent during the Tribulation Period:

1. Demon worship—2—Idolatry—3—Murder.
4. Drug related occult activities. The word "sorceries" in Revelation 9:21, comes from the Greek word *pharmakeia,* which means "pharmacy" and refers here to the practice of the occult with the use of drugs.
5. Porneia refers to all kinds of sexual activity outside of its Biblically sanctioned function between a married man and woman.
6. Theft. This included burglaries, (theft by breaking into houses and businesses), and robberies, (theft by threat of personal violence).

The Bible tells us that even after all these judgments are inflicted by these invaders, those who survive are still unrepentant!

This paints a grim picture! In the final days nothing will be sacred. Life, marriage, family, sex, one's health, nor the property and rights of others will not mean anything. We are seeing this in the twenty-first century.

CHAPTER 10

The interlude between the sixth and seventh trumpets

(1) Then I saw another mighty angel coming down from heaven. He was robed in a cloud, with a rainbow above his head; his face was like the sun, and his legs were like fiery pillars.

Christ's messenger is:

1. *"robed in a cloud,*
2. *with a rainbow above his head."*
3. *"His face was like the sun,*
4. *and his legs were like fiery pillars."*

This mighty angel has on his regal attire, and is sent to call mankind to account for breaking God's commandments. His legs were like fiery pillars declaring the supreme character of the angel and the message he delivers.

There may be a similarity between the portrayal of this mighty angel (vv1-6) and the description of the bronze statue of Colossus at Rhodes, an island to the southeast of Patmos. This statue erected around 280 BC, was 10 feet high, but an earthquake over 50 years later destroyed it.

(2) He was holding a little scroll, which lay open in his hand. He planted his right foot on the sea and his left foot on the land,

The angel standing on the land and the sea denotes the complete authority of God. In Lev. 25:23 God stated that *"The land must not be sold permanently, because the land is mine and you are but aliens and my tenants."*

Some think this is the same scroll mentioned in Chapter 5.

V3,4—and he gave a shout like the roar of a lion. When he shouted, the voices of the seven thunders spoke. (4) And when the seven thunders spoke, I was about to write; but I heard a voice from heaven say, "Seal up what the seven thunders have said and do not write it down."

John heard the seven thunders speak but was told not to write down what he heard. It was sealed from mankind.

Through the vision John received, he was able to write the book of Revelation, and he then passed on these divine revelations to the Church. In this instance John saw several things glorious about this angel's appearance:

1. He was heavenly—he came down from heaven. (V1).
2. He was robed in a cloud. (V1).
3. There was a rainbow above his head. (V1).
4. His face was as the sun in its brilliance. (V1).
5. His legs were like fiery pillars. (V1).
6. He held an opened scroll (book) in his hand. (V2).
7. He plants his right foot on the sea. (V2).
8. He plants his left foot on the land. (V2).

John was told not to reveal what he saw or heard. God, even though He has revealed much, He still has some secrets that He has not seen fit to reveal to mankind at this time. It could be that man, who has not reached his spiritual realm, would not understand.

In Job 26:14, we find *"How faint the whisper we hear of Him. Who then can understand the thunder of His power?"* And again in Chapter 37:5, *"God voice thunders in marvelous ways; he does great things beyond our understanding."* David in Psalm Chapter 29 verse 3 gives a description of the seven thunders of the Revelation. *"The voice of the Lord is over the waters; the god of glory thunders."* See Jer. 25:30; Isa. 29:6.

V5,6—Then the angel I had seen standing on the sea and on the land raised his right hand to heaven. (6) And he swore by him who lives forever and ever, who created the heavens and all that is in them, the earth and all that is in it, and the sea and all that is in it, and said, "There will be no more delay!"

101

This is a mighty angel, not Christ, standing with one foot on the sea and the other one on the land. He lifts up his right hand to heaven, and announces a solemn oath by God the Creator. There will be no more delay! A wave of divine judgments are about to come on the scene. When the Lamb opened the sealed book, the first six seals brought terrible judgments among men; and again after the seventh seal, six of the seven trumpets brought direct visitations from heaven upon impenitent men.

V7—but in the days when the seventh angel is about to sound his trumpet, the mystery of God will be accomplished, just as he announced to his servants the prophets.

The *"mystery of God"* appears to be God's commandments, counsels and dealings made known to the Old Testament prophets, with all of them looking forward to the arrival of the Messiah. We are still in the days of "mystery." We, like the Old Testament prophets are looking forward to the coming of the Messiah, but this time it will be His second coming.

There are several mysteries we do not know:

The Rapture—1 Cor. 15:51.
Israel's Blindness—Rom. 11:25.
God's Wisdom—1 Cor. 2:7.
Christ and the Church—Eph. 5:31, 32.
Christ in us—Colossians 1:26, 26.
Kingdom of Heaven—Matt. 13.
Godliness—1 Tim. 3:16.

There are those who think that the apostate papal church has been given centuries to mend its ways. It has been stated by one writer that Jesus came to Israel approximately 1500 years before its founding, and the Reformation came to the church about 1500 years after its founding.

V8-10—Then the voice that I had heard from heaven spoke to me once more: "Go, take the scroll that lies open in the hand of the angel who is standing on the sea and on the land." (9) So I went to the angel and asked him to give me the little scroll. He said to me, "Take it and eat it. It will turn your stomach sour, but in your mouth it will be as sweet as honey." (10) I took the little scroll from the angel's hand and ate it. It tasted as sweet as honey in my mouth, but when I had eaten it, my stomach turned sour.

The little book in Daniel 12:4, 9 was closed. This book is open. This could very well be the book Daniel was told to seal up until the end of time! The passage in Daniel 12:4, 9 appears to be the foundation of these verses. This is the reason the scroll was *"sweet as honey"* when first eaten, (Ezek. 2:8, 9; 3:1-3) but when digested, bitter (Jer. 15:10; 20:14-18).

Eating a scroll was symbolic of one accepting the message, which was sweet, because it came from God, and because it held the judgments of terrible suffering it became bitter.

John, like Ezekiel (Ezek. 2:9-3:3) was obedient to God and ate the "book."

(11) Then I was told, "You must prophesy again about many peoples, nations, languages and kings."

John is told to prophesy. The heavenly inhabitants are well aware as to God's earthly judgments and His prophetic programs. The blessings of all the nations on earth depend on their relationship with the Nation of God, Israel.

There are some who think eating of the book:

1. Represents the reception of the church of the Bible at the time of the Reformation. Having been starved for God's Word for hundreds of years, it was now as sweet as honey to the taste.
2. John was told to let the Word of God affect him before he ministered it to others.
3. The Gospel is in itself glorious and sweet, but its proclamation is always followed by bitter persecution.
4. God's Word is bitter in that it not only contains promises of grace but also contains in Revelation the divine judgments, which will be poured out on the earth.

CHAPTER 11

V1, 2—I was given a reed like a measuring rod and was told, "Go and measure the temple of God and the altar, and count the worshipers there. (2) But exclude the outer court; do not measure it, because it has been given to the Gentiles. They will trample on the holy city for 42 months.

The reed was a bamboo-like cane that often reached up to a height of 20 feet, which grew in abundance in the water along the banks of the Jordan River. They were straight, light, and were used for three things; a walking staff, a measuring rod, and a pen. Its size varied according to its use.

In Ezek. 40:3, Ezekiel sees *"a man whose appearance was like bronze,"* measuring the temple and all of its walls and courts. Herod, in the additions he made to the temple, built an outer court and called it the Court of the Gentiles, which was not a part of the Temple, whereas God would have no regard for it. According to Ezek. 40:17-19, the outer court contained thirty rooms facing the pavement. The outside court covered approximately 26 acres.

This prophecy of measurement not only speaks of Gentiles and Jews sharing holy places on the Temple Mount, but also predicts the awful last half of the tribulation.

Dr. Asher Kaufman, an archaeologist, upon carefully checking all of the evidence, found that the Dome of the Rock could not be over the Temple site (as had been almost universally believed) because of its proximity to the Eastern Gate. Every ancient document describing the Temple placed the Eastern Gate exactly on the east/west centerline of the Temple itself. The Dome of the Rock is at least 150 meters south of that centerline.

This could mean that the Temple could be rebuilt at any time without destruction of the third holiest shrine of the Moslem faith.

There are other archaeologists who disagree with this.

It is irrelevant whether the Dome of the Rock is on the Temple site or not. God will make the necessary arrangements to prepare the site for His Temple.

Daniel indicates that the temple will be rebuilt and in use by the middle of the Tribulation Period.

Christians of the day will probably not see the Temple being rebuilt. They will be *"caught up"* to be with the Lord. However, if Christians do see the Temple being started before the "rapture," then they had better be sure their "house" is in order!

During this period of forty two months (equivalent to three and one half years) Jerusalem will see nothing but war; one Gentile army after another will invade the city of Jerusalem and march up and down its streets. In Luke 21:24 Jesus predicted, *"Jerusalem will be trampled on by the Gentiles until the times of the Gentiles are fulfilled."* The "Times of the Gentiles" which began in 606 BC, will end with the return of Jesus Christ to the earth at the last battle of the Tribulation, the Battle of Armageddon.

Antiochus IV (Epiphanes), king of Syria, subdued Jerusalem for three and a half years beginning in 168 BC. During this time Antiochus desecrated the temple by sacrificing a pig (an unclean animal to the Jews), and ordered the Jewish people to abandon their faith, prophesied by Daniel in Chapters 7:25 and 9:27. There will be a desecration of the temple in the middle of the tribulation that will surpass what Antiochus did.

(3) And I will give power to my two witnesses, and they will prophesy for 1,260 days, clothed in sackcloth.

These two great prophets or *"witnesses'"* testimony will preserve Israel from doom and lay the foundation of *"the fear of the Lord"* in the remnant.

In the Old Testament the Mosaic Law required two witnesses to validate matters pertaining to Jewish religion.

Who are these two witnesses? Moses, and Elijah as seen at the transfiguration? Could it be Moses and Enoch? Maybe Elijah and Enoch!

In 1997, an epistle or letter, written about (306-73) was discovered. This discovery was called *Pseudo-Ephraem*. This document claims to have been written by Ephraem of Nisibis, who was considered to be the greatest figure in the history of the Syrian Church. This document divided into ten sections, states in section nine that 'the prophets Enoch and Elijah, who, while not yet tasting death, are the servants for the heralding of the Second Coming of Christ . . .' This document or sermon, also teaches the Pre-Tribulation Theory.

For someone to say that it has to be Enoch because Hebrew 9:27 says, *"Just as man is destined to die once, and after that to face judgment, . . . ,"* would be presumptuous on their part because when the rapture occurs, all believers in that time will not "die," but will be translated.

According to the writer Heb. 11:5, the purpose of Enoch's translation was *"that he did not experience death."* If it is literal, then Enoch cannot be one of the witnesses because they will die.

Tertullian and Irenaeus mention Enoch and Elijah as the two witnesses.

These two witnesses will have the power to send fire out of their mouths and to kill those who try to persecute them. They also have power to stop rain, turn waters to blood, and smite the earth with plagues.

The prophet Malachi in Chapter 4:5,6 predicted that Elijah would come before *"the coming of the great and terrible day of the Lord."* In addition to this, we find that the use of fire in the Old Testament was limited to Elijah, who called down fire to consume the altar of Baal (2 Kings 18:20-40.) He also withheld rain from the earth for three years.

Jude 14 and 15 states that Enoch prophesied that *"the Lord is coming with thousands upon thousands of his holy ones, to judge everyone . . ."*

John the Baptist stated that he was not Elijah, Jn. 1:19-23. Elijah must come back to fulfill Mal. 3,4.

God told Elijah He was going to translate him for a special ministry in the future and he, believing God, was translated by his faith.

Here are six reasons given why Moses and Elijah could be the two witnesses:

1. Both were present at the transfiguration.
2. Moses brought plagues down on Egypt,
3. Moses and Elijah combined represent the entire Old Testament.
4. Moses represents the law and Elijah represents the prophets.
5. Moses represents those who die and will be raised again.
6. Elijah represents those who will never die but will be caught up in the rapture.

God's witnesses who were dressed for mourning, clothed in sackcloth of humiliation, through their lamentations, prayer, mourning and warning were crying out on God's behalf. For 3 1/2 years they shall prophesy, then God will turn them over to the people to be slain.

There are some who think they will be two prophets raised up from among those who turn to Christ during the tribulation.

The importance is not who these witnesses are, but that they are men God is using to bring salvation to those who will respond to their preaching.

One thing we might want to remember is Matthew 11:14, *"And if you are willing to accept it, John himself is Elijah who was to come,"* NASB. Maybe this would eliminate Elijah as one of these witnesses, but John in John 1:21 said he only came in the spirit and power of Elijah, but he was not Elijah.

Luke 4:25 states that the famine of Elijah's day was 3 ½ years even though the Old testament never actually says how long it was.

There are still others who think:

1. Two witnesses—churches boldly proclaiming truth.
2. Who prophesy—proclaiming God's Word against sin.
3. In sackcloth—humble and repentant, mourning sin.
4. For 1,260 days—minister during the time of great suffering.

5. Two olive trees—empowered by the Spirit of God.
6. Two lamp stands—God's new people (rather than Israel).
7. *"he will make war against them,"* a further indication that the two witnesses are the whole church and not just two individuals.

(4) These are the two olive trees and the two lampstands that stand before the Lord of the earth.

Zechariah in chapter 3 and 4 made the two olive trees to be Zerubbabel (representing the royal line) and Joshua (representing the priestly line). These two are anointed to serve the Lord. These olive trees stand by a lampstand and provide oil (representing the Holy Spirit) for the lampstand. Some say the candlestick represents God and the olive trees the Spirit of God.

There is the thought that this verse gives evidence that these two witnesses have to be living in the Old Testament times. They are said to be "standing before God," back in the days of Zechariah.

Zechariah 4:14 had received a vision of a golden candlestick (lampstand) with seven lamps, surrounded by two olive trees yielding golden oil for the lamps. The olive trees were interpreted as the two anointed ones (or "the ones with the oil"), that stand by the Lord of the whole earth.

(5) If anyone tries to harm them, fire comes from their mouths and devours their enemies. This is how anyone who wants to harm them must die.

God has given these two witnesses protection from harm so they can announce His judgments. If we see Zechariah's vision as seeing the two olive trees as representatives of the Royal and Priestly lines, then it could be that these two witnesses are someone we do not know.

(6) These men have power to shut up the sky so that it will not rain during the time they are prophesying; and they have power to turn the waters into blood and to strike the earth with every kind of plague as often as they want.

These two witnesses have God's unlimited trust and faith in them. If we were given these same powers, how often would we abuse them?

In I Kings 17:1, we find that Elijah shut the skies up, so it would not rain. In Exodus Chapter 7-11, Moses afflicted the land with the authority of God.

These two 'witnesses', whoever they are, their power and conduct are spectacular. They are given the following power:

1. To kill their enemies.
2. Stop the rain.
3. Turn waters to blood,
4. And bring plagues upon the earth.

When we have been to Heaven only a short time, God's love and glory will consume us and will become a part of us.

V7,8—Now when they have finished their testimony, the beast that comes up from the Abyss will attack them, and overpower and kill them. (8) Their bodies will lie in the street of the great city, which is figuratively called Sodom and Egypt, where also their Lord was crucified.

These two witnesses finish their task and God removes His protection from them and allows the Beast to attack and kill them. The Beast that comes out of the sea is the world dictator. The beast that comes out of the land is the leader of that day (13:11). Who is this beast? John doesn't say. Perhaps it is one of Satan's minions.

Some say this great city is Rome, which may be spiritually called Sodom for its abominations, Egypt for its tyrannous cruelty, but Jerusalem itself is intended because of its persecution of Christians and because the 8th verse says here was the place our Lord was crucified.

In spite of the preaching and testimony of these two witnesses, the majority of the people reject God. This is reminds us of Luke 16:19-31 where the rich man died and in hell asked to go back so he could tell his brothers show terrible hell was. The reply was that if they did not hear Moses and the prophets, they would not listen to one who had returned from the dead.

V9-10—For three and a half days men from every people, tribe, language and nation will gaze on their bodies and refuse them burial. (10) The inhabitants of the earth will gloat over them and will celebrate by sending each other gifts, because these two prophets had tormented those who live on the earth.

The whole world will see their dead bodies, either in person or via television and will actually rejoice in the death of God's witnesses. They treat these witnesses worse than dead animals, showing the contempt and hatred the world has for these two witnesses. For 3 1/2 days they rejoice and exchange gifts. (See Esther 9:19, 22).

In the ancient world, exposing the enemy's dead body was the ultimate way of dishonoring and desecrating them. God had commanded the Israelites not to engage in this practice, and Christian burial was denied by papal decree to those who were declared heretics.

V11, 12—But after the three and a half days a breath of life from God entered them, and they stood on their feet, and terror struck those who saw them. (12) Then they heard a loud voice from heaven saying to them, "Come up here." And they went up to heaven in a cloud, while their enemies looked on.

V12-*"they heard."* After three and one half days God breathes life into the witnesses and they stand up and wait for God to call them up to Heaven. Those who heard the voice from heaven and saw them ascend to heaven were struck with awe.

If the multitude heard God's voice, we can see them standing there in amazement. Their eyes fastened upon the two witnesses as they ascend to heaven. Then suddenly within the same hour, probably as soon as the multitude watch the two witnesses disappear out of sight, there's a violent shaking of the earth, an earthquake so severe that 7,000 people of Jerusalem perish. God "shakes like a hut" this whole guilty earth, as He did at the time our Lord Jesus was slain by men in Jerusalem. Chapter 16:18-20 states that under the seventh bowl of wrath the greatest earthquake that has ever been, is yet to come. Men have forgotten to fear the Lord God who declares in Isa. 2:20,21-*"In that day men will throw away the rodents and the bats their idols of silver and idols of gold, which they made to worship. They will flee to caves in the rocks and to the overhanging crags from dread of the Lord, and the splendor of his majesty, when he rises to shake the earth."* In the last great earthquake of Revelation 16, the cities of the Gentiles will fall.

They were in a great stage of fear and their eyes were at a transfixed stare.

Lazarus lay in the grave three and a half days. We find that Christ delayed his trip to Lazarus's grave because the Jews believed the spirit (soul) hovered over the body for three days before leaving. Jesus wanted no one to doubt His power over death.

(13) At that very hour there was a severe earthquake and a tenth of the city collapsed. Seven thousand people were killed in the earthquake, and the survivors were terrified and gave glory to the God of heaven.

The King James Version and a couple of other translations say 7,000 men.

(14) The second woe has passed; the third woe is coming soon.

Another judgment has passed. There are more to come.

There is a belief by some that the two witnesses began their ministries at the start of the Tribulation.

Seventh Trumpet-The Third Woe.

(15) The seventh angel sounded his trumpet, and there were loud voices in heaven, which said: "The kingdom of the world has become the kingdom of our Lord and of his Christ, and he will reign forever and ever."

The saints and angels in heaven give loud and joyful acclamations.

(16) And the twenty-four elders, who were seated on their thrones before God, fell on their faces and worshiped God, saying:

Some say they are representatives of the universal Church of Christ, or as discussed earlier, they could be, as some think, the leaders of the twelve tribes and the twelve apostles.

Perhaps the most logical explanation is that they are representative of all the Old Testament Saints. It would not seem reasonable for John to see himself sitting on the throne. He said he saw twenty-four elders. The Bible says the Apostles will themselves sit on their own thrones.

V17,18—"We give thanks to you, Lord God Almighty, the One who is and who was, because you have taken your great power and have begun to reign. (18) The nations were angry; and your wrath has come. The time has come for judging the dead, and for rewarding your servants the prophets and your saints and those who reverence your name, both small and great—and for destroying those who destroy the earth."

The Bible and history tells us that since the beginning of time, nations have been determined to destroy God's Gospel, but they have and will always fail to do so. We see this happening in the world today, even in America, the nation which was founded on its belief in God!

(19) The God's temple in heaven was opened, and within his temple was seen the ark of his covenant. And there came flashes of lightning, rumblings, peals of thunder, an earthquake and a great hailstorm.

Heaven, now open, reveals God's Temple and in the temple is the Ark of the Covenant. From God's temple comes His divine judgment seen in flashes of lightning, thunder, an earthquake, and a great hailstorm.

The temple here on earth is a copy of the heavenly temple, Heb. 8: 2, 5. See Isa. 6:1.

CHAPTER 12

The central figure in chapter 12 is Satan, the motivator who has two counterparts described in Chapter 13, the beast from the sea and the beast from the land (earth). Since the sea often symbolizes the nations of the world, it is thought that the Antichrist will be both a Gentile and Jew. The second beast will be from the earth or land, since the land of Israel is often referred to as "the land," he could possibly be an apostate Jew. The beast's functions will be religious.

This trinity consists of Satan himself, the Antichrist, and the False prophet.

The Jews will be able to build a tribulation temple and establish a sacrificial system.

V1, 2—A great and wondrous sign appeared in heaven: a woman clothed with the sun, with the moon under her feet and a crown of twelve stars on her head. (2) She was pregnant and cried out in pain as she was about to give birth.

In Revelation a sign is a person or event that looks beyond itself to some greater significance. In John's gospel each sign pointed to the divinity of Jesus.

The sun, moon and stars remind us of Joseph's dream in Gen. 37:9. The woman clothed with the sun is Israel. The sun was Jacob, the moon Rachel, the crown of twelve stars represented their 12 children (the twelve tribes of Israel).

The moon is thought by some to represent here Satan, the lesser light and despiser of the woman.

The wondrous sign:

1. Woman clothed with the sun, moon under her feet, and a crown of 12 stars on her head.
2. Pregnant, cried out with pain.

Crying out in pain and giving birth could be a reference to two things:

1. Israel, under Jacob, Rachel and the twelve sons were about to come onto the scene.
2. Mary, from Israel, was going to give birth to the Messiah as verses 5 and 6 say she will give birth to a child.

Many suggestions have been offered to identify this *"woman clothed with the sun."* The Church of Rome has maintained that she represents the Virgin Mary. In 1678 the Spanish artist Murillo created his famous painting "Mystery of the Immaculate Conception," a painting of the "woman clothed with the sun." He did not, for his own reason, show her standing on the moon with a crown of twelve stars on her head. Thus the picture for some reason has been used to teach Mary's bodily assumption into heaven.

Isa. 9:6; Micah 5; Hebrew 7:14; and Romans 9 state that Israel, not the church, gave birth to Christ. It was Christ who gave birth to the Church.

Israel was often portrayed as a married woman in the Old Testament (Isa. 54:1), and as an adulterous divorced wife by her sin and rejection (Isa. 47:7-9; 50:1; Jer. 3:1-25; Hos. 2:1-23).

V3, 4—Then another sign appeared in heaven: an enormous red dragon with seven heads and ten horns and seven crowns on his heads. (4) His tail swept a third of the stars out of the sky and flung them to the earth. The dragon stood in front of the woman who was about to give birth, so that he might devour her child the moment it was born.

"a great red dragon." He is red because he was the one who motivated all the bloodshed throughout man's history, beginning with Cain and continuing until today.

The dragon will have seven heads symbolizing the seven Gentile World Governments that Satan will lead during the tribulation. It will also have 10 horns, symbolizing the ten kings that will reign with him during the 7 year Tribulation Period. The Antichrist will subdue three of those ten kings so that their power will ultimately be concentrated into seven crowns or divisions of the last world government.

Much is said about the number of nations that belong to the European Confederacy. There are 15 nations now that belong. There could be 20, 30, 40, nations, which would have no bearing on the final grouping of these nations. It would appear that regardless of the total number of nations that have joined this Confederacy, they would be consolidated into ten nations.

Stars are symbols of angels. Satan caused one third of the angels to fall. His mutiny was a great rebellion that involved millions of angels.

At the beginning of Jesus' ministry, Satan offered Him the kingdoms of the world if He would bow down and worship him.

The dragon is identical as that "old serpent," Gen. 3:1-10, called the devil (accuser) and Satan (opposer).

Ezekiel 28 states that the dragon seems to be the highest creature ever made, the anointed one of the cherubim, *"full of wisdom and perfect in beauty,"* and being of a higher order of being than angels, (Jude 8, 9), Michael the archangel *"did not dare to bring a slanderous accusation against him."* John 8:44 says of the dragon *"he was a murderer from the beginning."*

In the 80's, increasing scientific evidence that the great reptiles known as dinosaurs survived into fairly modern times, with maybe some marine dinosaurs surviving today in the inaccessible depths of the ocean and the deep lakes of the world. **Psalm 91:13** *You will tread upon the lion and the cobra; you will trample the great lion and the serpent.* **Isaiah 34:** *Thorns will overrun her citadels, nettles and brambles her strongholds. She will become a haunt for jackals, a home for owls.*

In Isaiah 14:4, Lucifer is also called the "King of Babylon," like the one described here, which applies to his future coming.

V5, 6—She gave birth to a son, a male child, who will rule all the nations with an iron scepter. And her child was snatched up to God and to his throne. (6) The woman fled into the desert to a place prepared for her by God, where she might be taken care of for 1,260 days.

Four things are declared:

1. His birth.
2. His destiny, which is to break His foes to pieces, Psa. 2:9, and then to rule in righteousness.
3. His crucifixion and ascension.
4. His position on God's throne. He is destined to rule yet Satan knows this and pursues the woman (godly Israel).

Israel's flight into the wilderness (probably to Petra), Matt. 24:16; Dan. 11:41, is to be sustained for 3 1/2 years during Satan's terrible persecution which he effects through the beast, 2 Thess. 2:3-7.

The ancient city Petra lies in a mountainous area about 20 miles south of the Dead Sea in the country of Jordan. The red and white sandstone mountains are simply a great volcanic crater where the Edomites lived in approximately 500 BC. The people carved temples, houses, and businesses directly out of the rock face. The name Petra means "the rock" and the city is often called the "Rose Red City" because of the red stone buildings and the red cliffs they are cut out of. The city has been deserted for a long time and is difficult to reach because of the narrow passage that serves as its only entrance. The passage, a mile long, is easily defended against an invading army.

This is where Christians of Jerusalem fled from Rome's armies during the three and one half years that Rome battled the Jews in Jerusalem. The "great eagle" that carried her into the desert could have been Rome. The imperial eagle was the insignia Rome carried on her standards.

Some have suggested that the "wilderness" would be all the nations of the world where the persecuted Jews would scatter and hide.

CHAPTER 12:6 IS THE MID-POINT
OF THE TRIBULATION

V7-9—And there was war in heaven. Michael and his angels fought against the dragon, and the dragon and his angels fought back. (8) But he was not strong enough, and they lost their place in heaven. (9) The great dragon was hurled down—that ancient serpent called the devil, or Satan, who leads the whole world astray. He was hurled to the earth, and his angels with him,

The *"ancient serpent called the devil,"* is in reference to Satan's first appearing in the Garden of Eden. The name used for the devil in the gospels, as mentioned earlier, means "slanderer" or "accuser." "Satan" means "adversary." The devil is the adversary of all God's children and an accuser of Christians (Job 1:1). He is in opposition to Christ as priest and prophet and is the one who brings forth the first beast, and the false prophet.

A WAR IN HEAVEN BETWEEN THE ANGELIC HOSTS:

Michael appears to be the commanding general of the heavenly hosts, and is the special protector of God's people, the Jews (Dan. 10:13-21; 12:1). When Satan's time draws near for his expulsion from heaven, Michael will be involved in the war to expel him. Satan and his angels have had access to heaven, even after their rebellion, but now it will no longer be available to them (Job 1:6; 2:1; Gen. 3:1-10; Eph. 2:2; 6:10-12).

Satan will enter heaven and make war with Michael the Archangel. Michael will defeat Satan and his followers, who will then be cast down to earth. Earth will be Satan's base of operations, he will immediately turn his rage and anger against the nation of Israel, pictured as a woman. There are two angels mentioned by name in Scripture, Michael and Gabriel. Gabriel is the announcing angel. Michael, suggested on the basis of Isaiah 14 and Ezekiel 28, was created lower than Satan, but is superior to the majority of angels. Jude 9 tells us Michael had a pervious confrontation with Satan where he contended with him and disputed about the body of Moses. Satan wanted the body of Moses, probably to use as a sacred shrine, a relic or an object of worship to further mislead the children of Israel. Michael preserved the body of Moses against that eventuality, but even he *"dared not bring against him (Satan) a railing accusation, but said, The Lord rebuke you."* Michael does not seem to have the power to contend with Satan himself but relies on the power of God for his defense. This is an excellent object lesson to Christians! If the archangel Michael, commander of God's heavenly host, is not adequate to take on Satan in conflict, neither are we!

His fall—*"his tail drew the third part of the stars of heaven and did cast them to earth."* This refers to Satan's original fall described in Isaiah 14. In the middle of the Great Tribulation he and one third of heaven's angels will be expelled and cast down to earth, 7-9, (Dan. 10:10-14). When Satan and his angels are expelled from heaven, there is great rejoicing in heaven.

V10-12—Then I heard a loud voice in heaven say: "Now have come the salvation and the power and the kingdom of our God, and the authority of his Christ. For the accuser of our brothers, who accuses them before our God day and night, has been hurled down. (11) They overcame him by the blood of the Lamb and by the word of their testimony; they did not love their lives so much as to shrink from death. (12) Therefore rejoice, you heavens and you who dwell in them! But woe to the earth and to the sea, because the devil has gone down to you! He is filled with fury, because he knows that his time is short.

This joyous shout is a prelude to the establishment of Christ's kingdom, which begins with the return of Christ. Victory over last day malignity will be on the basis of the accomplished sacrifice of Christ, by a faithful testimony and by martyrdom. Satan's expulsion means earth will face great trial and tribulation. Knowing his time is short, he and his demons will vent their fury on God's people on earth.

V13-14—When the dragon saw that he had been hurled to the earth, he pursued the woman who had given birth to the male child. (14) The woman was given the two wings of a great eagle, so that she might fly to the place prepared for her in the desert, where she would be taken care of for a time, times and half a time, out of the serpent's reach.

Satan and his followers are cast from Heaven. They can no longer go *"to and fro."* Satan now turns his anger against the godly remnant of Jews still in the land, (Isa. 1:9; 6:13; Rom. 11:5). These are individual godly Jews who had not escaped to safety when the Tribulation broke out, Matt: 24:15-20.

There are at least three reasons why Satan has hated Israel since the Garden of Eden:

1. Because they are God's people.
2. Because out of that nation came Christ (Romans 9:5) who will rule the kingdom.
3. Because Israel is the ever-lasting proof before the eyes of men that the Scriptures are true and that there is indeed an Almighty God.

Satan, knowing that his defeat was sealed when Jesus, the Son of God was exalted through His death and resurrection, now vents his fury upon the sun-clothed woman, Israel, who gave birth to the man-child. The eagle wings given to the woman to *"escape to the wilderness"* recall how the Lord delivered Israel from Egypt and bore her *"on eagle's wings"* Ex. 19:4; Deut. 32: 11-12.

Two is the number of union, division, and witnessing. One wing possibly represents the swift transport of the martyred souls to the "Sea of Glass," while the other represents the swift flight into the wilderness of Petra. The passage into Petra is by way of a grand rock formation called "El Cig." At the entrance to El Cig stand several old buildings, a hotel, café, and a museum. The Cig itself is 6,000 feet long with a width from 12 to 30 feet. The walls of the cliffs are almost perpendicular, reaching a height from 300 to 500 feet. The entire complex, including the Cig, is almost 20 square miles.

V15-16—Then from his mouth the serpent spewed water like a river, to overtake the woman and sweep her away with the torrent. (16) But the earth helped the woman by opening its mouth and swallowing the river that the dragon had spewed out of his mouth.

This could be an enormous nuclear explosion triggering a tidal wave to kill the Jewish refugees, followed by an earthquake provided by God to swallow the water, or perhaps Satan's army pursuing Israel.

This flood could come from the Med-Dead canal, an attempt to channel the water from the Mediterranean Sea to the Dead Sea. If this project is complete, the dam could be destroyed in an attempt to drown the Jews as they pass through the Dead Sea area, and the earthquake could open the ground up to swallow the water.

Perhaps this is Satan's army, like a great flood, attacking the Jewish people, or maybe this verse is literal, water coming out of Satan's mouth.

(17) Then the dragon was enraged at the woman and went off to make war against the rest of her offspring—those who obey God's commandments and hold to the testimony of Jesus. And the dragon stood on the shore of the sea.

Satan's hatred of Israel is vented out on her son Jesus and His followers during the middle of the Tribulation.

Israel has faced constant threats through-out history. In 722 BC Israel was destroyed as a nation and in 586 BC Judah followed.

From 1095-99 AD, we find that the first wide spread persecution of the Jewish people, took place. The Crusaders were on their way across Europe toward Palestine when mobs of unruly crusaders destroyed Jewish homes and villages and slaughtered the inhabitants. In 1099 they captured Jerusalem and herded the people into a synagogue and set it on fire. Most of the Jews perished, but those who survived were sold into slavery.

In 1290, King Edward I of England banished all Jews from England, giving England the dubious honor of being the first country to expel its Jewish population. Perhaps this is why "the kingdom on which the sun never sets" can no longer hold claim to that honor. The Jews were not allowed to return to England until the time of Oliver Cromwell.

In 1306, France and in 1492 Spain followed suit.

In 1348-50 the Jews were blamed for various diseases and disasters, especially the Black Death and were savagely persecuted.

In 1881 the Russian Tsar Alexander II was assassinated and the Jews were blamed. Within 40 years of "retaliation" against the Jews, tens of thousands of Jews were killed.

During Stalin's reign 3 million more Jews were killed.

In the 1930's the Nazi party came to power in Germany. Adolf Hitler had 6 million Jews slaughtered, which was more than half of the Jewish population in Europe.

What these men, along with Napoleon, Alexander the Great, tried to do but failed, Satan will rule the entire world and receive its worship, the thing he wanted in the beginning.

Eusebius, an early church historian, tells the story of a woman named Blandina. Blandina was subjected to torture by her persecutors who took turns torturing her. Blandina was with such power that those who took their turns to subject her to every king of torture from morning to night were exhausted by their efforts, and confessed themselves beaten, thinking of nothing else they could do to her. They were amazed that she was still breathing, for her whole body was mangled and her wounds were gaping open. This blessed woman grew in strength as she proclaimed her faith, uttering the words, "I am a Christian! We do nothing to be ashamed of."

Three young men, Marturus, Sanctus, Attalus, who had been captured earlier were taken into the amphitheatre along with Blandina. There they were run through the gauntlet of the whips again and in accordance with local custom, they were mauled by beasts, and endured every torment the frenzied mob in the amphitheatre demanded and howled for. Then finally, they were put in the iron chair, which roasted their flesh and suffocated them with the reek of their own burning flesh.

CHAPTER 13

(1) And I saw a beast rising out of the sea, with ten horns and seven heads, with ten diadems on its horns and blasphemous names on its heads.

Some thoughts:

1. The beast comes from the Mediterranean Sea area.
2. It is possible that the beast is a Gentile rising up from the Mediterranean Sea area.
3. The beast (Antichrist) comes from the great mass of humanity, a reference to the Gentile powers.
4. The beast is a reference to the ancient sea monster "leviathan," Dan. 7:1-7.

The two legs in the vision of Nebuchadnezzar in Daniel represent Rome, divided into the west and the east. The ten toes are said to represent: Rome which was comprised of ten subordinate kingdoms; (1) Anglo-Saxons, (2) the Franks, (3) the Alleman-Franks, (4) the Burgandic-Franks, (5) the Visigoths, (6) the Suevi, (7) the Vandals, (8) the Ostrogoths, (9) the Bavarians and (10) the Lombards.

The double prophecy would put the ten toes as the Revived Roman Empire, the European Commonwealth Economy.

II Thess. 2:4—*"He will oppose and will exalt himself over everything that is called God or is worshiped, so that he sets himself up in God's temple, proclaiming himself to be God."*

The Antichrist is known by several names:

1. "Assyrian"—Isa. 10:5-6; 30:27-33.
2. "King of Babylon"-Isa. 14:4.
3. "A little horn"-Dan. 7:8; 8:9-12.
4. "King of fierce countenance"-Dan. 8:2-3.

5. "Prince that shall come"-Dan. 9:26.
6. "The willful king"-Dan.11:36.
7. "Man of Sin"; "son of perdition"-II Thess. 2:3-8.
8. "Antichrist"-I Jn. 2:18.

BEAST OUT OF SEA—The First Beast

1. He will be a man.
2. He will rise out of the sea of humanity, a sea of troubled nations.
3. He will become a ruler of the 10 kingdoms that will be formed.
4. He will be a blasphemer. He will blaspheme God, slander the name of God, slander the church (the dwelling place of God), and he will slander those who live in heaven.
5. Some think he will not be assassinated and resurrected from the dead. They say it is one of the heads on the best that is wounded to death and is healed, not the beast himself.
6. He will revive the old Roman Empire.

Some think he will revive the old Grecian Empire.

Daniel along with John gives us some more insight as to the characteristics of Antichrist:

1. He will be an intellectual genius (7:20).
2. He will be an oratorical genius (7:20).
3. He will be a political genius (11:21).
4. He will be a commercial genius (8:25).
5. He will be a military genius (8:24).
6. He will be an administrative genius (Rev. 13:1-2).
7. He will be a religious genius (II Thess. 2:4).

There are several keys as to the identity of Antichrist.

1. He will rise to power in the last days (Dan. 8:19-23).
2. He will rule the whole earth (Rev. 13:7).
3. His headquarters will be in Rome (Rev. 17:8-9).
4. He is intelligent and persuasive (Dan. 7:20).
5. He will rule with international consent (Rev. 17:12-13).

6. He will rule by deception (Dan. 8:24-25).
7. He will control the world's economy (Rev. 13:16-17).
8. He will sign a peace treaty with Israel (Dan. 9:27).
9. He will break the treaty and invade Israel (Dan. 9:26).
10. He will destroy the religious system so that he can rule unhindered (Rev. 17:16-17).
11. He will claim to be God (II Thess. 2:4).
12. He will not regard the God of his fathers' (Dan. 11:37).
13. He will not have the desire of women (Dan. 11:37).
14. His god will be the god of power (Dan. 11:38).
15. He will do everything according to his own selfish will (Dan. 11:36).
16. He will profane the temple (Matt. 24:15).
17. He will be energized by Satan himself (Rev. 13:2).
18. He will be utterly crushed by the Lord at the Battle of Armageddon (Rev. 19).
19. He will be the first creature thrown into the lake of fire (Rev. 19:20).

In March 1957, based on the Treaty of Rome, the European Common Market was founded. Each year Europe's importance has grown. The European flag has twelve stars formed in a circle. These stars do not represent twelve nations. Presently (at the time of this writing) fifteen nations are full members and many more are yet to be added. But Europe's constitution requires that only twelve stars can represent all the nations that will be gathered into the Union. Why only twelve? It is possible Satan, the great deceiver, has them unconsciously imitating the twelve tribes of Israel and the twelve apostles of the Lord.

The first six founders of the European Economy were:

(1) Belgium   (4) Italy
(2) France   (5) Luxembourg
(3) Germany   (6) Netherlands

In January 1973, three more were added, (1) Britain, (2) Denmark, and (3) Ireland. In 1986 two more were added (1) Portugal, (2) Spain, giving Europe a total of 336 million people. On January 1, 1995 three more nations were added, (1) Austria, (2) Finland, and (3) Sweden. The total combined population of the European Union was now 362 million.

There will eventually be ten power structures in the European Union with perhaps more than ten nations. Some scholars say the ten power structures now are: (1) Europe, (2) The Far East, (3) Mideast, (4) North America, (5) South America, (6) South Asia, (7) Central Asia, (8) Austria and New Zealand, (9) Southern Africa and (10) Central Africa.

Some scholars have the following ten power structure: (1) Canada and the USA, (2) European Union—Western Europe, (3) Japan, (4) Eastern Europe, (5) Latin America-Mexico and Central South America, (6) North Africa and Middle East (Moslems), (7) Central Africa, (8) Australia, New Zealand, South Africa, and Pacific Islands, (9) South and Southeast Asia, (10) Central Asia.

Both structures are very close. Time will tell.

The seven heads of kingdoms are the following: See Daniel 7.

1. Egyptian,
2. Assyrian,
3. Babylonian,
4. Medo-Persia,
5. Greek,
6. Roman (Old Roman Empire), and
7. The Revived Roman Empire.

There are at least two things delaying the finalization of The Revived Roman Empire:

1. The Church of Jesus Christ, which is the light of the world, is one. As long as this light is on earth, darkness cannot fully develop and complete its work of deception. Therefore, we know that the rapture of the church of Jesus Christ must be at hand.
2. Israel. It is God's special chosen people and is incomparable to any other nation. Israel must become one with the Gentiles.

The creature has **seven heads and ten horns.** The "ten horns" will not be crowned until the final stage of the fourth kingdom (the Roman). This kingdom will continue until the final kingdom (Christ's) destroys and replaces it completely. The ten toes of the two feet of the image in Daniel also represent this last stage. Both dragon and creature wear crowns, but the crowns are on the dragon's heads, while they are here on the creature's horns.

Therefore, both heads and horns refer to kingdoms where the term "kings" represents the kingdoms, for they are the heads of their kingdoms.

We must conclude that the beast is a ruler of a kingdom for he will have ten horns and seven heads. The sea is symbolic of a great multitude of nations, as it corresponds with the four beasts of Daniel 6 (which rises out of the sea).

The Roman Empire was never dissolved, but in 1453 by Mohammed II, the Turkish sultan brought about the downfall of Constantinople. The bastions of Mistra fell in 1469, and Trebizond fell in 1461.

(2) And the beast that I saw was like a leopard; its feet were like a bear's, and its mouth was like a lion's mouth. And to it the dragon gave his power and his throne and great authority.

John said this beast resembled a leopard. It could (as some think) or could not be a coincidence that a leopard with its three colors of black, brown, and white is one beast that represents the tree major races.

The Leopard could be, as some think, the future Arab Coalition. 'Feet like those of a bear' could be Russia and her allies. The lion is thought by some to represent England. This theory would include the United States of America, as they came out of England.

It could be a metaphor for ancient Greece's swiftness and agility, the bear for ancient Medo-Persia depicting their ferocious strength, and the lion for ancient Babylonian Empire, depicting their fierce all-consuming power.

In Daniel 7:2-8, we see Daniel looking to the future and list the animals in this order: *² Daniel said: "In my vision at night I looked, and there before me were the four winds of heaven churning up the great sea. ³ Four great beasts, each different from the others, came up out of the sea. ⁴ "The first was like a lion, and it had the wings of an eagle. I watched until its wings were torn off and it was lifted from the ground so that it stood on two feet like a man, and the heart of a man was given to it. ⁵ "And there before me was a second beast, which looked like a bear. It was raised up on one of its sides, and it had three ribs in its mouth between its teeth. It was told, 'Get up and eat your fill of flesh!' ⁶ "After that, I looked, and there before me was another beast, one that looked like a leopard. And on its back it had four wings like those of a bird. This beast had four heads, and it was given authority to rule. ⁷ "After that, in my vision at night I looked, and there before me was a fourth beast—terrifying and frightening and very powerful. It had large iron teeth; it crushed and devoured its victims and trampled underfoot whatever was left. It was different from all the former beasts, and it had ten horns. ⁸ "While I was thinking about the horns, there before me was another horn, a little one, which came up among them; and three of the first horns were uprooted before it. This horn had eyes like the eyes of a man and a mouth that spoke boastfully.*

We see from Daniel the:

1. Lion with eagle's wings.
2. Bear with three ribs in his mouth.
3. Leopard with four wings of a fowl and four heads.
4. Beast-dreadful and terrible with great iron teeth, with ten horns,
5. And a little horn arising from among the ten horns.

We know that:

1. Lion is Babylon.
2. Bear-Medo-Persia.
3. Leopard-Greek.
4. Ten horns—Revived Roman Empire.

John sees these in reverse, looking back into the past:

1. Ten horns
2. Leopard
3. Bear
4. Lion

(3) One of its heads seemed to have a mortal wound, but its mortal wound was healed, and the whole earth marveled as they followed the beast.

To many this refers to Antichrist himself being killed & being raised to life. Some believe that an antichrist from the past, e.g., Hitler or Nero, will come back to life and rule the New Revived Roman Empire.

That "one of his head's received a deadly wound" does not indicate that the entire beast was dead, but rather that he appeared to be mortally wounded in one aspect of his being. When the resurrection does take place under Antichrist it will be as though an empire, not a person, came back from the dead. This will be a fake death and a fake resurrection, an imitation of Christ's death and resurrection.

Some think it is possible that the fatal wound of the beast is the Revived Roman Empire. This empire, the beast wounded, the Roman Empire was thought to be destroyed when in reality it has only been wounded as it will live again. The Roman Empire was never conquered, it rotted from within.

There are those who say Geopolitics comes into play here. Geopolitics is a systematic study of internal and continental geographical features, physical, economic, and anthrop graphical, as essential factors in shaping governmental policies for securing national security. We could say here it means:

1. Whoever rules East Europe rules the Middle East.
2. Whoever rules the Middle East rules Palestine.
3. Whoever rules Palestine rules the world.

V4-5 And they worshiped the dragon, for he had given his authority to the beast, and they worshiped the beast, saying, "Who is like the beast, and who can fight against it?"
(5) And the beast was given a mouth uttering haughty and blasphemous words, and it was allowed to exercise authority for forty-two months.

The "dragon," "Satan," gave him his power for 31/2 years, the last half of the Tribulation period.

(6) It opened its mouth to utter blasphemies against God, blaspheming his name and his dwelling, that is, those who dwell in heaven.

He blasphemes not only God, but heaven, the angelic beings, and the martyred saints in heaven.

Blasphemies:

Making one equal with God and claiming authority to forgive sins (John 10:33; Luke 5:21), impious speaking when applied to God. It's the prostitution of a sacred name to an unholy purpose. Many Roman emperors deified themselves, taking themselves the names "lord" and "gods."

1. Pope Leo XIII wrote an apostolic letter on June 20, 1894, claiming, "We hold the place of Almighty God on earth."
2. Pius X stated, "The Pope . . . . is Jesus Christ Himself, hidden under the veil of flesh."
3. Pope Pius XI on April 30, 1922 said, "You know that I am the Holy Father, the representative of God on earth, the Vicar of Christ, which means I am God on the earth."

(7) Also it was allowed to make war on the saints and to conquer them. And authority was given it over every tribe and people and language and nation,

Satan's hatred of Jesus and His people is so great that through the ages he has vented his hatred out on the Jews and Christians. Now he has been given limited power and will slaughter multitudes trying to wipe out all

Jews and Christians and establish his satanic reign and his one world religion.

V8-9 and all who dwell on earth will worship it, everyone whose name has not been written before the foundation of the world in the book of life of the Lamb who was slain.(9) If anyone has an ear, let him hear:

In verse eight we find the Book of Life belongs to the Lamb that was slain. He knows all things. He knows who will worship the Antichrist and who will not. Before the world was created, he intended to die for them.

Those who are not written in the Lamb's book of life are the only ones Satan shall subject entirely to his will.

These words were added to impress the reader with the awfulness of what had just been spoken.

(10) If anyone is to be taken captive, to captivity he goes; if anyone is to be slain with the sword, with the sword must he be slain. Here is a call for the endurance and faith of the saints.

God has appointed the various trials of those who are to be persecuted by the beast. Those who have been killed with sword shall themselves fall by the sword, and those who led the people of God into captivity shall themselves be made captive.

The difference between Jesus and the Antichrist was one was willing to die for the godly, the other willing to kill the godly. One died on the cross and one sent others to the cross.

One of the most frequently asked questions about the Antichrist concerns his nationality. There are several references as to the origin of the Antichrist. Rev. 13:1 indicated that he *"rises up out of the sea,"* meaning the sea of people around the Mediterranean. From this we may gather that he will be a Gentile. Dan. 8:8, 9 suggests that he is the *"little horn"* that came out of the four Grecian horns, signaling that he will be part Greek. Daniel 9:26 refers to him as the prince of the people that shall come, meaning that he will be of the royal lineage of the race that destroyed Jerusalem. Historically this was the Roman Empire; therefore he could be predominantly Roman. Daniel 11:36, 37 tell us that he regards not *"the God of his fathers."* Taken in context, this suggests he will be a Jew, and perhaps from the tribe of Dan. It could be possible that the Antichrist will appear to be a Gentile and, like Adolph Hitler and others who feared to reveal Jewish blood, will keep his Jewish ancestry a secret. The Antichrist could be both, a Roman and a Jew. Paul was both, his mother a Jew, his father a Roman by birth or had purchased his citizenship.

According to verse 8, "All that dwelt upon the earth shall worship him (the beast, or Antichrist)." This indicates that not only Roman Catholicism and Eastern Orthodoxy will be united, but the Protestants will join together with them, along with all the world's religions, including even the Muslims, to form one new world religion. It will involve emperor worship, as in the days of the Caesars, with the death penalty for those who refuse to comply, verses 14-15.

(11) Then I saw another beast, coming out of the earth. He had two horns like a lamb, but he spoke like a dragon.

The second beast has the outward appearance of a lamb, but inwardly he is a monster.

V12-15 He exercised all the authority of the first beast on his behalf, and made the earth and its inhabitants worship the first beast, whose fatal wound had been healed. (13) And he performed great and miraculous signs, even causing fire to come down from heaven to earth in full view of men. (14) Because of the signs he was given power to do on behalf of the first beast, he deceived the inhabitants of the earth. He ordered them to set up an image in honor of the beast who was wounded by the sword and yet lived. (15) He was given power to give breath to the image of the first beast, so that it could speak and cause all who refused to worship the image to be killed.

BEAST OUT OF THE EARTH

1. He will be a man. The Greek "allos" means another of the same kind.
2. He will come out of the earth.
3. He will come after the first beast and will be his prophet.
4. He will be a great imposter appearing on the scene as a religious person, coming with a lamb like appearance.
5. He will exercise all the power of the first beast or Antichrist before him.
6. He will cause men on earth to worship the first beast.
7. He will carry out his plans by lying and performing miracles.
8. He will gain control of the world not by war but by tricking the leaders of the world into the idea that he can offer peace and by gaining enough support from each of the ten kings of the earth.
9. He will become a leader of a one-world government dominating the world economy.
10. His true religion will be atheism, which has been increasing in prominence since the early days of German rationalism and today it is given the respectability of intellectualism.

V16-18 He also forced everyone, small and great, rich and poor, free and slave, to receive a mark on his right hand or on his forehead, (17) so that no one could buy or sell unless he had the mark, which is the name of the beast or the number of his name. (18) This calls for wisdom. If anyone has insight, let him calculate the number of the beast, for it is man's number. His number is 666.

The right hand represents human work and activity. The forehead represents human spirit and worship.

There are several scholars who believe that Nero is the beast. The name Caesar Nero spelled Kaisar Neron if written with Hebrew endings, has a corresponding numerical value in the K equals 100, S equals 60, R equals 200, N equals 50, R equals 200, O equals 6 and N equals 50. Whether or not the final antichrist is actually Nero or not, he will in effect be a Nero incarnate. Probably the simplest explanation here is the best that the triple

6 is the number of a man, each digit falling short of the perfect number seven. Six in scripture is man's number.

Goliath was six cubits tall, the head of his spear weighed six shekels and he had six pieces of armor. Nebuchadnezzar's image was sixty cubits high and six cubits wide. Man was created on the sixth day and worked six days a week. A Hebrew slave had to be redeemed after six years. The land had to have rest after six years.

An interesting note: Almost every (UPC) Universal Product Code on most grocery items sold has the "mark of the beast." In UPC language, one way to represent the number six is with two thin extended bars. These extended bars are at the beginning, the middle, and the end of the UPC code. These extended bars are called guide bars and are used by a computer scanner to bracket two sets of numbers that each code is composed of so the computer can "lock" onto the code of the product.

There is a possibility that the mark of the beast is a microchip implanted in the right hand or forehead. The 666 could be the scan code as mentioned above. Microchips are being used in animals today. This microchip, which will hold one's pertinent information, will be the mark of the beast. There will be in the future a chip for mankind that will hold everything about the person that is wearing that chip, their social security number, driving license number, bank account, etc. There will be no need for anyone carrying money. They will scan your hand or forehead as you checkout and your purchases will immediately withdrawn from your bank account. It will also contain all of your medical information. Perhaps the mark is spiritual and not physical.

In 1 Kings 10:14 we find that Solomon received each year 666 talents of gold from the Queen of Sheba

Perhaps this is why God said in Lev. 19:28 that tattoos are an abomination to Him. Those who are eager to tattoo their bodies are easy prey for Satan.

Many are looking for someone to come and bring peace. They are looking for a dictator. The only problem with dictatorship is that the price is freedom and that price will be as they find out, too high of a price to pay.

Americans who have lived in freedom will find that their freedom is taken away.

The Antichrist will not be revealed until after the "rapture."

Rev. 17:8-17 limits the kingdoms of Antichrist to the ten nations.

In Daniel 7:7-8, 23, 24 the future ten nations are to be inside not outside the Roman territory.

In Daniel 11:44-45 it is stated that the countries north and east of the ten nations under Antichrist will make war on him.

Antichrist will not rule America at the beginning or be a worldwide dictator. His kingdom will be limited to the Old Roman Empire.

CHAPTER 14

Irenaeus, (John trained Polycarp, who in return trained Irenaeus), understood the 666 to be the Greek word of 'Lateinos'. Lateinos means 'Latin Kingdom'. Papal Rome made Latin its official language. Rome's canons, missals, prayers, decrees, bulls, blessings, cursings are in Latin.

They make an open profession of their subjection. God has written "Mene, Mene, Tekel" upon all His enemies. He has numbered their days just as He had numbered Belshazzar's, and they shall be finished, but His kingdom shall endure forever, and those of us who accept Christ as our Lord and Savior, will abide with Him.

SEVEN DISTINCT SECTIONS IN THIS CHAPTER

1. Vision of 144,000. (1-5).
2. Angel proclaiming the Eternal Gospel. (6-7).
3. The prophetic announcement of Great Babylonian's fall. (8).
4. he angelic warning of the eternal doom of the Beast-worshippers. (9-12).
5. The proclamation of the Special Blessedness, for those who should "die in the Lord" from that time. (13).
6. The vision of the Harvest of the Earth. (14-16).
7. The vision of the Vine of the Earth and the Winepress of Blood. (17-20).

Six other angels.

V1-5—Then I looked, and there before me was the Lamb, standing on Mount Zion, and with him 144,000 who had his name and his Father's name written on their foreheads. (2) And I heard a sound from heaven like the roar of rushing waters and like a loud peal of thunder. The sound I heard was like that of harpist playing their harps. (3) And they sang a new song before the throne and before the four living creatures and the elders. No one could learn the new song except the 144,000 who had been redeemed from the earth. (4) These are those who did not defile themselves with women, for they kept themselves pure. They follow the Lamb wherever he goes. They were purchased from among men and offered as first-fruits to God and the Lamb. (5) No lie was found in their mouths; they are blameless.

144,000—Who are they? Are they the same mentioned in Chapter 7? Some think the repetition of the number 144,000, one of governmental completeness and fullness, is not necessary conclusive proof that the two companies are one and the same. Those in Chapter 14 are sealed on their foreheads, but the form of the seal is the Lamb's name and the name of His father, whereas those of Chapter 7 were sealed as *"the bondservants of our God."* Those of Chapter 14 were redeemed from the earth. They are not said to be of Israel's tribes.

These differences are not conclusive whether they are the same 144,000 or not. I believe they are the one and the same, but it is immaterial.

We see God's power in the sealing of a multitude of people. Those who perhaps had began to see Christ as the Messiah but had not made a profession of faith. After the rapture, they confessed God as their Lord and were sealed by God to proclaim the Gospel to others.

SEVEN THINGS TOLD OF THIS AMAZING COMPANY:

1. They had written on their foreheads the name of the Lamb and the name of His Father proclaiming they belonged to Jesus and His father. It exhibited their character. They were dedicated to God forever.
2. This 144,000 were the only ones who could learn and sing the "new song" that burst forth as the voice of many waters and as the voice of a great thunder of harpers harping with their harps. A "new song" began in Revelation 5:9, 10, where the Lamb took the seven sealed book of judgment, to celebrate His worthiness to do so, and was done in view of the earthly kingdom of priests. We are not informed what the words of the "new song" were, but we know it was of rushing, thunderous exultation. If we are in tune with heaven, what gives heaven such ecstasy, must move us deeply.

3. They have been purchased (redeemed) by and belong to God.
4. They were without blemish, no lie was found in their mouth. They are a public example and pledge of what the "all righteous nation of Israel will be in the millennium."
5. They will follow the Lamb of God wherever He goes.
6. Romans 11:15 says they *"were purchased from among men, the first fruits unto God and unto the Lamb."*
7. They had not defiled themselves with women.
8. They were blameless. There was no sin held against them. God created men in *"his own image,"* but six times in Revelation the worship of the beast is described as directed to his image.

The next three angels appear in a logical sequence.

The first angel in chapter 14 is preaching the gospel.

According to Matthew 24:14 the whole world will hear the gospel of the kingdom. Is this when it happens?

V6-7 Then I saw another angel flying in midair, and he had the eternal gospel to proclaim to those who live on the earth—to every nation, tribe, language and people. (7) He said in a loud voice, "Fear God and give him glory, because the hour of his judgment has come. Worship him who made the heavens, the earth, the sea and the springs of water.

Mid-heaven refers to a point in the sky where the sun reaches it meridian apex, or in other words, high noon.

Angels up to this point had not been allowed to preach the gospel. This was the responsibility of mankind. Now we find angels preaching to mankind! Never before in the annals of mankind have we seen this!

The second angel pronounces judgment.

V8—A second angel followed and said, "Fallen, Fallen, is Babylon the Great, which made all the nations drink the maddening wine of her adulteries."

The story is told that Semerimus was the wife of Nimrod. Some scholars think that she was his mother and that she married her own son. She was Queen of Babel, which later became Babylon. Semerimus devised a nice story that began a whole system of idolatry. In this story she came out of an egg in the Euphrates River. She cracked the shell and stepped out fully-grown. Babylon was the origin of false religion and has been the center of Satan's operations ever since the flood. It was here that idolatry began, and this Babylonian system was extended to all nations. It was Satan's plan to destroy the knowledge and worship of God. *"Fallen, Fallen"* indicated the coming of double destruction as Chapters 17 and 18 will show, a system, then a city.

The idolatry, which originated at Babylon will bring wrath on all the nations, and eventually cast Babylon down to the same doom as Sodom. See Jer. 50:40.

Zechariah 5:5-11 speaks of a temple being built in the land of Shinar, which is Babylon. This prophecy was given in 519 BC, 20 years after the fall of Babylon, indicating that this prophecy is futuristic. Before a temple can be built, it is reasonable to assume that a city would have to be built there.

There is much discussion about Babylon and its meaning. Ancient Babylon, even if it again becomes an inhabited and functioning city, though not very feasible, would not possibly be the Babylon to which the writing on the woman's forehead refers. Babylon could be the center of the Harlot "religion" for a short while, until it is destroyed by the Antichrist.

Nebuchadnezzar built his Babylon around the ruins of the Tower of Babel.

There are several theories concerning the identity of Babylon. Some think John was using Babylon as a "code" word for Rome. Some think John's use of the word Babylon was a metaphor for a worldwide system of evil.

Babylon in I Peter 5:13, is the code word for Rome. Peter writing from Rome says, "The church here in Babylon . . . . sends you her greeting."

The popes say they are successors of Peter. There is no record that Peter was ever Bishop of Rome and no Bishop of Rome could be his successor. Irenaeus, Bishop of Lyons (178-200), provided a list of the first 12 Bishops of Rome. Linus was the first on the list, with no mention of Peter.

Eusebius of Caesaria, the Father of the Church History, never mentions Peter as Bishop of Rome. He simply stated that Peter came to Rome "about the end of his days" and was crucified there. Paul, writing Romans, never mentioned Peter even though he greeted others by name. One would think that if Peter was Bishop of Rome, Paul would have acknowledged him.

The third angel promises eternal damnation.

V9-11 A third angel followed them and said in a loud voice: "If anyone worships the beast and his image and receives his mark on the forehead or on the hand, (10) he, too, will drink of the wine of God's fury, which has been poured full strength into the cup of his wrath. He will be tormented with burning sulfur in the presence of the holy angels and of the Lamb. (11) And the smoke of their torment rises forever and ever. There is no rest day or night for those who worship the beast and his image, or for anyone who receives the mark of his name.

The *"hour of trial,"* (the Tribulation) will be great and fearful. A warning is given that whoever takes "the mark of the beast" will receive the wine of God's fury. God, who has always been a God of mercy, now withdraws His mercy forever from those who take the mark of the beast. Once this mark is taken, it becomes permanent. One cannot change his mind once they have received the mark! They shall be tormented with fire and brimstone. Brimstone is one of the most terrible substance known in its action upon human flesh. Its torment, when it touches the body is unbearable. Combined with fire it becomes an agony that words cannot describe. The smoke of their torment (compare Gen. 19:24, 28) goes up forever. They will receive no rest during the day or night.

Psalm 75:8 (NIV).
[8] *In the hand of the LORD is a cup full of foaming wine mixed with spices; he pours it out, and all the wicked of the earth drink it down to its very dregs.*

V12-13 This calls for patient endurance on the part of the saints who obey God's commandments and remain faithful to Jesus. (13) Then I heard a voice from heaven say, "Write: Blessed are the dead who die in the Lord from now on." "Yes," says the Spirit, "they will rest from their labor, for their deeds will follow them."

"Blessed are the dead who die in the Lord from now on." It was not until now that these words could be spoken. It had been said that it was better to live one's life to benefit others and for the learning of obedience by daily discipline. Now, the fearful days of the Antichrist have arrived.

There are two reasons death is better than life:

1. In death they will receive rest from their labors. We are reminded of Luke 22:53 when Jesus said to the mob led by Judas in Gethsemane, *"This is your hour when darkness reigns."* He contrasted that hour with, *"every day I was with you in the temple courts, and you did not lay a hand on me."* It is no wonder that the next words were, *"Then seizing him, they led him away."* The only road left open for Jesus was death. This was the way for Him to go home to His Father. According to Revelation 3:10, there is an hour of trial coming on the whole world except the present church. Daniel 7:28 states that the Beast *"shall wear out the saints of the most high."* Revelation 13:7 tells us, *"He was given power to make war against the saints and to conquer them."* The only way they will receive rest is to die.
2. The second reason is that those who die in the Lord are *"blessed"* and their works will accompany them. They will leave their grief and torment behind them, enter heaven and rest in the presence of God.

In Matthew 24:22 Jesus describes this as a period of "great tribulation." Perhaps the 144,000 and the two witnesses do not begin their ministry until the last half of the tribulation, the "great tribulation."

V14—I looked, and there before me was a white cloud, and seated on the cloud was one "like a son of man" with a crown of gold on his head and a sharp sickle in his hand.

JOHN SEES TWO THINGS:

1. The angel looks *"like a son of man"* and was sitting on a cloud. The cloud was His chariot.
2. He was wearing a gold crown and holding a sharp sickle in his hand. He was adorned with the crown of righteousness and authority. He had come in that authority to reap the harvest, separating the sheep from the goats.

This is the fourth, fifth and sixth angel mentioned in this chapter.

V15-16—Then another angel came out of the temple and called in a loud voice to him who was sitting on the cloud, "Take your sickle and reap, because the time to reap has come, for the harvest of the earth is ripe." (16) So he who was seated on the cloud swung his sickle over the earth, and the earth was harvested.

"Take your sickle and reap." Many say this is reaping of both saints and sinners, but this looks more like the sickle of judgment for they are thrown into the great winepress of God's wrath (V19). Matthew 13 gives us the parable of the tares, which will occur at the consummation of this age. The sickle is used for cutting down the workers of iniquity. Only the wicked are gathered for the fire. The righteous will remain to go into the new kingdom, the Millennium.

Joel 3:9 says, *"Proclaim this among the nations: Prepare for war: Rouse the warriors! Let all the fighting men draw near and attack. Beat your plowshares into swords and your pruning hooks into spears."* Just the reverse of what Christ the Prince of Peace will do when He comes! Isaiah 2:4.

(17) Another angel came out of the temple in heaven, and he too had a sharp sickle. (18) Still another angel, who had charge of the fire, came from the altar and called in a loud voice to him who had the sharp sickle, "Take your

sharp sickle and gather the clusters of grapes from the earth's vine, because its grapes are ripe."

Some think V18 "the earth's vine," is a reference to Antichrist.

The Church Age is gone, false Christianity is swallowed up by the beast and his ten kings (Revelation 17:16, 17, 18) and all the earth but *"the elect"* of those days, of *"one mind to give their kingdom unto the Beast."* Thus comes, *"the vine of the earth"* Moses spoke about long ago, Deuteronomy 32:31-35.

All this earth is at war with God Almighty. And, although today is a time of salvation, and of restraining grace, when that salvation ceases and restraint is removed, Psalm 83 tells us that the whole earth will rush to cut off the name of Israel from the earth.

(19) The angel swung his sickle on the earth, gathered its grapes and threw them into the great winepress of God's wrath. (20) They were trampled in the winepress outside the city, and blood flowed out of the press, rising as high as the horse's bridles for a distance of 1,600 stadia.

The day of wrath begins when Jesus appears on earth as Son of Man, in Palestine, trampling the allied armies of all the earth (Rev. 14:20; 19:19-21).

This day inaugurates the thousand-year reign. All judgments seen under the seals, trumpets and vials are prior to this Great Day. They are preliminary visitations of wrath before the Great Day of Wrath at Christ's coming to earth.

When we read the four gospels we see:

1. Matthew setting forth Christ as Israel's Messiah.
2. Mark, as Jehovah's Servant;
3. Luke, as the Son of Man;
4. John, as Son of God; each book goes over the same period, each writer bringing out his own perspective on certain phases of the Lord's life on earth.

The movement of the nations to Armageddon will come from Satan's energy. God will allow Satan to entice man to Armageddon where they may be trampled as one mass by the Son of Man Himself (Isa. 63; Rev. 19:15).

Isaiah 34 tells us that Edom (where the slaughter begins) shall be *"made drunken with blood,"* and its very dust *"fat with fatness"* at that slaughter. *"Without the city"* means Jerusalem. Blood to the bridles of the horses, four feet of human blood from Edom to Carmel, 1600 furlongs or 200 miles, which is approximately the length of the Holy Land from the North to the South.

The question is asked, "is this verse symbolic or literal?" Many think this is literal. Whether it is or not, we see that many will die and the shedding of blood will be great.

Isaiah 63 declares it is a literal trampling of the enemies of the Lord.

"Unto the bridles of the horses." There is much discussion about this statement. Some think it is only figurative but Josephus wrote that when Titus took Jerusalem, the Roman soldiers obstructed the very lanes with dead bodies; and made the whole city run down with blood, to such a degree indeed that the fires of many of the houses were quenched with these men's blood, (Wars 6:8).

CHAPTER 15

Chapter 15 is an introduction that prepares the reader for the execution of the judgments described in chapter 16.

Hebrews 2:3; *"How shall we escape, if we ignore such a great salvation?"* Escape what? Escape the judgment! The purpose of the Great Tribulation is judgment!

We will see THE SEVEN LAST PLAGUES. "Pleges" literally means a blow or a wound. These are not really diseases or epidemics but powerful deadly blows that will strike earth. 2 Peter 3:9 says "the Lord is patient . . . . not wishing anyone to perish but for all to come to repentance." But those who refuse God's love, reject His grace, and scorn His mercy, will face His wrath.

V1—I saw in heaven another great and marvelous sign: seven angels with seven last plagues—last, because with them God's wrath is completed.

Plagues are associated with pain, not sickness.

In Exodus 34:10, *"I am making a covenant with you. Before all your people I will do wonders never before done in any nation in all the world."* John saw a *"great and marvelous sign,"* seven angels pouring out the seven bowls of wrath because *"with them God's wrath is completed."* Mankind has seen God's great signs for centuries, but God will now show this world even greater wonders.

In verses 2-4, God gives us a vision of the souls who triumph during these days of great tribulation when these terrible vials are poured out upon earth's inhabitants.

V2-4—And I saw what looked like a sea of glass mixed with fire and, standing beside the sea, those who had been victorious over the beast and his image and over the number of his name. They held harps given them by God

(3) and sang a song of Moses the servant of God and the song of the Lamb: "Great and marvelous are your deeds, Lord God Almighty. Just and true are your ways, King of the ages. (4) Who will not fear you, O Lord, and bring glory to your name? For you alone are holy. All nations will come and worship before you, for your righteous acts have been revealed.

In chapter 4 verse 6 John saw, what looked like, a *"sea of glass, clear as crystal,"* which spoke of the holiness of God. Here again the *"sea of glass"* comes into view, but this time mixed with fire which speaks of God's divine judgment which proceeds from His Holiness. This description is one of vastness. This sea looks like glass, which is calm and peaceful. It is settled, unruffled, and looks like crystal, denoting the purity of God's own throne.

In the sea of glass *"mingled with fire"* we see that:

1. These saints *"who had been victorious"* had been called to pass through the very worse trials ever known to man. It has been well said that while we are called on to oppose the world, the flesh and the Devil, these have had a fourth foe, even Satan's Christ, a being brought back from the abyss and known to be such, to whom all at the earth has been given over, and whose delusions were so strong as to deceive, if it were possible, the very elect.

The "sea" in the Old Testament was a brazen basin which stood between the altar and the Holy Place where the priests washed their hands and feet in preparation for the priestly ministry (1 Kings 7:23-26: 2 Chon. 4:2-6). It was 18 feet in diameter and 7 ½ feet in height and held 2,000 baths, possibly 12,000 gallons and stood on 12 brazen oxen, in four groups of three each, facing the 4 directions of the compass. Could this be the "sea" John saw? This time the "sea" was glass instead of brass.

The seven angels sing the song of Moses. The Song of Moses (the song of the Israelites) was sung beside the Red Sea (Ex. 15) by the Israelites celebrating their exodus from the harsh hand of the Pharaoh of Egypt.

Moses stands for the power of God who *"caused his glorious arm to go at the right hand of Moses,"* who brought Israel up out of the land of Egypt, out of the house of bondage by the outstretched arm of God's might. These plagues are acts of judgment of God's wrath and will bring doom to those who continue in their blasphemous disregard of the holiness and sovereignty of Almighty God.

V5-8—After this I looked and in heaven the temple, that is, the tabernacle of the Testimony, was opened. (6) Out of the temple came the seven angels with the seven plagues. They were dressed in clean, shining linen and wore golden sashes around their chests. (7) Then one of the four living creatures gave to the seven angels seven golden bowls filled with the wrath of God, who lives forever and ever. (8) And the temple was filled with smoke from the glory of God and from his power, and no one could enter the temple until the seven plagues and the seven angels were completed.

V5-8—In Heaven there is a literal temple of God. Moses was given instructions on how and when he was to make the Tabernacle, *"see that you make them according to the pattern shown you on the mountain,"* Exodus 25:40. Now these tabernacle things are distinctly called in Hebrew 9:23, *"copies of the heavenly things."*

We saw in Revelation 11:19 that, *"there was opened the temple of God that is in heaven; and there was seen in his temple the ark of His covenant."*

We find in the temple in 11:19, the ark of God's covenant. In 15:5, we find that remarkable expression *"the temple of the tabernacle of the testimony in heaven."* This indicates that God is about to *"fulfill"* His covenanted promises toward Israel, for the covenanted things belong to Israel, Romans 9:4.

John does not see a temple in the New Jerusalem. The reason is given that our Lord God, the Almighty, and the Lamb are the temple there of. In that city they will see His face directly.

What does a church building, and a human body have in common?? They are temporary dwellings.

CHAPTER 16

Seven angels are given a trumpet to blow in revealing the second quarter of the tribulation judgments. Now we see the seven angels to whom the judgments of the last half of the Tribulation Period are given.

Here in Chapter 16, we find seven bowls of wrath:

1- Upon the earth—loathsome & malignant & grievous sores (16:2).
2- Upon the sea—oceans polluted, death of all life (16:3).
3- Upon the rivers—fresh waters polluted, turned into blood (16:4).
4- Upon the sun—scorching heat (16:8-9).
5- Upon the seat of the beast—darkness and pain (16:10-11).
6- Upon the Euphrates River—kings of the east (16:12-16).
7- Most powerful & destructive earthquake in history, it is done (16:17-21).

V1—Then I heard a loud voice from the temple saying to the seven angels, "Go, pour out the seven bowls of God's wrath on the earth."

The voice from God's Temple that has been *"a house of prayer for all nations,"* now the issues of divine judgments are for the enemies of God.

First Bowl (Vial)—Upon earth—First Angel

V2—The first angel went and poured out his bowl on the land, and ugly and painful sores broke out on the people who had the mark of the beast and worshiped his image.

In Exodus 9:9, Moses and Aaron threw ashes from the furnace toward the sky in the sight of Pharaoh and said, *"It will become fine dust over the whole land of Egypt, and festering boils will break out on men and animals throughout the land."* God creates evil as well as good, as He says: *"I form the light and create darkness, I bring prosperity and create disaster; I, the*

Lord, do all these things" Isa. 45:7. God is not only saving the lost, He is also creating judgments.

Deuteronomy 28:15, 27, 35—*[15] However, if you do not obey the LORD your God and do not carefully follow all his commands and decrees I am giving you today, all these curses will come upon you and overtake you:*

(27) The LORD will afflict you with the boils of Egypt and with tumors, festering sores and the itch, from which you cannot be cured. (35) The LORD will afflict your knees and legs with painful boils that cannot be cured, spreading from the soles of your feet to the top of your head.

The seven bowl judgments are messages that warn the beast (the Anti-Christ) that his time is at hand. These judgments are crowded into a relatively brief space. We see when the darkness is poured out of the fifth bowl that the sores of the first bowl are still upon men. The sixth bowl involving the gathering of the hosts to Armageddon will not need more than a few months to bring to pass. It will be as it was in Egypt, one plague crowding upon another.

When the first angel pours out his bowl, sores or ulcers break out upon those who worship his image. These are not ordinary sores. They are abscessed, ulcerated, and malignant, and they not only smelled terrible but itched and were very painful. God's judgment is not poured out upon the animals, as in Egypt under the sixth plague, but upon men who have taken the mark of the beast. This universal and horrible judgment falls upon mankind who have allied themselves with Satan.

There are those who think that when bowl number 1 is poured out, it unleashes these sores which are the result of the implanting of a microchip underneath the surface of the skin. See chapter 13.

Second Bowl (Vial)—Upon the Sea—Second Angel

V3—The second angel poured out his bowl on the sea, and it turned into blood like that of a dead man, and every living thing in the sea died.

This corresponds to the first plague in Egypt when the Nile turned to blood, which is the mark of death and the ways of sin.

The sea covers a far greater portion of this globe. Myriads of shoals of sea creatures die, and come floating to the surface. The stench of their rotting flesh attests to the wickedness of men. There is no escaping these words of God: *"every living thing in the sea died."* Isaiah 24:1-13 gives us a look at God's judgment on the earth. When God cleared earth of mankind in the days of Noah, He left eight people. It will be *"as it was in the days of Noah."* God will allow the human race to have another thousand years on earth (Rev. 20:4-6), but the earth's population will be reduced through the rapture and the bowl judgments so that a *"few men will be left"* to start that 1,000 years.

The blood flowing through our veins, and animals, is made up of hemoglobin in the red corpuscles, due largely to its component of iron. In living flesh, these corpuscles transmit oxygen and other materials to all the cells of the body. This brings to mind Leviticus 17:11 where it says, "the life of the flesh is in the blood." In Genesis 1:21 we find that God created every living soul in the waters and here every living soul in the seas die.

There is a tiny organism called *Pfeisteria,* also known as "red tide." This organism produces a poison a thousand times more toxic than cyanide. As the deadly red tide approaches the shore, people see fish leaping out of the water in an effort to escape the excessive hot water and from being boiled alive. In laboratories, this "killer" has also shown a taste for human blood, causing those who come in contact with it to suffer symptoms like memory loss, crippling muscle weakness and extreme weight loss. *Pfeisteria* boils fish alive by acting as a microscopic piranha dubbed "Red Tide" or the "cell from hell."

Third Bowl (Vial)—Upon the rivers and springs—Third angel

V4-5—The third angel poured out his bowl on the rivers and springs of water, and they became blood. (5) Then I heard the angel in charge of the waters say: "You are just in these judgments, you who are and who were, the Holy One, because you have so judged;

Now, all the waters on earth have turned to blood.

For thousands of years God's messengers had warned mankind to repent. Underneath the altar there were myriads of martyrs, who had been praying for divine vengeance and now it must be answered. In answer to these prayers the angel pours his bowl on the rivers and springs and they become blood.

The seas and rivers do not merely turn to blood, they turn to that as verse 3 says, as a *"dead man."* In other words, it becomes a dark purple, coagulated blood. Nothing to drink or bathe in.

(6) for they have shed the blood of your saints and prophets, and you have given them blood to drink as they deserve." (7) And I heard the altar respond: "Yes, Lord God Almighty, true and just are your judgments."

If one could drink the water, drinking bloody salt water could be toxic, but drinking fresh water, though repugnant, would not.

They deserved to drink the bloody water because they had shed the blood of the saints. God's judgments are always just.

Fourth Bowl (Vial)

V8, 9—The fourth angel poured out his bowl on the sun, and the sun was given power to scorch people with fire. (9) They were seared by the intense heat and they cursed the name of God, who had control over these plagues, but they refused to repent and glorify him.

Compare Matthew 24:21 with Daniel 12:1: *"For then there will be great distress, unequaled from the beginning of the world until now—and will never to be equaled again."* . . . . *"At that time Michael, the great prince who protects your people, will arise. There will be a time of distress such as has not happened from the beginning of nations until then."*

God, who created all things, has absolute power and control over His creation. The Beast, the chosen one of earth, has no power at all to direct creation, or to deliver his followers from these troubles. The sad part is that he doesn't want to!

Scientist say that the sun is "cooling off" which reaffirms God's words, that *"the wisdom of men is foolishness with God."*

The fourth angel pours out his bowl on the sun, and now the welcomed warmth of the sun becomes an unwelcome furnace. Man through insecticides, pesticides, and other chemicals have finally depleted the ozone layer.

The sun when it is "normal," emits a continuous stream of high energy particles that race toward earth, its peak speed is at 3 million miles an hour.

Scientist say the earth is surrounded by a field of radiation called magnetosphere, which protects us from the sun's deadly assault.

When the protection is removed, the earth's inhabitants will be faced with highly intense heat. Since 1670, this magnetosphere is thought to have been reduced by 15% and at its present rate of decrease, it is predicted that it will disappear by 3990.

There is no guarantee that these predictions are even remotely accurate for they are based on its present rate of decrease. Accelerate the decrease and this date will be lowered.

These people are in agonizing pain because of their sores. And to add to their agony, the scorching heat of the sun makes them thirsty, but there is no water to drink. The strong heat of the sun will bear down upon them, and the sweat will fall from their bodies. Their thirst for water becomes more intense, but nothing to drink. They will get sunburned from the top of their head to the soles of their feet, and the painful sores will become more unbearable. Blisters, sunstroke, and extreme thirst will be God's punishment to the unbelievers.

Malachi 4:1 *"Surely the day is coming; it will burn like a furnace. All the arrogant and every evildoer will be stubble, and that day that is coming will* *set them on fire," says the LORD Almighty. "Not a root or a branch will be left to them.*

Isaiah 24:6 *Therefore a curse consumes the earth; its people must bear their guilt. Therefore earth's inhabitants are burned up, and very few are left.*

The intense heat of the sun will evaporate great quantities of water from the earth, lowering the sea level and water tables. It will also melt the ice of Antarctica creating still other problems. Will there be more water evaporating than melting? Even the angels of the winds, Chapter 7:1, are no longer restraining the winds. It is estimated that there is enough ice, if melted, would increase the sea level 200 feet. Ps. 147:17-18 *He hurls down his hail like pebbles. Who can withstand his icy blast? ^{18} He sends his word and melts them; he stirs up his breezes, and the waters flow.*

It is interesting to note that no one repents. Men will blaspheme God and their blasphemy will increase until the Lord comes. Man will then, as he does now, fail to take responsibility for his own sins.

We can readily see the extreme heat from the sun not only scorching earth's inhabitants, but also melting the polar ice caps raising the level of the ocean waters. This would inundate many of the major cities of the world and disrupt ocean travel. We are told that even today there is melting of the polar ice caps.

Fifth Bowl (Vial)—Upon the throne of the beast—Fifth Angel

V10-11—The fifth angel poured out his bowl on the throne of the beast, and his kingdom was plunged into darkness. Men gnawed their tongues in agony (11) and cursed the God of heaven because of their pains and their sores, but they refused to repent of what they had done.

Zech. 5:5-11 says that Babylon, which was once Satan's throne, will be rebuilt to house a temple for Satan in the *"land of Shinar,"* where *"wickedness"* is to be set on its base in the end time. Shinar was an ancient name for the district in which the cities of Babel (Babylon), Erech, Accad, and Calneh were located, Gen. 10:10; 11:2. The fact that a house was built for the woman suggests that the removal of wickedness in V8, from Israel was permanent.

The bowl of darkness that is poured out is not ordinary darkness, but one that penetrates, much like the one in Egypt in the ninth plague in Exodus, suddenly falls upon the throne and kingdom of the Beast. Satan, try as he may, cannot believe it! "Thick Darkness" that could be felt was on Egypt three days; while God's people had *light in their dwellings."* (Ex. 10:21-23).

We find that men, in excruciating pain, are shut in with their horrid sores, for there is no relief. They gnaw their tongues from the agony they are in.

These lost souls are set in their evil ways and works, *"they repented not."*

It should be noted that this darkness is not that darkening of the sun and moon just before our Lord's arrival in the Great Day of Wrath of Revelation 19:11-15.

Job lost his sons, daughters, help and livestock, and then he was afflicted with sores, but unlike these people, he would not blaspheme God.

When Jesus, the Light of the World (John 8:12), gave His life on the cross, God plunged the world into darkness for three hours. Jesus passed from this realm to His heavenly realm, just as all believers will. Christ is alive forevermore. His death was, like ours will be, only physical.

Some think the kingdom of the beast does not refer to the whole world but only to his particular kingdom, the base from which he later will acquire control over all the other kingdoms.

Sixth Bowl (Vial)—Upon the Euphrates—Sixth Angel

V12-14—The sixth angel poured out his bowl on the great river Euphrates, and its water was dried up to prepare the way for the kings of the East. (13) Then I saw three evil spirits that looked like frogs; they came out of the mouth of the dragon, out of the mouth of the beast and out of the mouth of the false prophet. (14) They are spirits of demons performing miraculous signs, and they go out to the kings of the whole world, to gather them for the battle on the great day of God Almighty.

According to the Jewish dietary laws, frogs were unclean animals. These, unlike the frogs in Ex. 8:5, were not literal frogs but frog-like apparitions as spirits of demons, revolting and disgustingly slimly, coldblooded and vile.

In verse 12 this great army is designated as "kings of the East." This indicates that there will possibly be a coalition of powers from the Eastern countries and many agree it will probably be led by Red China. It is said that this has been made possible by Russia constructing a dam near the headwaters of the Euphrates. God does not need a dam constructed to stop the flow of water.

He is capable of doing that without help from mankind. It is possible that He may use this dam for His purpose.

Turkey has built several dams on this great river, the Euphrates (1780 miles long, from 300 to 1200 yards wide, and its depth is from 10 to 30 feet) allowing them to raise or lower the water level. The Euphrates flowed through the center of Babylon.

Cyrus, according to history was an engineering genius. He used these engineering skills to divert this river into a lake, thus, drying up the Euphrates so he could enter Babylon under its wall.

A road constructed several years ago from China through the Himalayas of Kashmir to Pakistan has made it possible for a great Oriental invasion.

Three evil spirits gather the kings of the world. This will be an alliance of all nations. They will all gather with one thing in mind, to go to war. This will be a union of all the earth. It would appear that all nations were not united until now. They will attempt to abolish God from the earth. How can man abolish God from the earth, when Satan, a more powerful adversary, tried and failed! Oh how foolish is the foolishness of man!

V15-16—"Behold, I come like a thief! Blessed is he who stays awake and keeps his clothes with him, so that he may not go naked and be shamefully exposed. (16) Then they gathered the kings together to the place that in Hebrew is called Armageddon.

The valley of Megiddo is located about fifteen miles southeast of modern Haifa.

We have seen:

- First Bowl—The worshippers of the Beast receive horrid sores.
- Second bowl-The waters of the sea are turned into blood.
- Third Bowl-The rivers and the fountain waters are turned into blood, giving the inhabitants of the earth nothing but blood to drink.
- Fourth Bowl-Power, that has never been known, is given to the sun. The sun's devastating heat will affect earth and mankind.
- Fifth Bowl-Utter darkness surrounds the throne of the Beast and his kingdom.

According to some there are several stages involved in the military maneuvers, which will be involved in the last military conflict of the world, The Battle of Armageddon. (Daniel 11:40-45).

1. The Arab-African Confederacy called "the king of the south," launches a massive attack against Israel.
2. The immediate full-scale invasion against Israel and the Middle East by Russia called ("the king of the North" in Daniel 11:40-45) and her satellites.
3. Russia will quickly return from Egypt to regroup her forces in Israel. According to Daniel 11:44-45, their command post will be set up in the Jerusalem area.
4. The Russian army is completely annihilated in Israel and its environs by the European forces of the Roman Antichrist (Daniel 11:45; Ezekiel 38:18-39:5). Zechariah 14:12 predicts the plague that will inflict the soldiers who attack Jerusalem. He predicts that *"their flesh will rot while they are still standing in their feet,*

their eyes will rot in their sockets and their tongues will rot in their mouths." This sound like the results of a nuclear war.

ARMAGEDDON

Here God will allow Satan's agency to gather the host of the earth. Just as Ahab, by God's command, was deceived by an evil, lying spirit, to go to battle, there to be slain (I Kings 22).

The Mount of Megiddo is a large hill just west of the Jordan River, in the Plain of Esdralon.

What is Armageddon, or more accurately, Har-Magedon? Its name means "Mountain of Megiddo."

SIGNIFIANCE OF ARMAGEDDON:

1. Barak overthrew the Canaanites with the help of the Lord (Judges 19).
2. This region is name from Megiddo, a royal Canaanite city (Joshua 12:21).
3. Mt. Carmel lies to the northwest, where at the mouth of the Kishon River Elijah killed Baal's prophets.
4. King Saul was killed at Mt. Gilboa located to the southwest.
5. Mt. Tabor located to the northwest is where Barak gathered the troops against the enemies.
6. From Judges 4:6, 12,14, and Jeremiah 46:18, the mountain (Hebrew Har) in Har-Megedon is Mt. Tabor.
7. Josiah fell in the same region, trying to defend Babylon against Egypt (II Chron. 35:22-25), and Zechariah 12:11 tells of the mourning for him.

Megiddo is named twelve times, the governmental number in scripture.

Ezekiel 38:8, 21; 39:2, 4, 17 says the final victory will be in the mountains. God brings the nations here for destruction. God will deal with this earth according to man's sins, until a man shall be *"more rare than fine gold,"* and until the land is *"drunken with blood."* The battle starts in the plains but as men are killed and the armies are down to a remnant, they will retreat to the mountains, there to be slain.

Seventh Bowl (Vial)—The final outpouring of God's wrath.

V17-21—The seventh angel poured out his bowl into the air, and out of the temple came a loud voice from the throne, saying, "It is done!" (18) Then there came flashes of lightning, rumblings, peals of thunder and a severe earthquake. No earthquake like it has ever occurred since man has been on earth, so tremendous was the quake. (19) The great city split into three parts, and the cities of the nations collapsed. God remembered Babylon the Great and gave her the cup filled with the wine of the fury of his wrath. (20) Every island fled away and the mountains could not be found. (21) From the sky huge hailstones of about a hundred pounds each fell upon men. And they cursed God on account of the plague of hail, because the plague was so terrible.

With the exception of the final judgment on rebellion at the end of the Millennium, this bowl completes God's wrath.

While this great battle of Armageddon is raging, the greatest earthquake since the creation of man, occurs and has the following effects on the world:

1. It will split Jerusalem into three parts, and every city in the world is leveled.
2. Great flashes of lightning will explode to the ground, and the thunder will rattle the earth.
3. Fires will break out as this tremendous earthquake shatters the land. The earth could be shaken either by a literal earthquake or by a full-scale nuclear exchange.
4. All islands and mountains disappear.

GREAT HAIL;

And as if this was not enough, great hail stones, approximately 100 lbs., fall from the sky. This reminds us of the "Law" as stated in Lev. 24:16, which stated that the "blasphemer" shall be stoned to death. These men and women had blasphemed God and now is the time of retribution. The biggest hailstones recorded weighed 2 lbs.

The splitting of Jerusalem into three parts (Zech. 14:4) will change her topographically and furnish her with additional water, 19:11. In the Roman Triumphal processions, the victorious general rode his white horse up the Via Sacra to the temple of Jupiter on the Capitoline Hill. This splitting will be an improvement, preparing her for her central place in the Millennium kingdom.

An oil company doing seismic studies of the Mt. of Olives area discovered a fault running east and west precisely through the Mt. of Olives area. The fault is so severe it could split at any time. It is now waiting for the pressure of our Lord's foot, Zech. 14.

The sixth and seventh bowls of wrath, reveal to us two terrible things that happen:

1. The gathering of the nations to Palestine to war against God, the great and fearful shaking of the earth in divine retributive anger so long prophesied, which divides Jerusalem into three areas. This great shaking of the earth, an earthquake or nuclear warfare, destroys all the cities of the nations, the restored Babylon, the last great world capital, banishes all islands and mountains and casts terrible hailstones down to earth, have been reserved *"for the day of battle and war,"* Job 38:22, 23.
2. The seventh bowl is the final outpouring of God's wrath on the sinners on earth. This bowl will pour out the worst calamity in the history of the world. It will contain the most complete and devastating catastrophe the earth will ever experience. This angel did not dump this bowl upon the earth, but poured it out upon the air.

After the angel pours out the seventh bowl, a loud voice from the Throne says, *"It is done!"* Men refused to accept the Savior's *"It is finished!"* on Calvary; so they must have the awful *"It is done!"* from the one they crucified! Men today refuse to hear the warning to flee from the coming storm!

It has been said that the early church unanimously viewed "Babylon" as Rome. They viewed is as symbolic of the Roman Empire in general.

CHAPTER 17

This chapter is referred to by some as the Ecclesiastical Chapter.

Characteristics in Chapter 17 and 18 of the Apocalyptic Babylon:

1- Rich and prosperous (17:4).
2- Immoral and drunken (17:2).
3- Associated with Satan and the beast (17:7-8).
4- City that sits on seven hills (17:9).
5- Leader of a 10-nation confederacy with Roman European roots (17:10-11).
6- City that rules over many nations (17:15-18).
7- Center of commercial enterprise (18:3,11-13).
8- Sailors cross the sea to get there (18:17-18).
9- An entertainment capital (18:22-23).
10- Burns up in one hour (18:9-10; 17-19).

V 1, 2—One of the seven angels who had the seven bowls came and said to me, "Come, I will show you the punishment of the great prostitute, who sits on many waters. (2) With her the kings of the earth committed adultery and the inhabitants of the earth were intoxicated with the wine of her adulteries.

In Rome the prostitutes in public brothels wore a frontlet on their forehead bearing their names. Here this prostitute has four names:

1. V1—the great prostitute.
2. V5—the mother of prostitutes.
3. The abominations of the earth.
4. V15, 16—the prostitutes.

Babylon is named in Scripture over 260 times, 37 times in one prophecy.

The only city mentioned more in the Bible than Babylon is Jerusalem.

The great prostitute is synonymous with apostate religion and its false religion of the last days. The greatest expression of false religion will be the uniting of all religions. This has been discussed in our time by religious leaders.

This great harlot is portrayed as the mother of prostitutes and of the abominations of the earth. Satan uses the religious system to control men by its doctrines. Satan, in his subtle ways, synthesizes man's conscious through T.V., etc., and man walks in his natural lusts.

Many waters had been identified as multitudes of people. Perhaps this is the meaning here.

(3) Then the angel carried me away in the Spirit into a desert. There I saw a woman sitting on a scarlet beast that was covered with blasphemous names and had seven heads and ten horns.

John's spirit is carried away to a desert. This is a description of the region surrounding both Babylon on the Euphrates and Rome on the Tiber.

We see that Babylon is two things, a woman and a city. As a mother she is a failure. Instead of raising her children to follow God, she, being a prostitute, has raised her children as prostitutes, and to follow false religions.

The Scriptures inform us that a prostitute is more than just a woman who physically commits sexual sins. A prostitute is a person who has spiritually stopped following the one and only true God and has turned to idol worship.

(4) The woman was dressed in purple and scarlet, and was glittering with gold, precious stones and pearls. She held a golden cup in her hand, filled with abominable things and the filth of her adulteries.

The woman sitting on a scarlet beast is arrayed in purple and red, adorned with gold, precious stones, and pearls. It has been stated that there is a great similarity in the trappings of ecclesiastical pomp today and especially of high officials in the Roman Catholic Orthodox Churches.

(5)—This title was written on her forehead: Mystery-Babylon The Great-The Mother Of Prostitutes-And Of The Abominations Of The Earth.

Peter wrote in I Peter in Babylon, I Peter 5:13. We find in Rev. 18 that *"Babylon, the great city, shall be cast down, and shall be found no more at all."*

Babylon (the city) will open her doors to a one-world government, one-world religion and global trade. She will be filled with adulterous kings.

Ancient Babylon is in modern Iraq and part of Iran. The Bible says it will be absolutely destroyed, and as of yet this has not happened.

When Jeremiah prophesied the final destruction of Babylon, a literal city, (Rome?) he gave God's final solemn warning to His people to flee from Babylon: *"Flee from Babylon! Run for your lives! Do not be destroyed because of her sins, it is time for the Lord's vengeance . . . Come out of her, my people! Run for your lives! Run from the fierce anger of the Lord."* (Jer. 51: 6, 45).

Babylon, Satan's capital, built in the Land of Shinar, was located on the Euphrates River. It had in its middle a gigantic temple dedicated to Belus, later know as Baal. A tower was erected that rested on a base of stone 300 feet square, and 110 feet high. Upon this stone they built the second stage, which was 260 feet square and 60 feet high. The third stage was smaller, with each section becoming smaller. The sixth stage was 110 square feet and 20 feet high. On top of this, 300 feet in the air, was the sanctuary in which the statue of the Babylonian god was housed.

Babylon was a city of idolatrous worship, which began almost shortly after the flood, in the days of Nimrod, and as the people spread out throughout the earth they took this worship of idols with them. The beginning of Babylon's evil form was in opposition to God's Holy Word.

The same idolatrous system that opposes God's saints of the church age can be found in Babylon and Rome.

Babylon spread over an area of fifteen square miles, covering 2,500 acres, was superbly constructed. Herodotus, a famous historian, said a wall surrounded the city that was 350 feet high and 87 feet thick. It was wide enough for six chariots to drive abreast. Around the top of the wall were 250 watchtowers place in strategic locations. The city had a hundred gates of iron and brass with the Euphrates River flowing diagonally through the city. A large ditch, or moat, was outside the high wall which surrounded the city and was kept filled with water from the Euphrates River. The large ditch was meant to serve as an additional protection against attacking enemies, for any attacking enemy would have to cross this body of water first before approaching the great wall.

Revelation 17 reveals the primary importance of Babylon in its relationship to religion. In addition to materials given in the Bible itself, ancient accounts indicate that the wife of Nimrod, who founded the city of Babylon, became the head of the so-called Babylonian mysteries, which consisted of secret religious rites, and were developed as a part of the worship of idols in Babylon. She was known by the name of Semerimus and was a high priestess of idol worship. According to extra biblical records, which have been preserved, Semerimus gave birth to a son who she claimed was conceived miraculously. This son, given the name of Tammuz, was considered a savior of his people and was, in effect, a false messiah, purported to be the fulfillment of the promise given to Eve.

Semerimus instituted a religious system, which made both her and her son the objects of divine worship. From Babylon it spread to Phoenicia under the name of Asheroth and Tammuz. In Egypt it was known as Isaiah and Horus, In Greece it became Aphrodite and Eros. In Rome they were worshipped as Venus and her child.

Tammuz was said to have been killed by a wild boar and miraculously brought back to life forty days later. His mother wept for forty days. Forty days of lent memorialized the forty days of weeping over the death of Tammuz and at the end of forty days, the feast of Ishtar was observed to celebrate the resurrection of Tammuz. The term Easter is derived from the word "Ishtar." Ezekiel protests against the ceremony of weeping for Tammuz in Ezekiel 8:14. Jeremiah mentions the heathen practices of making cakes for the queen of heaven (Jer. 7:18) and offering incense to the queen of heaven (Jer. 44:17-19, 25).

(6) I saw that the woman was drunk with the blood of the saints, the blood of those who bore testimony to Jesus. When I saw her, I was greatly astonished.

John knew that religion would wield great authority, so why was he astonished? Perhaps because he saw that the church had become a prostitute. She had committed fornication with the world.

An early Christian writer had this to say, in part, about Christians: "They exist in the flesh, but they live not after the flesh. They spend their existence upon earth, but their citizenship is in heaven. They obey the established laws, and in their own lives they surpass the laws. They love all men, and are persecuted by all."

(7) Then the angel said to me: "Why are you astonished? I will explain to you the mystery of the woman and of the beast she rides, which has the seven heads and ten horns.

The true church was a mystery hidden by God for centuries and finally was revealed to the apostle Paul. II Peter 3:15, 16, tell us that John and Peter had read and studied these letters of revelations written by the Gentile apostle. Matt. 27:28 tells us that scarlet was one of the colors of imperial Rome. Jesus was adorned with a scarlet robe (Mark 15:16, 20), not because they accepted His Kingship, but in mockery of His title as King. After His death they would come face to face with the one whom they mocked.

This woman is the whore and is seen in both purple and scarlet. The emperor wore purple clothing, the senators wore a broad purple band, and the knights wore a narrower band, so this woman in John's eyes would be exercising all the power of the Roman Empire, though she was not crowned, and she was not a queen in her own right.

(8) The beast, which you saw, once was, now is not, and will come up out of the Abyss and go to his destruction. The inhabitants of the earth whose names have not been written in the book of life from the creation of the world will be astonished when they see the beast, because he once was, now is not, and yet will come." (9) "This calls for a mind with wisdom. The seven heads are seven hills on which the woman sits.

Some think Chapter 17 covers the first part of the Tribulation before Antichrist comes out of the Abyss.

Rome originally included seven small mountains along the Tiber River, and they were given the names; Palatine, Aventine, Caelian, Equiline, Viminal, Quirinal and Capitoline. As Rome grew, however two more hills were added, Janiculum and Pincian.

Although Rome is considered by some to be mentioned, it is said that the muddy Tiber River that flows through it is not big enough to sustain the enormous maritime traffic portrayed in Chapter 18.

We found in verse nine and ten that the seven heads are not only hills but also are kingdoms on which the woman sits.

John could be referring to Rome, even though there are nine hills. Rome was always depicted as a city on seven hills. Perhaps it is 7 kingdoms!

Rome claims to be the "Eternal City" and the "Holy City," titles which the Bible has given to Jerusalem. Rome claims to be "The New Jerusalem," putting her in direct conflict with God's promises concerning the true city of David.

Salvation, as taught by the Bible, comes when we accept Jesus as our Lord and Savior. According to the Catholic Church, the only way you can obtain salvation is through them and you "earn" it through works.

In 1564, the Roman Catholic Council of Trent declared that Rome believes that the truth concerning salvation, etc. is determined solely by the popes and church councils, not the Bible as the Word of God. Cardinal D'Allen declared "The Reformation was a Protestant revolt disrupting the unity of the church. Union will take place when the rebels accept the authority of the Pope and abandon the authority of Scripture. Rome can accept nothing short of this." The Council of Trent, though not surprising, has never been rescinded.

Rome has laid claim that it has never changed, but history informs us that there have been several changes since 1190.

Let me say that even though Catholicism has set itself on a plane equal with God, contrary to the Bible, there are many Christian Catholics.

It was by order of the Popes, through subservient governments, over a period of 500 years, that unnumbered multitudes of Christians were tortured and murdered for the 'heresy' of reading the Bible. Thus, God's Word was driven out of circulation, and became an unknown book. Martin Luther, in nailing his thesis, started the reformation, and restored the Bible to the people.

In 303, what would be known as The Great Depression began under the Emperor Diocletian and his co-emperor Galerius. Under their persecution all Bibles had to be surrendered to the authorities, all churches were to be destroyed, all Christian worship was forbidden, all the clergy were imprisoned, and all citizens of the empire were to sacrifice to the pagan god. Failure to do so meant torture or death.

A blood-bath ensued where in Phrygia "where the whole population was Christian, a whole town was wiped out."

In 313, Constantine took control of the West, while his ally Lecinius, conquered the East. Together they signed the Edict of Milan restoring Christians the full rights of citizenship.

A writer once noted that Christianity had merged with paganism. Statutes of Isis and Horus were renamed Mary and Jesus. The Roman Lupercalia and the feast of purification of Isis became the Feast of the Nativity. Soon the people and priests would use the sign of the cross as a magic incantation to expel or drive away demons.

Gregory I (590-607), was basically a good man. He consolidated Christendom after Rome's fall in 476, and was considered by some to be the first real pope. He is the first to institute the idea of purgatory. He had the bright idea that he could raise money by selling, for a price, the entrance into Heaven from hell and that people would be willing to pay to get their loved ones from hell to heaven. His body is buried in St. Peter's basilica in Rome.

Sergius III (904-911). Fathered illegitimate children with a notorious harlot named Marozia, and raised their children to be popes and cardinals.

Benedict IX (1033-1045), became pope when he was twelve years old. He committed murders and adulteries in broad daylight and robbed graves. Finally the enraged people of Rome drove him out of the city.

Gregory VI (1046), Benedict IX and Sylvester III were three rivals who laid claim to the throne at this time. Rome was filled with hired assassins, as each pope was trying to cut the throat of the other. Emperor Henry III decided to put a stop to the killing, stepped in, kicked all three out, and appointed his own pope, Clement II. It is actions like this that dispel the idea that all popes descended from Peter.

Innocent III (1198-1216). He was the most powerful of all the popes. He condemned England's Magna Carta, and Bible reading was forbidden.

John XXII (1316-34) set a price for every crime under the sun. For a price you could be forgiven and retain salvation. Julius III (1550-5) followed suit as did Pope Leo X (1513-21).

Once the church had "freed" you the civil authorities could not persecute you.

The following is a list of some of the pagan beliefs that crept into Catholicism.

709-Kissing the Pope's foot.
786-Worshipping of images and relics.
850-The beginning of the use of "holy water."
995-Canonization of dead saints.
998-Fasting on Friday and during Lent.
1079-Celibacy of the priesthood.
1090-Prayer beads.
1184-The Inquisition. (Tribunal for suppressing heresy and heretics).
1190-Sale of Indulgences. (Remission of punishment still due for a sin after the guilt has been forgiven).

1215-Transubstantiation. (Bread and wine becomes the body and blood of Jesus).
1220-Adoration of wafer (Host).
1229-Bible forbidden to laymen.
1414-Cup forbidden to people at communion.
1439-Doctrine of purgatory decreed.
1439-Doctrine of seven sacraments affirmed.
1508-The Ave Maria approved.
1534-Jesuit order founded.
1545-Tradition granted equal authority with Bible.
1546-Apocryphal books put into the Bible.
1854-Immaculate conception of Mary.
1865-Syllabus (study) of Errors was proclaimed.
1870-Infallibility of Pope was declared.
1930-Public schools were condemned.
1950-Assumption of the Virgin Mary. (Pure, holy, without sin).
1965-Mary proclaimed Mother of the Church.

Petrarch, who had observed for many years the Roman Curia, concluded that Rome was the fulfillment of John's vision in Rev. 17. He said, "She was the apocalyptic woman drunken with blood, the seducer of Christians, and plague of the human race."

St. Bonaventure in his commentary on the Apocalypse declared that "the harlot who makes kings and nations drunk with the urine of her "whoredom," was Rome.

Roman Catholics were taught that they had replaced the Jews as God's chosen people.

John Paul II has stated that he consecrated and dedicated himself "as priest, as bishop, and as cardinal to Mary." God has never commanded or permitted the worship of anyone other than Himself.

(10) They are also seven kings. Five have fallen, one is, the other has not yet come; but when he does come, he must remain for a little while. (11) The beast who once was, and now is not, is an eight king. He belongs to the seven and is going to his destruction."

There are those who think this is a reference to the following:

1. Augustus, 31 B.C.-AD-14
2. Tiberius, 14-37 AD.
3. Caligula, Gaius, 37-41.
4. Claudius, 41-54, and
5. Nero, 54-68.
6. One at present: Vespasian, 69-79.
7. Another to come for a short time: Titus, 79-81.
8. The Beast that was: Nero.

If we follow Chapter 13, the seven hills are kings: *"Five are fallen, and one is and the other is not yet come."* The five represented the kings of the nations until John's lifetime.

The existing king Domitian, was the sixth, thus we have the five that were, the sixth that is, and the seventh to come (the Antichrist at the end time).

The seven hills (kingdoms) according to Daniel were:

1. Egypt—earliest persecutor of the church. (Tried to destroy God's chosen people by ordering the slaughter of all male babies (Ex. 1).
2. Assyria—destroyed the 10 northern tribes of Israel (722 BC).
3. Babylon—destroyed the 2 southern tribes (586 BC).
4. Medo-Persia—came very close to destroying the Jews during the time of Esther.
5. Greece.
6. Roman reign.
7. The revived ten kingdoms of modern Europe.

The leaders or kings of these kingdoms were:

1. Egypt—The Pharaohs
2. Assyria—Sennacherib
3. Babylon—Nebuchadnezzar
4. Medo-Persia—Darius and Cyrus
5. Greece—Alexander the Great
6. Domitian (during John's time)
7. Antichrist

V12-18—"The ten horns you saw are ten kings who have not yet received a kingdom, but who for one hour will receive authority as kings along with the beast. (13) They have one purpose and will give their power and authority to the beast. (14) They will make war against the Lamb, but the Lamb will overcome them because he is Lord of lords and King of kings—and with him will be his called, chosen and faithful followers." (15) Then the angel said to me, "The waters you saw, where the prostitute sits, are peoples, multitudes, nations and languages. (16) The beast and the ten horns you saw will hate the prostitute. They will bring her to ruin and leave her naked; they will eat her flesh and burn her with fire. (17) For God has put it into their hearts to accomplish his purpose by agreeing to give the beast their power to rule, until God's words are fulfilled. (18) The woman you saw is the great city that rules over the kings of the earth."

Verse 12 tells us the end time world government will be 10 kingdoms (nations) for a while.

Daniel in Chapter 7 tells us that the beast will overtake 3 kings and will be the ruler of 3 nations. Then he will take over the other 7, or rather they will relinquish their control to the beast.

The ten horns are ten kings—the European Common market—the Antichrist Confederacy of Nations.

One might ask, "Where is the United States in all of this?" Psalm 33 says, *"Blessed is the nation whose God is the Lord."*

The Bible does make mention of a nation remote from Babylon that will play a role in the Great War. In Ezekiel we find *"I will send fire upon those who dwell securely in the coastland."*

We find that God has warned us not to sacrifice our sons or daughters in the fire. Although here in America we do not legally throw living babies into the fire, we do kill 4,000 of them every day in an equally repugnant ceremony called abortion.

In just a few short years from 1973 to the present, we will have aborted approximately thirty times as many babies than the number of Americans lost in all US wars.

Another failure of our nation is our disobedience to God's Word where in Deuteronomy, He warns us against divination or sorcery. Today divination and sorcery are found in many New Age activities, and among other so-called "Christians." Astrology, or observing times, is a contemporary myth that America widely accepts. A Gallop poll taken in 1988 showed that ten per cent of evangelicals believed in astrology. These are, supposedly learned men of the Bible, who are blatantly disobeying the Word of God. The years that followed have seen a great increase in the study of astrology.

A wizard is a person who has a familiar spirit. In the Old Testament, a (familiar spirit) was a spirit that had frequent communication with the wizard. New Agers call this practice "channeling." This is a term for spirit possession. A familiar spirit, called a "spirit guide," speaks through the channeler (automatic speaking) or writes through him (automatic writing).

Our nation's spiritual root, from which this nation was built, has eroded from every vestige of society. The Bible has been removed from public life and replaced by occultist and pagan ideas of the past, even though America achieved greatness because it was founded upon Christian principles and values. If God brought judgment upon nations in the past that turned to occultism, how can He ignore a land where thirty per cent of our children are born out of wedlock, where 1.5 million unborn babies are murdered in their mother's womb each year, where an estimated thirty million people belong to cults and another sixty million believe in or practice some form of occultism? But God will not be mocked!! Judgment day is coming!

These are a few possibilities given concerning the future of the US:

1. America will have been destroyed. Russia has an ABM protection system around its major city, Moscow, whereas America does not.

2. America will have been blackmailed into non-participation. America may have simply been discounted and considered a paper tiger.
3. America may simply lose its prestige, acceptance, financial leadership, and many other things in the world because of its present inattention to moral things. There is little doubt that America has been in the process of forsaking the Lord, much as the Russians did over 80 years ago. Today we are allowing homosexual marriages and ordaining homosexuals for Pastoral positions. According to God's Word, homosexuality is an abomination to God. He destroyed Sodom and Gomorrah for their homosexual acts, why would He allow The U.S. to get by?
4. Another possibility may be the rapture of the Church. The rapture of the Church would take a high percentage of the leadership class out of the U.S. In one day there would be a crisis of leadership in America that could be governmentally fatal.
5. It may be that when the Tribulation begins, America will not be affected until later. It may be that only the 10 Union Confederacy of Europe will be affected.

It would serve America to look at the history of Great Britain. In Ezekiel 36:6-10, Ezekiel tells us that God says that because Nations have scorned Israel, they too will be scorned.

In March, 1939, the British Government became hostile toward the Jews and asked Germany to discourage the Jews from traveling. This helped seal the fate of the Jews and also of Great Britain. Gen. 12:3 says. *"I will bless those who bless you and I will curse those who curse you."*

The Jews were slaughtered like cattle, their corpses became rendering for soap, their skin became lampshades, and the women's hair became stuffing for mattresses. As if this wasn't enough, gold was taken from their teeth, and their bones ground for fertilizer.

The United Kingdom "on whose flag the sun never sets," was progressively destroyed. Today, it has been said, they are only a mere shadow of their greatness.

There seems little doubt that America, because the "light" that has been given her has been so brilliant and so revealing, is to receive punishment greater than any other nation. She also turned Jews away during World War II.

Dr. Wim Malgo, founder of Midnight Call Ministry, was asked a question in 1967. The questionnaire wanted to know if America would become a communist nation. He replied, "America will not become communist, but rather Catholic." He went on to say, "America's strength does not lie in her military force, but this indefinable power is due to the existence of a strong, independent church. As the years will go by, powerful deceptive movements will sweep the nation with the aim to bring the church back to Rome."

We find in Genesis 10, the Table of Nations, and a reference to a tribe called the Senites. Sinim is derived from a root suggesting thorns. China? Probably derives from Ch'in, the feudal state in China from 897-221 BC, which unified China in the third century BC, and built the Great Wall.

Perhaps America will not be ruled by the Antichrist. Some feel that the "all" in Rev. 13:7, 8, 16, and 17 is a synecdoche, a figure of speech. Rev. 13 limits the kingdom of the Antichrist to the Old Roman Empire that will consist of the 10 European Kingdoms.

Daniel 7:7, 8; 8:23, 24 gives the indication that the location of the future 10 kingdoms will not be outside but inside of the Old Roman Empire. No country outside of the 10 kingdoms will be ruled by Antichrist.

In Daniel 9:27; 11:40-45, the Antichrist breaks his seven-year covenant with Israel and takes over Palestine and many other countries, "but these shall escape out of his hand, Edom, and Moab, and the chief of the children of Ammon," (modern Jordan, Arabia). If these countries escape Antichrist, and those on the border of Palestine that do not escape him, then it is surely conceivable that many countries across the vast oceans will also escape him.

CHAPTER 18

This is called the Economic Chapter.

Isaiah 13:19-22 indicates that ancient Babylon will be rebuilt and destroyed, and this destruction is mentioned in this chapter.

V1-3—After this I saw another angel coming down from heaven. He had great authority, and the earth was illuminated by his splendor. (2) With a mighty voice he shouted: "Fallen! Fallen is Babylon the Great! She has become a home for demons and a haunt for every evil spirit, a haunt for every unclean and detestable bird. (3) For all the nations have drunk the maddening wine of her adulteries. The kings of the earth committed adultery with her, and the merchants of the earth grew rich from her excessive luxuries.

John saw a different angel with features that revealed his importance and great power:

1. He came from Heaven with great authority. He was sent by God with the delegated authority from God.
2. The earth was illuminated with his glory. The world had been plunged into darkness by the outpouring of the fifth bowl.
3. He cried with a mighty voice. No one was able to ignore him.

Babylon had become a dwelling place of demons and a prison of every unclean spirit. It was in this vicinity that 200 million mounted troops had been bound and were released at the sound of the sixth trumpet.

Verse 2 indicates that Babylon is where demons of the spirit world and unclean birds of the physical world will be incarcerated during the Millennium. Confirmation of this is found in Isaiah 13:19-22; Jeremiah 50:38-40.

Babylon fell in one night to Cyrus the Persian in 539 BC. Later in 482 BC, the Persian king Xerxes (the Ahasuerus who married Esther) demolished Babylon and burned it. In 333 BC, Alexander the Great attempted to rebuild Babylon and in 173 BC Antiochus IV Epiphanes tried to rebuild this great city, but both failed.

Ancient Babylon was never totally destroyed, as prophesied in Isaiah 13:19. Babylon is said to be destroyed during the day of the Lord, which is an Old Testament term referring to the Tribulation, Isaiah 13:6. Archaeological discoveries have shown that bricks and stones from ancient Babylon have been reused for building purposes, contrary to the prophecy of Jeremiah 51:26. This prophecy is yet to be fulfilled.

Scripture indicates (Zech. 5:9-11) that Babylon will literally be rebuilt during the Tribulation. It is reported that Saddam Hussein, before he was removed from power, had spent over 850 million dollars rebuilding it. Some do not feel Babylon is a literal city but is symbolic.

Some think it is impossible for Babylon to be rebuilt. They say there is not enough time. I have seen a whole city "per se" built in less than five years, hotels, service stations, churches, banks, shopping malls, hundreds of homes, restaurants, etc. To say that there is not enough time is ludicrous.

If Babylon is a code word for Rome, as some think, then Babylon will not be rebuilt.

Babylon has a very long history. It is said it became prominent under Hammurabi (1728-1686 BC) who was the guiding light to the empire during the old Babylonian period. Babylonian's greatness was achieved under Nebuchadnezzar who lived during the Neo-Babylonian period about 600 years before Christ. Daniel the prophet wrote his book at that time. The story of the city and empire has been deciphered from thousands of cuneiform tablets unearthed by archaeologists.

The cost of constructing this military defense was estimated to be in excess of one billion dollars. When we consider the value of a billion dollars in those days, plus the fact that it was built with slave labor, one can imagine something of the wonder and magnificence of this famous city. But in addition to being a bastion for protection, Babylon was a place of beauty.

The famous hanging gardens of Babylon are still on record today as one of the Seven Wonders of the World. Arranged in an area 400 feet square, and raised in perfectly cut terraces one above the other, they soared to a height of 350 feet. Viewers could make their way to the top by means of stairways, which were ten feet wide. Each terrace was covered with a large stone slab topped with a layer of asphalt, two courses of brick cemented together, and, finally, plates of lead to prevent any leakage of water. On top of all this was an abundance of rich, fertile earth planted with vines, flowers, shrubs, and trees. When viewed from the level plains of the valley, a long distance away, these hanging gardens gave the appearance of a beautiful mountainside. The estimated cost to build this thing of beauty ran into hundreds of millions of dollars.

The tower of Babel with its temples of worship presented and imposing sight. The tower itself sat on a base 300 feet in breadth and rose to a height of 300 feet. The one chapel on the top contained and image alone reported to be worth $17,500,000 and the sacred vessels used in worshipping Babylonian gods, were estimated at a value of $200,000,000.

Others Thoughts:

Reasons Babylon will be rebuilt:

1. Isaiah 13:19, Jeremiah 50:40—Babylon will be overthrown by God as He overthrew Sodom and Gomorrah. This has never happened.
2. Babylon will never be inhabited after it final overthrow, Isa. 13:20; Jer. 50:40; 51:29, 37, 43.
3. Arabs and Shepherds will never live there, Isa. 13:20.
4. There will be no remains of materials to be used again as they are now, Jer. 51:26.
5. Babylon will sink into the earth and will be one of the openings of hell on earth, Jer. 51:62-64; Isa. 14:9-17; 66:22-24; Rev. 18:21; 19:3.

Babylon fallen:

1. Spiritual Babylon (Papal Rome).
2. Rome in 476.
3. Fall of Jerusalem in 70.

V4,5—Then I heard another voice from heaven say: "Come out of her, my people, so that you will not share in her sins, so that you will not receive any of her plagues; (5) for her sins are piled up to heaven, and God has remembered her crimes.

In Jeremiah 51:45, *"come out of her, my people! Run for your lives! Run from the fierce anger of the Lord,"* we see the similarity between how the people were asked to leave Babylon in ancient days.

The purpose of leaving Babylon was twofold:

1. By separation from her they would not partake of her sin, and
2. they would not have her plagues inflicted upon them.

The fact that their sins have reached unto heaven is an allusion to the tower of Babel, which began the wicked career of ancient Babylon (Gen. 11:5-9).

Sheshach was the ancient name of Babylon.

V6-8—Give back to her as she has given; pay her back double for what she has done. Mix her a double portion from her own cup. (7) Give her as much torture and grief as the glory and luxury she gave herself. In her heart she boasts, 'I sit as queen; I am not a widow, and I will never mourn.' (8) Therefore in one day her plagues will overtake her: death, mourning and famine. She will be consumed by fire, for mighty is the Lord God who judges her.

Isaiah 63:1-4 says that in Christ's second coming He is seen coming from Edom with blood sprinkled garments.

The law of retribution is to pay back a debt, an "eye for an eye," but here the cup of iniquity which Babylon filled, is now to be filled twice with the measure of her judgment.

We find three sins of Babylon mentioned:

1. She was proud and glorified herself.
2. She pursued self-gratification and lived sensuously.
3. She was guilty of self-sufficiency.

Her blatant sin against God is now to be rewarded with torment and sorrow.

Babylon's judgment comes in one day and reminds us of the fall of Babylon in Daniel 5, which fell in the same hour that the finger traced its condemning words upon the wall. Before the sun rose, the ancient power of Babylon had been destroyed. The rich fool in Luke 12:16-20 lost his barns and his soul in one night. When it is time for God's judgment, there will nothing nor no one that can stop it.

V9-10—"When the kings of the earth who committed adultery with her and shared her luxury see the smoke of her burning, they will weep and mourn over her. (10) Terrified at her torment, they will stand far off and cry: "Woe! Woe. O great city, O Babylon, city of power! In one hour your doom has come!"

God will accomplish in one day what no earthly army could ever do.

Four major things will happen that day:

1. The angel of death will pass over Babylon.
2. This city, which first finished saying, "I will never mourn" will grieve bitterly.
3. The rich city will suddenly run out of food, and
4. it will be burned to the ground.

Some think the term "one hour" means a short time or a short space of time. Most think it will happen instantaneously.

The kings of the earth, now mourn the destruction of Babylon in its political and economic aspects. The very kings who participated in the wickedness and wealth of Babylon now mourn her passing, symbolized in the burning of the capital city.

Some believe that rebuilt Babylon is the political and commercial capital, and Rome will be the ecclesiastical capital.

V11-19—"The merchants of the earth will weep and mourn over her because no one buys their cargoes any more—(12) cargoes of gold, silver, precious stones and pearls; fine linen, purple, silk and scarlet cloth; every sort of citron wood, and articles of every kind made of ivory, costly wood, bronze, iron and marble; (13) cargoes of cinnamon and spice, of incense, myrrh and frankincense, of wine and olive oil, of fine flour and wheat; cattle and sheep; horses and carriages; and bodies and souls of men. (14) "They will say. 'The fruit you longed for is gone from you. All your riches and splendor have vanished, never to be recovered.' (15) The merchants who sold these things and gained their wealth from her will stand far off, terrified at her torment. They will weep and mourn (16) and cry out: "'Woe! Woe, O great city, dressed in fine linen, purple and scarlet, and glittering with gold, precious stones and pearls! (17) In one hour such great wealth has been brought to ruin!' "Every sea captain, and all who travel by ship, the sailors, and all who earn their living from the sea, will stand far off. (18) When they see the smoke of her burning, they will exclaim, 'Was there ever a city like this great city?' (19) They will throw dust on their heads, and with weeping and mourning cry out: "'Woe! Woe, O great city, where all who had ships on the sea became rich through her wealth! In one hour she has been brought to ruin!'

The reasons for Babylon's fall are tenfold:

1. Pride,
2. Oppression of Israel,
3. Pleasures,
4. Sin,
5. Luxuries,
6. Idol worship,
7. Fornication,
8. Spiritualism,

9. Sorceries, and
10. the martyrdom of saints.

The merchandise lost are:

1-Gold.
2-Silver.
3-Precious stones.
4-Pearls.
5-Fine linen
6-(purple,
the purple dye
came from a
shellfish called
Murex).
7-Silk.
8-Scarlet cloth.

9-Citron wood.
10-Items made from ivory.
11-Costly wood.
12-Bronze.

13-Iron.
14-Marble.
15-Cinnamon.
16-Spice.

17-Incense.
18-Myrrh.

19-Frankincense.
20-Wine.
21-Olive oil.
22-Flour.

23-Wheat.
24-Cattle.
25-Sheep.
26-Horses.
27-Carriages.
28-The bodies of men,
29-and the greatest loss,
the souls of men.

The commercial character of the city of Babylon is indicated by the fact that the merchants also weep and mourn for her. They weep not over the loss of life, or the loss of souls sent to hell, nor even for their own sins, but over their loss of income. Their weeping is not one of compassion for the city or the lost souls, but was for those who had lost the means to their wealth through shipping.

Citron (Thyine) wood was a fragrant wood corresponding to cypress and was used for expensive furniture in Roman times along with other precious materials. The use of vessels made of ivory, brass, iron, and marble as well as precious wood was symbolic of the luxury and wealth of Babylon before its destruction.

The above perfumes mentioned, so treasured by its inhabitants, could only be afforded by the wealthy. All the great riches of the city, described again as fine linen, purple and scarlet, gold, precious stones, and pearls, are brought to ashes.

Standing far off watching the smoke ascending up to the skies, mourning over the demise of Babylon are four classes of people,—1—monarchs 2—merchants—3—sea captains—4—mariners. History tells us when the second time the beautiful city of Tyre was destroyed, Ezekiel 27:32, their lament was similar to the weeping now heard over the lost of Babylon. When Nebuchadnezzar wiped Tyre out the first time, it was on the mainland. The Phoenicians later rebuilt it on an island. They made it their capital and turned it into a big trading center. Then along came Alexander the Great, and laid siege on Tyre. He had his troops push the ruins of the old city into the sea, making a causeway out to the island. His troops then walked on dry land and destroyed the rebuilt city. This reminds us of the Civil War when Fort Sumter was fired upon. The Confederate soldiers built a causeway out to the fort.

How sad when we fail to heed the word of Christ, when He said, *"Lay not up for yourselves treasures upon earth . . . But lay up for yourselves treasures in heaven."* Matt. 6:19-21.

Chapter 18 gives us five reasons for the destruction of Babylon:

1- The city will become the headquarters of all demonic activity during the tribulation. (V2).
2- Her devilish pride (V7).
3- Her gross materialism. This evil city will import and export twenty-eight principal items of merchandise, beginning with gold and ending with the bodies of men. (V12, 13).
4- Her drug activities (V23).
5- Her blood shedding (V24).

V20-24—Rejoice over her, O heaven! Rejoice, saints and apostles and prophets! God has judged her for the way she treated you. (21) Then a mighty angel picked up a boulder the size of a large millstone and threw it into the sea, and said, "With such violence the great city of Babylon will be thrown down, never to be found again. (22) The music of harpists and musicians, flute players and trumpeters, will never be heard in you again. No workman of any trade will ever be found in you again. The sound of a millstone will never be heard in you again. (23) The light of a lamp will never shine in you again. The voice of bridegroom and bride will never be heard in you again.

Your merchant s were the world's great men. By your magic spell all the nations were led astray. (24) In her was found the blood of prophets and of the saints, and of all who have been killed on earth."

THREE CLASSES OF PEOPLE REJOICE:

1. Saints.
2. Apostles
3. Prophets.

There are three events in the tribulation that cause all of heaven to rejoice:

1. When Satan is cast out.
2. When Babylon is destroyed, and
3. when the Lamb is married to the Church.

There are five things said to have brought about the fall and decline of the Roman Empire:

1. The undermining of the dignity and sanctity of the home, which is the basis of a human society.
2. Higher and higher taxes; the spending of public money for free bread and circuses for the populace.
3. The mad craze for pleasure; sports becoming more exciting, more brutal, and more immoral each coming year.
4. The building of great armaments when the real enemy was within—the decay of individual responsibility.
5. The decay of religion; faith fading into mere form, losing touch with life, losing power to guide the people.

There is a great parallelism between Rome's society and America's.

Ancient Babylonian's religion was saturated with magic, fortune telling, astrology and occultism.

Through the years there has been an increase in interest, not only in America but also in the world, in the same ideologies that made up the culture of the Babylonians. Politicians and businessmen are having their astrological charts drawn up. Leaders in Russia and Saudi Arabia are reportedly using blackmagic, or consult soothsayers for their political ends. Even the leaders of America are having their charts read, or consulting mediums.

In his vision John sees a *"mighty angel"* throw a stone like a great millstone into the sea, portraying the violent downfall of the great city. We find a similar instance found in Jeremiah 51:61-64. Jeremiah tells of Seraiah, a prince who accompanied Zedekiah into Babylon who is instructed after reading the book of Jeremiah to bind a stone to it and cast it into the midst of the Euphrates with the words *"So will Babylon sink to rise no more because of the disaster I will bring upon her. And her people will fall."*

The downfall of Babylon was a most impressive clue to the fact that her greatness was the secret of her rise in influence and power. As introduced in Genesis 11:1-9, Babylon, historically symbolized by the tower reaching to heaven, proposed to maintain the union of the world through a common worship and a common tongue. Man was united as one and their goal was to reach the heavens. God defeated this purpose by confusing the language and scattering the people, because man failed to heed God's word when He told them to go out into the world. Babylon, ecclesiastically symbolized by the woman in Revelation 17, proposed to unite a world church, thus uniting a common worship and a common religion. Babylon, politically symbolized by the great city of Revelation 18, attempts to achieve its domination of the world by a world common market and a world government. Christ will destroy these at His second coming (Rev. 19:11-21).

CHAPTER 19

Chapter 19 is thought by some to be one of the most dramatic, if not the most dramatic, chapters in the Bible.

John focuses only on the fact that we will rule with Christ on earth. Luke 16:19-24 tells us that the unsaved people go to hell (Hades) when they die. But hell (Hades) is not the end. It is only the holding place while they await their final trial at the Great White Throne Judgment.

The Hallelujah Chorus:

V1-6—After this I heard what sounded like the roar of a great multitude in heaven shouting: "Hallelujah! Salvation and glory and power belong to our God, (2) for true and just are his judgments. He has condemned the great prostitute who corrupted the earth by her adulteries. He has avenged on her the blood of his servants." (3) And again they shouted: "Hallelujah! The smoke from her goes up forever and ever." (4) The twenty-four elders and the four living creatures fell down and worshiped God, who was seated on the throne. And they cried: "Amen, Hallelujah!" (5) Then a voice came from the throne, saying: "Praise our God, all you his servants, you who fear him, both small and great!" (6) Then I heard what sounded like a great multitude, like the roar of rushing waters and like loud peals of thunder, shouting: "Hallelujah! For our Lord God Almighty reigns.

We can divide chapter 19 into four sections:

1. V1-6—The Hallelujah Choruses. (Alleluia-praise ye—jah—Jehovah).
2. V7-10—The announcement of the Marriage Supper of the Lamb.
3. V11-16—The announcement of the Advent of Christ.
4. V17-21—The announcement of Armageddon.

Hallelujah is taken directly from the Hebrew and is made up of two words *hallel,* meaning 'praise,' and *jah,* a basic word for God.

There are three additional words here used to express this praise to the Lord:

1. Salvation—signifies deliverance.
2. Glory—God's moral glory in judgment.
3. Power—His might was displayed in the execution of the judgment upon the harlot. God is omnipotent.

The extent of her judgment is seen in verse 3 in that *"her smoke from her goes up forever and ever,"* indicating that this judgment upon Babylonian religion, politics, and commerce will last until the world is destroyed by fire.

Tradition has it that Babylon, whether the old Babylon rebuilt, or Rome, hell will open up and swallow it and its smoke will ascend to the heavens forever.

Here again we see the twenty-four elders praising God.

V7-10—The announcement of the marriage supper of the Lord:

V7-10—Let us rejoice and be glad and give him glory! For the wedding of the Lamb has come, and his bride has made herself ready. (8) Fine linen, bright and clean, was given her to wear." (Fine linen stands for the righteous acts of the saints). (9) Then the angel said to me, "Write: 'Blessed are those who are invited to the wedding supper of the Lamb!" And he added, "These are the true words of God." (10) At this I fell at his feet to worship him. But he said to me, "Do not do it! I am a fellow servant with you and with your brothers who hold to the testimony of Jesus. Worship God! For the testimony of Jesus is the spirit of prophecy."

Fine linen, the brides' array stands for the righteous acts of the saints. The wedding garment of the bride will be made up of the righteous acts or deeds done in our life. We are the bride because of Christ's righteousness, and are clothed for the wedding because of our acts.

Ephesians 5:25-32 reveals that each person who believes in Christ becomes a member of His body, of His flesh and bones.

In Jewish custom a marriage contract was negotiated between the parents, usually when the children were still too young to assume their adult roles. This contract was a binding agreement: it meant that the two parties were legally married even though they would have no sexual contact with each other, sometimes for several years. This condition was known as a "betrothal," but it was a much stronger tie than our present day engagement period. It gave the two betrothed parties a chance to grow in their relationship before the actual consummation of their marriage vows.

The second step in the marriage process took place when the couple had reached a suitable age of maturity. The groom accompanied by his friends, would go to the home of his bride and escort her to the house he had prepared for them to live in. There usually was an exchange of gifts as the bride presented her dowry and the groom gave gifts to his new bride. Christ, on the cross, gave His life as a gift for us.

Finally there would come the consummating event, the wedding feast. Many guests would be invited to this gala event to share in the celebration of the happy bride and groom's union.

The Greek word for servant is Syndoulos, which indicates that not only men are redeemed by these token bond-slaves of Jesus, but angels also have similar obligation of obedience to God.

God alone is worthy of worship. The heavenly hosts do not deserve our worship, nor can they mediate our prayers. Man or angels cannot forgive us of our sins, (only when we sin against them). We must pray to God, and He alone will hear our prayers and He alone can forgive us of our sins.

V11-16—I saw heaven standing open and there before me was a white horse, whose rider is called Faithful and True. With justice he judges and makes war. (12) His eyes are like blazing fire, and on his head are many crowns. He has a name written on him that no one knows but he himself. (13) He is dressed in a robe dipped in blood, and his name is the Word of God. (14) The armies of heaven were following him, riding on white horses and dressed in fine linen, white and clean. (15) Out of his mouth comes a sharp sword with which to strike down the nations. "He will rule them with an iron scepter."

He treads the winepress of the fury of the wrath of God Almighty. (16) On his robe and on his thigh he has this name written: "King of Kings and Lord of Lords."

History tells us that most wars are fought for the love of conquest or to enlarge one's territory, but this war is neither of these. This war is to put down evil and to enthrone righteousness on earth, in order that there may be peace on earth. The rider on the white horse has eyes *"like flaming fire"* which denotes His omniscience. His penetrating eyes see all things. The rider on this white horse is Jesus, our Lord and Savior! He judges and makes war in righteousness, and will settle the destinies of the world and its inhabitants. This rider is a mighty warrior, conqueror, a righteous judge, and has the blood of His enemies splashed upon His garments.

The Greek text for "crowns" conveys "diadems." A diadem in John's day was individual ribbons tied around one's head. Here the many diadems represent Christ's supremacy.

See Genesis 49:11 in comparison to verse 13.

In verse 15 the sword is not a literal sword but the words of Christ that flows from His mouth. See 2 Thess. 2:8.

The Norwegian Academy of Sciences with help of the historians from Britain, Egypt, Germany, and India, using an electronic computer, has found that since 3600 BC, the world has know only 292 years of peace.

After the rapture three things will happen to Christians:

1. They will appear at the Judgment Seat (I Cor. 3:12-15; II Cor. 5:10).
2. The Marriage (Rev. 19:7-10).
3. They will return with Jesus to reign in the Kingdom (Rev. 20:6).

The announcement of Armageddon:

V17-21—And I saw an angel standing in the sun, who cried in a loud voice to all the birds flying in midair, "Come, gather together for the great supper of God, (18) so that you may eat the flesh of kings, generals, and mighty men, of horses and their riders, and the flesh of all people, free and slave, small and great." (19) Then I saw the beast and the kings of the earth and their armies gathered together to make war against the rider on the horse and his army. (20) But the beast was captured, and with him the false prophet who had performed the miraculous signs on his behalf. With these signs he had deluded those who had received the mark of the beast and worshiped his image. The two of them were thrown alive into the fiery lake of burning sulfur. (21) The rest of them were killed with the sword that came out of the mouth of the rider on the horse, and all the birds gorged themselves on their flesh.

God in preparing for this great feast has increased His invitations to the many guests. Every spring and fall 15 million raptors, (birds of prey) commute through Israel on their way to or from their homelands. There are reportedly nearly 300 different species, with an estimated 15 million birds, that annually migrate from Europe and Asia south to Africa along a narrow land corridor called Eretz Yisroel. There are European buzzards, eagles, falcons, jackdaws, storks, and numerous other birds migrating yearly. This takes place in late September and early October. God allows 15 million raptors to fly over Eretz Yisroel every Feast of Tabernacles, ready for this tremendous feast predicted more than 2300 years ago. This would give an indication that Armageddon will happen around late September and early October, but there is one thing to remember, God can change the migration time of these birds to fit His time frame.

Israel is in preparation for the coming of the King. They are looking for the red heifer without blemish. They are gathering wood and cutting stone for the new temple. Israel now possesses an ancient jug of balsam oil that could be used to anoint their messiah. God had hidden this oil away for 2000 years. In 1989 it was recorded that Israeli archeologists, searching caves near the Dead Sea, had discovered what they believe is a 2,000-year-old jug of once fragrant oil, the kind used to anoint the ancient Israelite kings. Even though the oil, thought to have been placed in its earthen container at the time of Jesus, had lost its fragrance, it was still fluid and had maintained its original chemical composition.

A farmer in America, who breeds red heifers, has sent a red heifer to Israel. A red heifer must be born and raised in Israel. Israel must now breed or clone red heifers to get one without blemish. I think it is highly improbable that God will accept a heifer that has been cloned.

Why a red heifer? Numbers 19:2 tells us that a young female cow had to be slaughtered outside the camp on the Mount of Olives. The priest would then take some of the blood from the red heifer and sprinkle it seven times in front of the tabernacle. Then the heifer was burned in the sight of the priest. While the heifer was being burned, the priest would toss cedar, hyssop, and a scarlet thread into the fire. The scarlet thread called, *Iashon Zehurit,* spoke of the great sin sacrifice and the need for atonement. When the heifer, cedar, hyssop, and scarlet thread were completely consumed by the fire, the ashes were used to prepare the water of purification, "for purifying from sin." When it is time to rebuild the Temple in Jerusalem, the ashes of the red heifer will be needed to produce the water of purification that will purify the Temple Mount before the new Temple can be built.

Isaiah 34:18 speaks of this time and says the land will "be soaked with blood."

CHAPTER 20

The great white horse and his rider appeared in Chapter 19. In chapter 20 the White Throne of judgment and justice appears.

In chapter 20 we will see four major things:

1. The binding of Satan. He will be imprisoned for 1,000 years.
2. The reign of Christ and the saints for one thousand years.
3. Satan will be loosed for a short time to test those who are born during the Millennium.
4. We will see the judgment of the wicked dead.

V1-3—And I saw an angel coming down out of heaven, having the key to the Abyss and holding in his hand a great chain. (2) He seized the dragon, that ancient serpent, which is the devil, or Satan, and bound him for a thousand years. (3) He threw him in the Abyss, and locked and sealed it over him, to keep him from deceiving the nations anymore until the thousand years were ended. After that, he must be set free for a short time.

The majority of the theologians take the 1,000 years to be literal. There are a few who hold to the symbolic approach, and there are some who take it metaphorically.

Those who hold to the symbolic approach say it refers to an indefinite period between the ascension of Jesus and His return, but this does not fit in with scripture and its definition of the last days.

There are some who think this angel is Christ, but all indications are that this is another great angel operating at God's command and authority. *"Dragon"* represents cruelty, and murder. *"Serpent"* signifies guile and cunning treachery. *"Devil"* is the deceiver, slanderer, and the tempter of men. *"Satan"* means the opponent, the enemy of Christ and His Church, (His people).

(4)—I saw thrones on which were seated those who had been given authority to judge. And I saw the souls of those who had been beheaded because of their testimony for Jesus and because of the word of God. They had not worshiped the beast or his image and had not received his mark on their foreheads or their hands. They came to life and reigned with Christ a thousand years.

Verse 4 reveals (1) thrones of judgment (2) souls of martyrs and (3) a millennium of living and ruling with Christ.

The scriptures do not teach that angels or heavenly creatures will reign here on earth. I Cor. 6: 2,3 says, *"Do you not know that saints will judge the world? And if you are to judge the world, are you not competent to judge trivial cases? Do you not know that we will judge angels? How much more the things of this life!"*

(5) (The rest of the dead did not come to life until the thousand years were ended.) This is the first resurrection. (6) Blessed and holy are those who have part in the first resurrection. The second death has no power over them, but they will be priests of God and of Christ and will reign with him for a thousand years.

When Jesus comes in the rapture, only the righteous will be raised. (I Thess. 4:13-18), but when He comes at the end of the ages, the wicked will be the only ones raised and will appear before the great White Throne to be judged.

Jesus is the resurrection and the life. In John chapter 11, John gives us the story of the raising of Lazarus. Jesus walked toward the tomb, stopped and said *"Lazarus, come forth."* He called Lazarus by name. Had He simply said, "Come forth," every dead person would have come forth, but He called out the name of one man, and only one man came forth from the grave.

When this present Church Age ends, the rapture of the church will take place, the dead in Christ will be raised, and at the end of the great tribulation, the tribulation saints will also be raised from the dead. Just as there are two kinds of deaths, namely, the first death which results in burial, and the second death which is described as being cast into the Lake of Fire (20:14). There are two kinds of resurrection, a first resurrection having to do with the resurrection of the righteous, and a second resurrection having to do with the wicked, or the resurrection of life, and the resurrection of damnation. The resurrection of the wicked is a resurrection unto eternal damnation, not a resurrection unto life.

Verse 5 reveals that there will be a thousand years between the two. The word "resurrection" in Greek is "anastasis" meaning literally "standing again."

Verse 6 is the only beatitude with a double predicate, blessed and holy. It is also singular but applies to all of God's people.

The eleventh chapter of Isaiah gives us a beautiful picture of peace and harmony during the Millennium. Verse 6-9 says: *"The wolf will live with the lamb, the leopard will lie down with the goat, the calf and the lion and the yearling together; and a little child will lead them. (7) The cow will feed with the bear, their young will lie down together, and the lion will eat straw like the ox. (8) The infant will play near the hole of the cobra, and the young child put his hand into the viper's nest. (9) They will neither harm nor destroy on my holy mountain, for the earth will be full of the knowledge of the Lord as the waters cover the sea."*

This is a picture of the original Garden of Eden. All living creatures are vegetarians.

Verse six tells us six things about those who will have a part in the first resurrection:

1. Blessed—Happy in their eternal state.
2. Holy—Separated and identified as God's Special people.
3. Priests—Will minister to and serve God.
4. Reign—Both political and royal priests.
5. A thousand years—Length of their reign.
6. Second death has no power—Will never suffer the lake of fire.

(7)When the thousand years are over, Satan will be released from his prison

A thousand years of peace! Sickness and disease will not exist and people will be able to live hundreds of years. People will be born. The population will increase greatly. God, no respecter of person, will test those born during the millennium. They will be tested as everyone before them.

(8) and will go out to deceive the nations in the four corners of the earth— Gog and Magog—to gather them for battle. In number they are like the sand on the seashore.

Satan will try one more time, as he did at the Battle of Armageddon to become greater than God by gathering a great army from all over the world, including those, as some think, from God and Magog. Russia will try again to destroy Israel, under the leadership of the Antichrist, but will fail again.

Magog—He was the grandson of Noah and the second son of Japheth. Magog is credited with founding the great kingdom north of the Black and Caspian Seas, which became known as Scythia and eventually known as Russia. His name seems to be preserved in the name of the ancient nation of Georgia.

Meshech and Tubal were his brothers. They also migrated into these northern regions, and are probably still slightly recognizable in the names Moskva (Moscow) and Tobalsk.

Gog and Magog is a description of the last rebellion against God and has no relationship with the battle of Gog and Magog in Ezekiel 38, 39.

(9) They marched across the breath of the earth and surrounded the camp of God's people, the city he loves. But fire came down from heaven and devoured them. (10) And the devil, who deceived them, was thrown into the lake of burning sulfur, where the beast and the false prophet had been thrown. They will be tormented day and night forever and ever.

They shall be tormented day and night, a continuous, unceasing torment. The lake of fire was prepared for the devil and his wicked angels, and is also the destiny of those who follow Satan. If one has not accepted

Christ as his Lord and Savior, and made a profession of faith, then they are followers of Satan.

V11-12—Then I saw a great white throne and him who was seated on it. Earth and sky fled from his presence, and there was no place for them. (12) And I saw the dead, great and small, standing before the throne, and books were opened. Another book was opened, which is the book of life. The dead were judged according to what they had done as recorded in the books.

These "books" contain the record of every thought, word, or deed of every unsaved person who has ever lived.

The Book of Life is a list of every person that has ever lived, less the names of those who were removed because of their sins against God, through blasphemy, denying Jesus, or adding to or taking away from the Scriptures.

V13-15—The sea gave up the dead that were in it, and death and Hades gave up the dead that were in them, and each person was judged according to what he had done. (14) Then death and Hades were thrown into the lake of fire. The lake of fire is the second death. (15) If any one's name was not found written in the book of life, he was thrown into the lake of fire.

Verse 13 states that everyone will stand before God's judgment seat, even those from the depths of the sea.

As mentioned before, the Bible (Heb. 9:27), *"Just as man is destined to die once, and after that to face judgment,"* teaches us that man or woman is destined to die once, and then he or she will face the judgment. This also dispels the theory of reincarnation.

Believers will face the Judgment Seat of Christ to receive their rewards. Non-believers will face the Great White Throne Judgment to be sent to their everlasting abode.

There are those who think God did not mean people will be tormented. They believe that all the unsaved will just die and no longer be in existence because God is a God of love and no one will be tormented. This is known as "Universalism."

The Bible from Genesis to Revelation says that all those who die rejecting God will be cast into a never consuming eternal fire, where there shall be *"gnashing of teeth."*

If God had not created a place of torment then there would be no scripture saying He had!

At the beginning of the Millennium there was a great judgment poured out upon the living. Now at the close of the Millennium there is another great judgment, which is the judgment of the dead.

The judgment in Matthew 25:31 has to do with nations; the great White Throne judgment has to do with individuals.

We find in heaven that there are three great thrones:

1. In heaven (Rev, 4:2), from where the universe is governed.
2. On earth (Matt. 25:31). The nations will be judged here in respect to their treatment of the preachers of the Kingdom set forth in Matthew 25:40-45.
3. The Great White Throne, where the wicked dead will be judged (Rev. 20:11).

In the Great White Throne judgment, some think the judge is our crucified Lord and Savior, Jesus the Christ. The despised man from Nazareth, this Nazarene (He was a Nazarene, one from Nazareth, not a Nazarite), who was hated, and crucified, (to be called a Nazarene was an insult to a person) is now about to judge "the quick (living) and the dead" (II Tim. 4:1).

The clouds, the atmosphere, and the earth are gone. The guilty will stand before God and there will be no caves or mountains for them to hide. They will come face to face with God, who sits upon the throne!

Everyone on earth has his life recorded in God's book. Every thought, every word, and every deed is recorded. This should make us hesitate before we say, think, or do anything.

We will not receive our full reward until the end of all things. When the righteous die, the spirit returns to God its creator, and rests . . . but *"their works do follow them."* (Rev. 14:13). Therefore, the righteous cannot receive their full reward until the last soul has received or rejected the Lord Jesus.

Scripture gives us 6 definitions of hell:

1. A place of total darkness Matt. 8:12; 22:13.
2. A place where the worm (the accusing conscious) devouring the wicked Isa. 66:24.
3. A place of banishment from God's kingdom.
4. A place of unending sorrow Matt: 25:30.
5. A place where there is wailing and gnashing of teeth Matt. 8:16, Luke 13:28.
6. The second death, the lake of fire. This is the only place where the Lake of Fire is mentioned.

CHAPTER 21

We find seven new things in the next two chapters that give us an insight to the eternal future God has prepared for those who love him.

1. A new heaven (21:1).
2. A new earth (21:1).
3. A new Jerusalem (21:2).
4. New things (21:5).
5. A new paradise (22:1-5).
6. A new source of light (22:5), and
7. a new place for God's throne.

V1-2—Then I saw a new heaven and a new earth, for the first heaven and the first earth had passed away, and there was no longer any sea. (2) I saw the Holy City, the new Jerusalem, coming down out of heaven from God, prepared as a bride beautifully dressed for her husband.

Both in the Old Testament and the New Testament the words for "new" mean new in respect of freshness.

We will also find that the earth has been or will be, destroyed at least three times. The first time was during Noah's time when the world was destroyed by water. The second time will be by fire, after which God will restore all things (Isa. 65:17-20). The third destruction will be the Heaven and earth, for John tells us that he sees a new heaven and a new earth; for the first heaven and the first earth were passed away, and there was no more sea. There is an indication in the Scripture that the earth was destroyed before it was created for mankind. Earth was created first for the angels, the second time for mankind. The third time will be for Christians.

This earth as we know it will be done away with. Both Isaiah and Peter graphically describe the dissolution of this material universe. II Peter 3:10 says, *"the heavens will disappear with a roar; the elements will be destroyed by fire, and the earth and everything in it will be laid bare."* This earth we are told is 25,000 miles in circumference and 8,000 miles in diameter. Two thirds of the earth is covered with water, which leaves only one third of the earth that is land, with a large portion being worthless land. Only a small percent of the earth is inhabitable. The new earth will contain no seas, just land, but the Bible does not tell us how big this new earth will be. The only water mentioned is the one river in chapter 22 verse 2.

Our Lord went to prepare for His saints a new Jerusalem that will come in all of its glory. We could never imagine how beautiful this new city will be.

When John saw the new heaven come down, *"from God out of Heaven,"* he does not say, or suggest, that it came to rest upon the earth's surface, nor did he suggest it didn't. He said it came down. There are some who think that the new Jerusalem will be suspended over the earth until after the final conflict.

V3—And I heard a loud voice from the throne saying, "Now the dwelling of God is with men, and he will live with them. They will be his people, and God himself will be with them and be their God.

Just think, one day we will dwell with God. No longer will we have to pray through faith. We can commune and see God in all of His Glory! God will "tabernacle" with us, walking in and out among us.

V4, 5—He will wipe every tear from their eyes. There will be no more death or mourning or crying or pain, for the old order of things has passed away." (5) He who was seated on the throne said, "I am making everything new!" Then he said, "Write this down, for these words are trustworthy and true."

No more sadness, no more pain or death. All old things have passed away, everything will be new. Christ, through His death and resurrection has conquered death, pain, and sadness. We now will know eternal peace and joy forever, for the old things have passed away. God has brought an end to the curse that sin brought to mankind first through Eve and then Adam.

V6-8—He said to me: "It is done. I am the Alpha and the Omega, the Beginning and the End. To him who is thirsty I will give to drink without cost from the spring of the water of life. (7) He who overcomes will inherit all this, and I will be his God and he will be my son. (8) But the cowardly, the unbelieving, the vile, the murderers, the sexually immoral, those who practice magic arts, the idolaters and all liars—their place will be in the fiery lake of burning sulfur. This is the second death."

The word for beginning means the first in the source of all things. The word for end means the goal. In the beginning all things were created with the goal being new life with God, face to face.

When Christ was hanging on the Cross, His life fading away, He said, *"It is finished"* (John 19:30). Jesus has conquered death and the grave through His death and resurrection. Again, He says, *"It is done."* Jesus' purpose for coming to earth in the form of a human was to die on the cross for the sins of mankind and after three days to be resurrected. He had reached His goal! A new heaven and a new earth prepared for the saints, just as He had promised. No one who has not accepted Him as their savior will inherit the Kingdom of God. They will be able to see heaven, see the saints there. I think it is quiet ironic that the people who ridiculed and hated Christians here on earth, will one day, from their abode in hell, see these same people basking in the light of God's love! Ironic, but very sad!

Anyone who is thirsty can be satisfied at the fountain of life. The fountain is God, the water is promised to all who are thirsty. The water of life is God's gift freely given. It cannot be bought for Christ paid the price at Calvary. We who are *"overcomers"* will not only inherit all things, but we will have a very close and personal relationship with God.

The following is a list of those who will enter into their abode, the fiery lake according to I Cor. 6:9-11 and Revelation 21:6-8:

1. Cowardly—without faith, embarrassed, ashamed, or afraid (for their life) to accept Jesus as the Lord of their life.
2. Unbelieving—they reject the truth.

3. Abominable—those who profess a faith in God and still practice evil.

4. Murderers—the deliberate taking of one's life.

5. Sexually immoral (whoremongers)—those who practice any kind of sexual impurity or sexual immorality, (homosexuality, bestiality, etc.).

6. Sorcerers—those who practice magic arts, reading of tarot cards, the use of poisons, drugs, and magic potions, tattoos, often in the name of religion.

7. Idolaters—those who worship false gods or put something else in the place of God.

8. All liars—those who are false prophets, as well as those who deny Christ is Lord, and those who are untruthful.

V9-15—One of the seven angels who had the seven bowls full of the seven last plagues came and said to me, "Come, I will show you the bride, the wife of the Lamb." (10) And he carried me away in the Spirit to a mountain great and high, and showed me the Holy City, Jerusalem, coming down out of heaven from God. (11) It shone with the glory of God, and its brilliance was like that of a very precious jewel, like a jasper, clear as crystal. (12) It had a great, high wall with twelve gates, and with twelve angels at the gates. On the gates were written the names of the twelve tribes of Israel. (13)There were three gates on the east, three on the north, three on the south and three on the west. (14) The wall of the city had twelve foundations, and on them were the names of the twelve apostles of the Lamb. (15) The angel who talked with me had a measuring rod of gold to measure the city, its gates and its walls.

In verse 9, 10, and 11, as John was in the spirit, standing on a very high mountain, he gives his account of the great city, the Holy Jerusalem coming down out of Heaven. We read the description about the light of the city, the foundations, walls, streets, gates, etc.

There is nothing said about the New Jerusalem resting on the new earth. It could remain suspended above the earth. Just because it doesn't say it rested on earth does not necessarily mean it didn't, as mentioned earlier.

The wall is of jasper and the city is pure gold, so pure that it is transparent, as clear glass, measuring 144 cubits, or, 216 feet thick.

The wall had 12 gates (twelve tribes of Israel), with 12 angels at the gates. The twelve tribes of Israel written on the gates. It had 12 foundations with the names of the 12 apostles on them. The apostles were the foundation of Christianity. Christ is the Chief Cornerstone.

Some have asked why angels are stationed at the 12 gates. Does the Holy City need security? It has been suggested it is a symbol that not everyone has access to God. Maybe they are there because they are the guardian angels of the apostles. Chapter 22:14 says that we will go in and out of the gates, so the angels are not there for security!

A cube has 12 edges. Since each edge measured 12,000 Stadia, the total length of the edges is 144,000, exactly the same number of the followers of the Lamb, 14:1. It was an ancient symbol of perfection. The Most Holy Place in the OT Tabernacle and in the Temple were cubic in design.

V16-17—The city was laid out like a square, as long as it was wide. He measured the city with the rod and found it to be 12,000 stadia in length, and as wide and high as it is long. (17) He measured its wall and it was 144 cubits thick, by man's measurement, which the angel was using.

A reed in John's day was approximately ten feet long. A furlong is 582 feet. Multiply 582 by 12,000, then divide by 5,280 feet in a mile, and we find the city is 1,500 miles long, 1,500 miles wide, 1,500 miles high. The walls are 216 feet wide. Some say 1,380 miles and others 1,400 miles.

V18-20—The wall was made of jasper, and the city of pure gold, as pure as glass. (19) The foundations of the city walls were decorated with every kind of precious stone. The first foundation was jasper, the second sapphire, the third chalcedony, the fourth emerald, (20) the fifth sardonyx, the sixth carnelian, the seventh chrysolite, the eight beryl, the ninth topaz, the tenth chrysoprase, the eleventh jacinth, and the twelfth amethyst.

1. Jasper—blue/white diamond. (Unity).
2. Sapphire-deep blue stone. (Division).
3. Chalcedony-green copper silicate. (Holy thing, Trinity).
4. Emerald-bright light green.(Number of the world).

5. Sardonyx-red sard and white onyx layered. (Picture of God's divine providence and abundant life given to man).
6. Carnelian (Sardius)-blood red. (Represents the blood shed for man).
7. Chrysolite-yellow topaz. (Perfection, completeness).
8. Beryl-sea green. (New beginning or "new" order of things).
9. Topaz-greenish gold. (Impurities).
10. Chrysoprase-translucent apple green. (10 commandments, 10 virgins).
11. Jacinth-bluish. (Number of judgment or disorder).
12. Amethyst-clear purple or blue violet, glossy quartz. (God's government by Divine appointment).

The new earth will be occupied by Israel and the saved nations. This Great City of precious stones will be the home of the New Testament Church, the Bride of Christ.

When the Rapture takes place God will not be finished with His Church. The Church will be the seat of eternal government, light, and knowledge throughout eternity. See Isaiah 9:6, 7.

It has been calculated that this city would extend from Maine to Florida and from the east coast to 600 miles west of the Mississippi River and that around 20 billion people could be accommodated spaciously.

(21) The twelve gates were twelve pearls, each gate made of a single pearl. The great street of the city was of pure gold, like transparent glass. (22) I did not see a temple in the city, because the Lord God Almighty and the Lamb are its temple. (23) The city does not need the sun or the moon to shine on it, for the glory of God gives it light, and the Lamb is its lamp. (24) The nations will walk by its light, and the kings of the earth will bring their splendor into it. (25) On no day will its gates ever be shut, for there will be no night there. (26) The glory and honor of the nations will be brought into it. (27) Nothing impure will ever enter it, nor will anyone who does what is shameful or deceitful, but only those whose names are written in the Lamb's book of life.

The question is "why 12 gates?" There will be people who will live outside of the city. It is believed by many that these will be Jews. See Isa. 60:21. They will have kings over them.

These are the children of Israel saved during the Tribulation.

There is no need of the sun or the moon to shine in it, because God's glory gives it light.

CHAPTER 22

V1-2—Then the angel showed me the river of the water of life, as clear as crystal, flowing from the throne of God and of the Lamb (2) down the middle of the great street of the city. On each side of the river stood the tree of life, bearing twelve crops of fruit, yielding its fruit every month. And the leaves of the tree are for the healing of the nations.

John sees the river of the water of life. The water we drink today is chemically treated water. The river of life is pure water with no chemicals.

Did John see not one tree of life, but at least two, possibly several? The Greek is plural. He said that on each side of the river was a tree. On each side, this makes two, at least. If we consider the enormity of the New City, and the numerous people, there probably are several trees of life with twelve different kinds of fruit on each tree. This is possibly the same kind of tree that Adam and Eve had in the Garden of Eden, and had they not sinned, they could have eaten of the tree and lived forever. Perhaps it is only one tree with the water running under the trunk. Ezek. 47:12, Ezekiel sees several trees on both sides.

Scripture seems to indicate that we will not have to eat to survive, but that we will be able to. Jesus, after His resurrection, did physically eat food.

V3-4—No longer will there be any curse. The throne of God and of the Lamb will be in the city, and his servants will serve him. (4) They will see his face, and his name will be on their foreheads.

When Eve and Adam sinned, God placed a curse upon His creation. Women were cursed with pain in childbirth; men would find weeds (thorns) in the field. Both would suffer sickness. Both would face both physical and spiritual death.

There will be no more curses. Satan has been sent to his abode, never more to tempt mankind.

Both Moses and Philip wanted to see the face of God. They were not allowed to, because if they did they would have died. Now we all will see the face of God and will stand in His Holy presence.

V5—There will be no more night. They will not need the light of a lamp or the light of the sun, for the Lord God will give them light. And they will reign forever and ever.

There will be no more night, for God will illuminate His city with His Holiness.

The Water of Life is thought by some to represent the activity and blessings of the Holy Spirit flowing from God's Throne in the heart of the believer.

V6-7—the angel said to me, "These words are trustworthy and true. The Lord, the God of the spirits of the prophets, sent his angel to show his servants the things that must soon take place." (7) "Behold, I am coming soon! Blessed is he who keeps the words of the prophecy in this book."

John assures us that we can depend on the truth of what is written. The Book of Revelation is real, regardless of what the modernist, liberals, secularists, and haters of God say.

Revelation is perhaps one of the most important books in the Bible. We should study this book because Christ says that the reader who does will be blessed (happy).

V8-11—I, John, am the one who heard and saw these things. And when I had heard and seen them, I fell down to worship at the feet of the angel who had been showing them to me. (9) But he said to me, "Do not do it! I am a fellow servant with you and with your brothers the prophets and of all who keep the words of this book. Worship God!" (10) Then he told me, "Do not seal up the words of the prophecy of this book, because the time is near." (11) Let him who does wrong continue to do wrong; let him who is vile continue to be vile; let him who does right continue to do right; and let him who is holy continue to be holy."

John says that he was not just told of these things, but that he saw and heard these things personally.

John bowed down before this angel, but was told not to, because he was a fellow servant. God is the only one worthy of our worship, not a statue of Mary holding the baby Jesus, not a cross, not a pope, nor any other craven image, but God Himself.

Revelation could possibly be the book that Daniel was told to seal up. John, unlike Daniel, was told not to seal up this book.

When eternity dawns, all non-believers will be condemned and cast into the Lake of Fire. There to be tormented for eternity, without hope because their eternal condition will never change.

A great chasm will separate the Lake of Fire from the Holy City. No one will be able to cross this chasm. The only ones who would want to would be those in Hell. Those in Heaven will have no knowledge of Hell.

V12, 15-"Behold, I am coming soon! My reward is with me, and I will give to everyone according to what he has done. (13) I am the Alpha and the Omega, the First and Last, the Beginning and the End. (14) "Blessed are those who wash their robes, that they may have the right to the tree of life and may go through the gates into the city. (15) Outside are the dogs, those who practice magic arts, the sexually immoral, the murderers, the idolaters and everyone who loves and practices falsehood.

If we accept Christ as our personal Savior, and keep God's commandments, we are blessed and have the right to the tree of life, and may enter in through the gates into the city. If we do not, then we will not be allowed to enter God's Kingdom, but shall spend the rest of eternity in hell.

V16-17—"I, Jesus, have sent my angel to give you this testimony for the churches. I am the Root and the Offspring of David, and the bright Morning

Star." (17) The Spirit and the bride say, "Come! And let him who hears say, "Come!" Whoever is thirsty, let him come; and whoever wishes, let him take the free gift of the water of life."

Jesus was born the King of the Jews and was crucified. He shall reign as the King of the Jews. Jesus the Bridegroom stirs the slumbering affections of the bride. He has kindled a fire in her soul which no one can put out.

V18-21—I warn everyone who hears the words of the prophecy of this book: If anyone adds anything to them, God will add to him the plagues described in this book. (19) And if anyone takes words away from this book of prophecy, God will take away from him his share in the tree of life and in the holy city, which are described in this book. (20) He who testifies to these things says, "Yes, I am coming soon." Amen. Come, Lord Jesus. (21) The grace of the Lord Jesus be with God's people, Amen.

In the beginning of Revelation it tells us that anyone who reads and studies the Book of Revelation would be blessed. We now read a solemn warning that if anyone adds anything to the book, God will add unto that person the plagues that are written in the book. This warning is even stronger in Deut. 4:2; and Prov. 30:6.

Chapter one, verse one, tells us Revelation was given by God, and it is His Word alone. He, no one else, has authority over it.

There are some today who teach that God is love, but refute the message of salvation, the wrath of God, the judgment of God, the Tribulation Period and Hell. Some teach that hell is only the grave; humans who are worthy will have to become a member of their belief. Some teach that Jesus is really the Archangel Michael and some teach that God, rather than Jesus, was once a mortal human being and the newer belief states that God is a cosmic force, not a personal being.

In 1966, a church in England joined a denomination in America in rejecting the medieval image of Hell, calling it a distortion of 'the revelation of God's loving Christ'.

If anyone tampers with Revelation, he has canceled his right to any part of eternal life and the joys of heaven beyond the grave. Gal. 1:8 says this is true with all of God's word.

The Old Testament closes with the promise of the first coming of Christ; the New Testament closes with the announcement of the grand and glorious second coming of our great God and our Savior, Jesus Christ.

SOURCES

Agee, M. J.—Revelation 2000.

Angley, Ernest W.—Raptured.

Biederwolf—The Second Coming.

Bloomfield, Arthur E.—The End of the Days.

Davis, James L.—Unveiling Revelation.

Dehaan, M. R.—The Second Coming of Jesus; Studies in Revelation.

Duck, Daymond—Revelation; Prophecies in the Bible.

Dyer, Charles H.—World News and Bible Prophecy.

Fogle, Lerry W.—Revelation Explained.

Graham, Billy—Till Armageddon.

Greene, Oliver B.—Revelation.

Gregg, Steve—Revelation.

Hagee, John—Beginning of the End; Final Dawn over Jerusalem; From
    Daniel to Doomsday.

Haggith, David—End Time Prophecies of the Bible.

Hindson, Ed—Earth's Final Hour.

Hitchcock, Mark—Bible Prophecy.

Horton, Stanley M.—The Ultimate Victory.

Hyles, Dr. Jack—Let's Study the Revelation.

James, William T.—Foreshocks of Antichrist; Raging into Apocalypse
    (with G. Jeffrey, J. Walvoord, D. Breeze, and C. Missler).

Jeffrey, Grant R.—Armageddon; Appointment with Destiny; Earth's Last
    Days; Messiah; and Final Warning.

Jeremiah, David R.—with C. C. Carlson—Escape the Coming Night.

Johnson, Carl G.—Prophecy made Plain.

Jones, R. Bradley—The Great Tribulation.

Kirban, Salem—Revelation Unveiled; Revelation; Rapture (under attack);
    Understanding the Last Days.

Lahaye, Tim, with Jerry B. Jenkins—End Times, Are we living in?

Lindsey, Hal—The Late Great Planet Earth; The Road to Holocaust; The
    Promise; There's a New World Coming; Planet Earth; Final Battle;
    Planet Earth 2000 AD.; Apocalypse Code; Combat Faith; Satan;
    The Promise of Bible Prophecy; Vanished; The Final Battle; The
    1980's Countdown to Armageddon.

Lynn, Betty—Pathways to Armageddon.

SOURCES

Marrs, Texe—Millennium.
Marrs, Texe, with Tim Lahaye, David Breeze, David A. Lewis—Storming Toward Armageddon.
McGee, J. Vernon—Revelation.
Morris, Henry M.—The Revelation Record.
Newell, William R.—Revelation, Chapter by Chapter; Revelation, The Book Of.
Price, Randall—The Coming Last Day's Temple.
Robertson, Pat—The New Millennium.
Ryrie, Charles C.—The Rapture.
Seiss, J. A.—The Apocalypse.
Swindoll, Charles R., John F. Walvoord, J. Dwight Pentecost—The Road to Armageddon.
Taylor, Robert—What the Bible Says About The End Times.
Thompson, Leonard L.—Revelation.
Vigeveno, H. S.—In The Eye of the Apocalypse.
Walvoord, John F.—Armageddon; Oil and the Middle East Crisis; The Revelation of Jesus Christ.
Yerbury, Ray W.—Vital Signs of Christ's Return.

OTHER SOURCES

Boyd's Bible Handbook.
Crusade New Analytical Study Edition Bible.
Disciples Study Bible.
Egemier's Bible Story Book.
Globe Digest Series—What the Bible Says about the End Times.
Hagee, John—Prophecy Study Bible.
Haley's Bible Handbook.
Josephus.
Kirban's Prophecy New Testament.
Lost Books of the Bible.
Nelson's Bible Handbook.
Our Living Bible.
Prophecy Study Bible.
Quest Study Bible.

OTHER SOUCES

Rainbow Study Bible.
Richard's Complete Bible Handbook.
Ryrie Study Bible.
The Chosen Word.
The Key Bible.
The Marked reference Bible.
Thompson's Chain Reference Bible.
Tyndale-Life Application Study Bible.
Unger's Bible Handbook.
Westminister's Introduction to the Bible.
Wilmington's Guide to the Bible.
Zondervan-NASB Study Bible.

COMMENTARIES

Adam Clark's Commentary on the Bible.
Irwin's Bible Commentary.
Jamieson, Fausset, and Brown Commentary on the Whole Bible.
Liberty Bible Commentary.
The Bible Knowledge Commentary by Walvoord and Zuck.
The Interpreter's Commentary of the Bible.
The New Layman's Bible Commentary by Howley, Bruce and Ellison.
The Matthew Henry Commentary.
The Wycliffe Bible Commentary.